GOLFERCISE

The Golf Fitness Manual

TIMOTHY D. CONWELL, DC, FACO

ADJUNCT CLINICAL PROFESSOR
LOGAN COLLEGE OF CHIROPRACTIC
ST. LOUIS, MISSOURI

HEAD PAIN & NEUROLOGY CENTER
DEPARTMENT OF MANUAL MEDICINE
SWEDISH MEDICAL CENTER
ENGLEWOOD, COLORADO

DIRECTOR OF COLORADO INFRARED IMAGING CENTER
SPALDING REHABILITATION HOSPITAL
SWEDISH MEDICAL CENTER
AURORA, COLORADO

FOREWORD BY MIKE MCGETRICK

PEAK PERFORMANCE
PUBLICATIONS

For information contact:
Peak Performance Publications
11290 W. Alameda Avenue
Suite 202-A
Lakewood, Colorado 80226
(303) 985-7565

ISBN: 0-887669-00-0

Cover Design by Shadow Canyon Graphics and Maddog Studio
Interior Design by Shadow Canyon Graphics and Maddog Studio
Cover Photos by Maddog Studio, John Bonath
Interior Photos by Maddog Studio, John Bonath
Models:

> *Mike McGetrick, Head PGA Teaching Professional*
> *David K. Detweiler, Head PGA Teaching Professional*
> *John Golden, Colorado Senior Amateur Player of the Year '93, '95*
> *Kelly Moore, Personal Trainer*
> *Richard Byars, Professional Water Skier*

The trademark Golfercise® is registered in the U.S. Patent and Trademark Office.

Golfercise® Patent Pending (exercise equipment)

THE INFORMATION CONTAINED IN THIS BOOK IS NOT INTENDED AS SUBSTITUTE FOR THE MEDICAL ADVICE OF A TRAINED PROFESSIONAL. THE AUTHOR STRONGLY ADVISES AND RECOMMENDS THAT THE READER CONSULT WITH THEIR HEALTH CARE PROFESSIONAL PRIOR TO ENGAGING IN ANY OF THE EXERCISES OR EXERCISE PROGRAMS CONTAINED IN THIS BOOK TO DETERMINE WHETHER OR NOT THE READER HAS ANY MEDICAL CONDITIONS THAT MAY PREVENT THEM FROM ENGAGING IN ANY OR ALL OF THE EXERCISES DESCRIBED HEREIN.

First Edition
1 2 3 4 5 6 7 8 9

Printed in the United States of America

Dedication

*This book is dedicated to
my Mother and Dad
who, by example, taught me
the virtues of hard work,
to strive for excellence,
to vigorously pursue knowledge,
and to remember to laugh and laugh often.
Through their love this legacy
will be passed on to our children!*

Contents

● ●

● ●

Foreword

• •

by Mike McGetrick

Director of Instruction, Mike McGetrick Golf School, Denver, Colorado
Teaching Professional to some of the nation's top touring players, including: Tom Purtzer,
Gary Hallberg, Brandt Jobe, Meg Mallon, Juli Inkster, Kristi Albers, and Lauri Merten

If you want to improve your game of golf, this book is for you. During my professional teaching career, I have read many books about how to improve this or that aspect of your game, but nothing has hit home like Dr. Tim Conwell's *Golfercise*. In these pages, you really get an in-depth understanding of how muscles work to produce each and every action of the golf swing, from the takeaway to the follow-through.

To my knowledge, this is the first book that addresses a golf-specific strength and conditioning program. Golf instructors and professionals like myself have been hoping that someone like Dr. Conwell would come along to provide us with a series of exercises that would enhance our own training programs, and he has succeeded admirably in *Golfercise*.

I am particularly impressed with Dr. Conwell's attention to details. This is not just some book with a few exercises here and there to get you limbered up to play the game. It gives you specific information that isolates the golf muscles and biomechanics, and it presents this information in an easy-to-follow format. I especially enjoyed the last two chapters, where he gives you the basic top-ten upper- and lower-body routines along with a pre-swing warm-up routine. I like it when a book covers all of the basics, but then goes farther to explain why a certain move is important, and how it affects my game.

I hope I don't even need to say how important it is for every golfer — no matter what your age — to have a golf-specific exercise program. And this is precisely what *Golfercise* does for you. Everyone benefits from the exercises in this book — touring professionals, amateurs, and low handicappers. Don't think that just because you're young, you don't need golf-specific exercise. And if you are a senior golfer, the stretching maneuvers in this book will help you develop the flexibility that you need for better results in your game. The exercise program will improve your power, distance, and accuracy. The Golfercise program will give you the "edge" you have been looking for.

●●●●●●●●●●●●●●●●●●●●●●●●●●●●●●●●●●●●●●

I also like the fact (and here is another way in which Dr. Conwell has paid attention to detail) that certain exercises provide a cautionary statement in case you have a problem with your lower back, or some other concern. The exercises in *Golfercise* will definitely give you the workout that you need to improve your game, but you can also feel comfortable that you won't be doing a movement that might further aggravate any problem area.

In addition to this timely book, Dr. Conwell has developed a unique, patented piece of exercise equipment, also called Golfercise. This equipment is easy to use and gives you the kind of workout you need for a golf-specific strength and conditioning program. It is an advanced piece of equipment, computer designed and engineered, that has been thoroughly researched and proven. You'll learn more about how to use the Golfercise equipment as you work your way through the book. Just one added benefit of becoming involved with Dr. Conwell's golf-specific program.

Because my golf career has taken me virtually all around the world, I would be remiss if I didn't mention the value of this book to golfers everywhere — from the United States, to Europe, to the Pacific Rim countries. Everyone, no matter where they live, can benefit greatly from following Dr. Conwell's golf-specific exercise prescription.

I hope that by picking up this book, reading it, and following its instructions, you will greatly lower your golf scores and, just as important, increase your enjoyment of the game. You simply can't help but enjoy your game more when your body has been warmed up and conditioned properly for all of the moves your muscles are required to make. So — your best bet is to pick up this book and make the most of it. Then, take what you have learned to the golf course and surprise everyone — perhaps even yourself — with your new level of performance.

Acknowledgements

● ●

This book was made possible only by the contributions of many individuals. To write a book such as this one, although undertaken by one person, is in reality bringing together numerous ideas from colleagues, physical trainers, and experts in the field of strength conditioning and rehabilitation, and numerous works by top PGA touring professionals and dedicated teaching PGA instructors. I am most grateful for those who came before me and provided the foundation for this book. Without the hard work of these dedicated professionals, this book would not have been possible.

I wish to express my sincere appreciation and thanks to the following individuals who read the manuscript and made significant contributions in improving the quality of the work. I am most grateful to Bob Leid, whose timely enthusiasm and support were most appreciated during some of the more difficult times in drafting this manuscript. My appreciation to Dr. William Ellender, whose critical critique of the work tremendously improved the chapters on principles. A special thanks to Fred Ramey, who was there at the beginning and who provided tremendous insights, encouragement and assistance. His editorial comments and direction were most valuable.

I owe a special thanks to John Golden, Colorado Senior Amateur Player of the Year '93, '95, who made significant contributions through his in-depth evaluation and critique of the manuscript. I also thank John for spending numerous hours in front of the camera demonstrating some of the stretches in this book. John incorporated the Golfercise program into his workout routine and provided helpful suggestions for improving the routine for the senior player.

I am most indebted to Dave Detweiler, Head PGA Teaching Professional, Raccoon Creek Golf Course, for his friendship, continued support throughout the development of this project, and invaluable recommendations that were instrumental in improving the exercise routines. Dave participated in the initial pilot study in developing the stretches and exercises specific for the golfer. I will always be indebted to him for his contribution to this project.

I wish to express a special appreciation to Mr. Joseph Spoonster. Joseph was kind enough to allow me to utilize the trademark Golfercise. Joseph's father was a touring PGA Professional who taught Joseph the marvelous game of golf.

●●●●●●●●●●●●●●●●●●●●●●●●●●●●●●●●●

Joseph has dedicated much of his life to helping the blind play golf. It is through this work that the trademark Golfercise arose. I will forever be grateful for his willingness to allow this project to bear the trademark of Golfercise.

I wish to express immense appreciation to Mike McGetrick, Head PGA Teaching Professional at the Mike McGetrick Golf School. Mike, being one of the top recognized PGA Teaching Professionals, has been very enthusiastic. Through his encouragement, this work will hopefully improve the games of many golfers. It is most enjoyable to have a top teaching professional with Mike's credentials provide his strong support.

I owe a special thanks to my editor, Dianne Borneman of Shadow Canyon Graphics. Her enthusiasm, technical skills, and encouragement are deeply appreciated. I am also especially indebted to John Bonath, Maddog Studio, who gave his all during a very tight deadline to produce the magnificent photographs used in this book.

It is difficult to express adequately my thanks and appreciation to my office manager, Kerry Koury, who worked diligently on the project from its inception. She worked an inestimable number of hours in transcribing the initial dictations of all of the paragraphs, retyping the numerous chapter edits, and organizing the manuscript for publication. In addition to these activities, she was most valuable in coordinating all of the activities related to completing the book. I am also indebted to her for her editorial suggestions. Without her continued support, marvelous attitude, and uncompromising work ethic, this work would have been impossible. I also wish to express my appreciation to Deb Heisler, my office secretary and technician, who is a most valuable assistant to Kerry and myself.

My deepest appreciation goes to my family, who never complained when I left for the office on numerous Saturdays and Sundays over a four-year period to work on this book. Their understanding was a source of inspiration for me. And finally, I give my thanks to my parents, teachers, and colleagues, who encourage me to strive toward excellence in my field. Without their help and encouragement, this book would never have been written.

About the Author

During the past fifteen years, Dr. Timothy D. Conwell, DC, FACO, has treated hundreds of athletes from professionals to top amateurs and weekend warriors. The sports medicine portion of his private practice focuses on sport-specific biomechanics, sport-specific strength-conditioning programs, and rehabilitation. His primary goal for the athletes under his care is to improve their overall condition so as to maximize their personal performance and reduce the risk of injury. Out of this goal evolved this work.

Dr. Conwell is an Adjunct Clinical Professor at Logan College of Chiropractic in St. Louis, Missouri. He lectures internationally on orthopedics, advanced clinical examination procedures, and case documentation/management. He is the Director of Colorado Infrared Imaging Center, Aurora Presbyterian Hospital. He consults and treats patients with musculoskeletal conditions at the Head Pain and Neurology Center, Department of Manual Medicine, Swedish Medical Center.

Dr. Conwell is board certified in chiropractic orthopedics and medical infrared imaging. He is a Fellow of the Academy of Chiropractic Orthopedists and is recognized as a leader in his field by being honored as a Fellow of the International College of Chiropractors by his peers.

In addition to his private practice and teaching responsibilities, Dr. Conwell has authored numerous journal articles and two texts on clinical examination procedures and case documentation. He has authored a chapter in the well-received *Chiropractic Family Practice*. As part of Dr. Conwell's work as an adjunct clinical professor, he frequently presents postdoctoral continued education courses throughout the United States and Canada.

Dr. Conwell graduated Cum Laude in 1981 from the Logan College of Chiropractic. He holds a Bachelor of Science degree from Ohio State University and conducted postgraduate studies in Microbiology and Microscopic Anatomy at Colorado State University. He served as a member of the Board of Directors of the Colorado Chiropractic Association (honored as the association's Young Chiropractor of the Year) and Colorado's State Delegate to the American Chiropractic Association.

Golf runs in Dr. Conwell's family, and it was due to the fact that he had difficulty over the years beating his own father and brother (a low handicapper) that he decided to find his own "edge." That edge, of course, was evaluating the golf swing to identify the primary muscles used during the four phases of the swing and to develop a golf-specific strength-conditioning and flexibility program. As a result, *Golfercise* became a reality and is proving to be *the edge* for many golfers around the world.

Section I

Introduction

A golf-specific strength and conditioning program is essential for peak performance.

Golfercise : The Missing Link

● ●

Why You Should Read This Book

This book is a fitness guide for all golfers, regardless of your age or level of play. The golf-specific physical-conditioning and training exercises described here will significantly lower the score of the high-handicap golfer and will shave strokes for the more advanced, low-handicap player.

Even players in the professional ranks use conditioning routines to improve their level of performance. This book, and the Golfercise System on which it is based, will teach you how to condition the specific muscles used in proper swing biomechanics. You will learn the stretching and strengthening exercises that will improve your flexibility, endurance, and power.

The muscles that are identified in this book as being active during the four phases of the golf swing are based on research by Frank W. Jobe of the Centinela Medical Center, the official hospital of the PGA and Senior PGA tour, and on research performed in my own clinic. I also gained information by evaluating numerous amateur and low-handicap golfers over my years of practice. By identifying the golf-specific muscles involved in each of the four swing phases, I have developed a sport-specific physical-conditioning and training program to improve your performance and decrease the potential for injury.

Understanding the Biomechanics of the Swing

The first step in establishing an effective and sports specific physical-conditioning and training program for the golfer is to understand the biomechanics of the joints and muscles of the upper and lower body during the swing. We do this by breaking the motion down into four swing phases which are:

1. Takeaway Phase: The takeaway begins when you address the ball and ends at the top of the backswing.
2. Forward Swing Phase: The forward swing begins at initiation of the downswing and ends when the club shaft is horizontal.
3. Acceleration Phase: The acceleration phase begins when the shaft of the club is in the horizontal position during the downswing and ends just after impact with the ball.
4. Follow-through Phase: Follow-through begins after impact with the ball and ends with the club at the top at the end of motion.

The primary muscles, as well as the stabilizing muscles for each swing phase, are identified in this book with clear descriptions of how to stretch and exercise them so that you can improve their flexibility, endurance, and power.

Importance of a Conditioning Program

Physical conditioning and training are prerequisite for any sports participation if you want a high level of performance.

Why should you participate in a stretching and strengthening conditioning program? Although the answer to this question seems obvious, few of the golfers I have treated and observed over the years understand the need to do so. Indeed, most amateur golfers do little or no stretching off the course and, prior to teeing off, generally do only rudimentary stretching, most of which is detrimental to their performance and may even cause injury. If you watch touring professionals on the practice range prior to play, you will rarely, if ever, see them performing a *structured* stretching routine. Yet physical conditioning and training are prerequisite for *any* sports participation if you want a high level of performance. Coaches, athletic trainers, and skilled athletes have recognized for years that improper conditioning, regardless of the sport, lowers your performance level and is one of the major causes of sports injuries.

Golf is not a benign sport. If you do not prepare for play, there is a strong likelihood of injury.

Although most players feel that golf is not a strenuous sport, the golf swing is physically demanding and may be the underlying cause of various types of injuries among both amateurs and professionals. Golf is simply not a benign sport. If you do not prepare for play as other athletes do, there is a strong likelihood of injury. Golf injuries could be greatly reduced or prevented by:

- using a pre-swing warm-up routine
- participating in a golf-specific physical-conditioning program
- utilizing proper swing biomechanics and
- knowing when to stop on the driving range.

Studies on Golf Injuries

The literature on golf injuries is sparse. McCarroll evaluated injuries in 226 male and female professional players through a survey. His results showed that at least 50% of the touring professionals had sustained at least one injury that required them to stop play for an average of three to ten weeks. This study showed that the most common injury sites for the professional were the back, wrist, and shoulder.

McCarroll also evaluated injuries in approximately 1,100 male and female amateur players through questionnaires. The average amateur in this study played about two rounds per week. More than 60% had sustained one or more injuries. The overall incidence of injuries among men and women was essentially the same: men, 62%; women, 61%. Although a slightly higher percentage of injured golfers were over age 50, a significant number of golfers under age 50 (58%) had been injured. The injuries required approximately five weeks for recovery, producing lost playing time. The most common injury site for men was the low back, followed by the elbow, hand, wrist, shoulder, and knee. The most common injury site for women was the left elbow, followed by the low back, shoulder, hand and wrist, and knee. Fewer than 10% of the injuries occurred to the hips, knees, and ankles.

In another study evaluating approximately 400 amateur golfers, Jobe and Yocum found that the back was the most commonly injured area, followed by the shoulder, elbow, and knee. These researchers felt that the primary cause of injury was excessive practice (repetitive strain injuries).

McCarroll found that, in amateurs, low-back pain occurred most frequently during the takeaway (21%) and follow-through (29%) phases. The elbow was the most common site of pain at impact. Injury to the elbow often occurred when taking a divot or using poor swing mechanics. Pain in the outer elbow was five times more prevalent than inner-elbow pain. Despite this fact, injury to the tendons of the outer elbow (lateral epicondylitis) is commonly called "tennis elbow," while injury to the tendons of the inner elbow (medial epicondylitis) is commonly called "golfer's elbow." The primary risk factors among amateur players were low handicap (poor biomechanics) and age (senior players in poor shape). The most frequent cause of injury to the professional was overuse.

The most commonly injured area in men professionals was the low back, followed by the left wrist and left shoulder. Among women professionals, the most commonly injured area was the left wrist, followed by the low back. McCarroll found that there were approximately an equal number of injuries to the left wrist and low back of both men and women professionals. The left hand, shoulder, and knee were injured far less frequently than the wrist and

The primary risk factors among amateur players are low handicap (poor biomechanics) and age (senior players in poor shape).

The most commonly injured area in men professionals is the low back, followed by the left wrist and left shoulder. Among women professionals, the most commonly injured area is the left wrist, followed by the low back.

low back. In addition, the incidence of injuries to the right arm was low in this group. This study suggests that the left side of the body in the right-handed player is far more prone to injury than the right side.

Areas Most Vulnerable to Injury During the Swing Phase

The back, which is a highly vulnerable area for both professionals and amateurs, appears to be most bothersome during the end of the takeaway and follow-through swing phases as well as during putting and chipping. To relieve the back pain that occurs during putting and chipping, try standing in a more erect posture. In addition, do not bend over from the waist to pick your ball out of the cup if you have low-back pain. Instead, bend down with one knee while keeping your back straight when retrieving your ball.

Low-back pain can occur from the twisting at the waist during the takeaway and follow-through phases of the swing. This twisting motion produces considerable stress on the muscles and joints of the low back. This action is exaggerated during the "modern" golf swing when the shoulders turn more than the hip at the end of the follow-through, producing the "C" curve of the low back. If you experience low-back pain, use a more "classic" swing in which your shoulders and hips turn almost equally. If you are an amateur player who experiences low-back pain, try a more upright posture with less hip rotation. This will help to decrease the aggravation and reinjury to an existing low-back condition.

In the takeaway phase, the wrists, right shoulder, left elbow, and low back are high-risk areas for injury. During the acceleration-through-impact phase, the left shoulder and left elbow (predominantly the lateral elbow region) and wrists are common areas of injury. During the follow-through phase, the right elbow and low back are the primary areas for injury. Should you find pain in any of these areas during the four phases of the golf swing, consult your teaching professional. Changes in your swing biomechanics can be very beneficial in decreasing your pain and preventing further injury.

Preventing Injuries

Prevention is of the utmost concern for amateur and professional alike. A pre-swing muscle-and-joint warm-up routine (refer to Chapter 14) is essential in preventing injuries. A warm-up routine prior to hitting balls either on the driving range or at the first tee will greatly reduce the chance of injury and will improve your play. Most amateur golfers—and many professionals—rarely par-

> *In the takeaway phase, the wrists, right shoulder, left elbow, and low back are high-risk areas for injury. During the acceleration-through-impact phase, the left shoulder and left elbow and wrists are common areas of injury. During the follow-through phase, the right elbow and low back are the primary areas for injury.*

ticipate in a structured muscle-and-joint warm-up routine. But if you are to prevent injuries, as well as decrease the degree of exacerbation to existing injuries, a warm-up routine prior to teeing up is essential. A structured sport-specific physical-conditioning program is also essential in preventing injuries (refer to Chapters 11, 12, and 13).

Poor conditioning can lead to injury. When muscles are weak and deconditioned and joints are inflexible, you are prone to injury during any of the four phases of the golf swing. This is particularly true in the major sites of injury, including the low back and left elbow. If the stomach and low-back muscles are weak, they are unable to support the low back during the golf swing. This greatly enhances your chance of injury. Likewise, if the forearm muscles of the left arm are weak, there is a greater tendency toward injuring the tendons of these muscles, which causes "tennis elbow" or "golfer's elbow" of the high-risk left elbow.

Poor swing biomechanics or technique can also lead to injury. Mechanical flaws in your golf swing place undue stresses on the muscles and joints. These stresses often produce injury, particularly when accompanied by poor conditioning and excessive practice. Should you experience continuing pain that does not respond to proper treatment, physical conditioning, and a structured warm-up routine, consult your teaching professional for an evaluation of your swing mechanics, because technique may be causing your continued problems. Making minor changes in your swing mechanics may resolve nagging injuries. This is particularly true if you suffer from chronic low-back pain.

> *To prevent injuries, a warm-up routine prior to teeing up is essential. A structured sport-specific physical-conditioning program is also essential in preventing injuries.*

Treating Injuries

Although some touring professionals who injure their backs require surgery for herniated discs, golf injuries primarily involve the muscles and tendons. These injuries, characterized as strain or sprains, are treated with a basic five-step approach, including: 1) rest, 2) ice (to the area of complaint), 3) compressing the area with an elastic bandage, 4) elevating the area to reduce swelling, and 5) judiciously using over-the-counter anti-inflammatory medication, i.e., aspirin or ibuprofen. This treatment regimen will alleviate most of the pain for the more common golf injuries. If the injury is severe enough, there may be a need for supports or braces to help stabilize the injured area, i.e., low-back corsets, wrist supports, tennis-elbow supports, etc. Should the above-mentioned conservative treatment regimen, including supports, not provide relief of either short- or long-term discomfort, you should consult your doctor for evaluation and treatment.

The Golfercise System

The Golfercise System uses unique, patented exercise equipment that incorporates the revolutionary *progressive resistance* exercise tubing. The Golfercise equipment is specifically designed to stretch and strengthen <u>all</u> the muscles used in golf. Four parts make up this highly efficient exercise unit:

1. Progressive variable resistance exercise tube
2. Exercise handle with exercise tube connectors at:
    position(s) A — ends of handle and
    position B — apex of handle
3. Exercise tube anchor with adjustable strap lock
4. Door hinge anchor

This book divides the golf-specific physical-conditioning and training program into three sections:

1. The systematic golf-specific stretching and strengthening exercises of the upper and lower body.
2. A basic Top-Ten upper- and lower-body physical-conditioning program.
3. A specific pre-swing warm-up routine that is designed to prepare your golf muscles for play.

The objective of this exercise program is to describe specific stretches and exercises for each individual muscle used during the golf swing so that you can achieve and maintain maximum muscular flexibility and strength.

The systematic, golf-specific stretching and strengthening exercises involve all the primary and stabilizing muscles required for proper swing biomechanics during all four swing phases. The objective of this systematic exercise program is to describe specific stretches and exercises for each individual muscle used during the swing so that you can achieve and maintain maximum muscular flexibility and strength. By analyzing your potential weaknesses in each of the four swing phases, you will be able to stretch and exercise specific muscles to help improve upon any specific problems. This book identifies in each muscle section the action of the muscle during each swing phase and clearly describes specific stretching and exercise maneuvers. The stretch section for each muscle includes a description of a self-stretch, a stretch-contract-relax (PNF) technique, and special stretches you can perform with the Golfercise System. The strength exercise for each muscle includes descriptions of exercises for strengthening the specific muscle, including self-exercise and exercises using the Golfercise System (refer to Chapters 11 and 12).

The basic Top-Ten upper- and lower-extremity physical-conditioning program describes ten golf-specific stretches and exercises for the upper and lower body which target the *primary* muscle groups used during the four swing phases. The objective of the Top-Ten exercises is to improve flexibility, endurance, and strength of the most active muscles used during the swing (refer to Chapter 13).

This golf-specific conditioning and training program is designed to be performed on a daily or alternating daily routine to prepare your body optimally for play. Individual exercises from the systematic program can be selectively added to this conditioning program to address any areas of weakness.

If performed consistently, the Top-Ten conditioning exercises should lower your score and decrease your potential for injury. This golf-specific physical-conditioning and training program, accompanied by working on your swing mechanics on the driving range, is the optimal approach to perfecting your game. One will not replace the other. You must perform both routinely if you are serious about lowering your scores and improving your performance.

The basic Top-Ten chapter contains recommendations for the number of exercise repetitions per set and recommendations on stretching routines. The exercise and stretching routines are divided into three levels that correspond to the starting or beginning point for three categories of players.

Level I is designed for the out-of-shape player who is just beginning an exercise program for the first time. This level may also include the injured player beginning the rehabilitation process and the senior player who is inactive.

Level II is designed for the younger player who is in average shape and the senior player who has actively performed the Level I routine for four to eight weeks and is ready to progress to Level II. Level II is designed to increase flexibility, strength, and endurance.

Level III is designed for the player who is in good physical condition from a very physical lifestyle. Level III is also designed for the player who has achieved maximum benefit from Level II. Level III will not only increase flexibility, strength, and endurance, but will enhance rapid strength or the explosive power of your muscles. Level III is not recommended for senior players unless they are very active and in excellent physical condition.

Warm-up procedures prepare you physiologically and psychologically for physical performance. Warming up also greatly reduces the potential for muscle and tendon injuries.

LEVEL	I	II	III

Speed of Contraction
    Concentric (Contract)
    Eccentric (Relax)
	Slow
	Slow
		Slow
		Slow
			Rapid
			Slow

Range of Motion	Short	Full	Full
Resistance	Mild—Moderate	Moderate—Full	Maximum

If used correctly and diligently, the Golfercise System will lower your scores and improve your performance on the course. This guide is the missing link for lowering the score of the low handicapper.

Once you are in good condition from exercising your golf-specific muscles and have developed good swing technique by working on the driving range and applying the techniques taught by your teaching professional, you are ready for the best golf of your life. However, all this conditioning and training can be lost if you don't engage in a pre-swing warm-up routine.

This book provides a seven- to twelve-minute pre-swing warm-up routine that will properly prepare your golf muscles for play (refer to Chapter 14). This routine is not designed to improve overall flexibility, endurance, or power, but rather to prepare your already conditioned and flexible muscles for play. It would seem foolish for any professional athlete to suit up, walk out on the field, and begin play without first warming up. The same is true for any golfer who is serious about his or her performance.

If used correctly and diligently, the Golfercise System will lower your scores and improve your performance on the course. This guide is the *missing link* for lowering the score of the low handicapper. It is vital to improving the performance of the average golfer and a must for any golfer who wishes to reduce injury or lower the chance of aggravating an existing injury.

The conditioning drills in this book are based on sound scientific principles, extensive study of swing biomechanics, and my own clinical experience in treating golfers of all levels of play. I am convinced that if you utilize the methods described in this book, you will very shortly begin to enjoy golf to its fullest, and you also will improve your overall condition. So shake off any pre-existing attitudes about golf and athletics and begin exercising!

REFERENCES

1. Jobe, F. W., D. R. Moyne, and D. J. Antonelli. "Rotator Cuff Function during a Golf Swing." *The American Journal of Sports Medicine*, 1986;14(5):388-392.
2. Pink, M., F. W. Jobe, and J. Perry. "Electromyographic Analysis of the Shoulder during the Golf Swing." *The American Journal of Sports Medicine*, 1990;18(2):137-140.
3. McCarroll J.R., and T.J. Gioe. "Professional Golfers and the Price they Pay." *Physical Sportsmedicine*, 1982;10(7):64-70.
4. McCarroll J.R., A.C. Rettig, and K.D. Shelbourne. "Injuries in the Amateur Golfer." *The Physician and Sportsmedicine*, 1990;18(3):122-126.
5. Jobe, F., L. Yocum. "The Dark Side of Practice." *Golf,* 1988;30(3):22.

Section II

Conditioning Principles

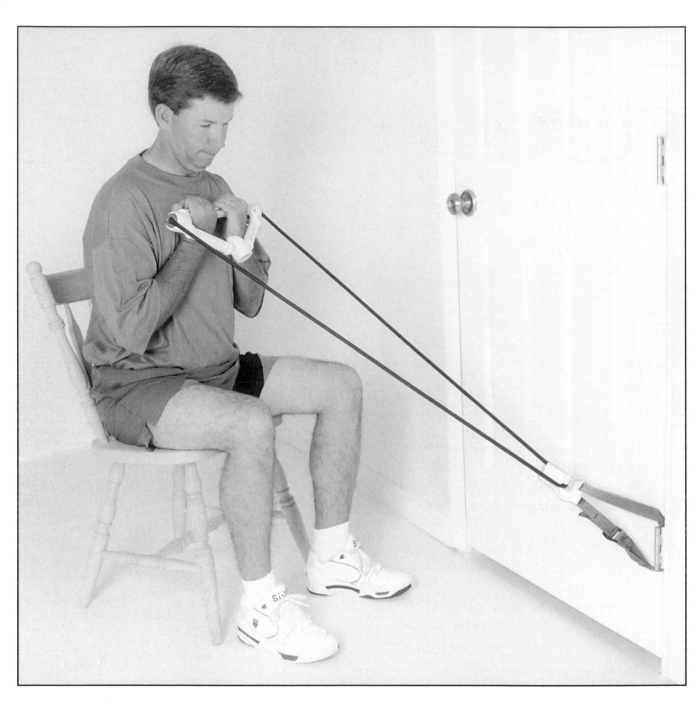

Strengthening your low-back muscles will allow you to play longer and with less discomfort.

Principles of Physical Conditioning

• •

2

Golf, like every other sport, requires you to be in the best possible physical shape in order to reach the top of your game and to avoid injuries. Poor physical conditioning will significantly limit the quality of play, regardless of handicap. But poorly designed and unfocused physical training will not help you avoid high scores or injuries. Only golf-specific routines designed to improve the flexibility, endurance, and strength of the specific joints and muscles used in golf will increase your performance, lower your scores, and lessen your chance for injury.

Successful physical conditioning requires a systematic routine of repetitive and progressive exercise. When you improve your voluntary muscle movement through constant repetition, you also improve your conscious movements so that your golf swing becomes more automatic and consistent. By being in good physical shape, you eliminate unnecessary movements. This will reduce the amount of energy that you must expend during your swing and will improve your endurance noticeably.

The golf-specific routines described in this book have been designed to reach all of these goals by reducing the concentration level required during your swing. This should help you to lower your scores.

In any physical conditioning and training program, certain principles should be followed to ensure maximum benefit and minimize the likelihood of injury. These principles are:

1. Always warm up before exercising and cool down afterwards.
2. You need to maintain a high level of motivation, which is so necessary for consistency.

3. Adhere to consistency, progression, and intensity in your workout. Exercising regularly and consistently is *vital*. You should also steadily increase the workload and the intensity of your exercise to ensure maximum conditioning. It is a mistake to prolong your workout rather than increase the tempo of the workload. This is based on the overload principle, which states that a program must be continually upgraded in workload to produce maximum results.

4. Make your workout specific and individual for your sport, and set concrete conditioning and training goals *prior* to beginning your program. Each specific muscle and joint used during each phase of your golf swing should be conditioned and trained.

5. Practice safety first. Your conditioning and training routine, as well as your workout environment, should be as safe as possible.

Warming Up

Most physicians, trainers, and exercise physiologists recommend warm-up procedures prior to beginning an exercise routine. The same is true of a cool-down routine. Warm-up procedures prepare you physiologically and psychologically for physical performance. Warming up also greatly reduces the potential for muscle and tendon injuries.

The main purpose of warming up is to raise both the general-body and deep-muscle temperatures by increasing the amount of blood flow to the muscles, tendons, and ligaments. For each degree of internal temperature rise, there is a corresponding rise in the metabolism rate by approximately 13 percent. With higher muscle temperature, more oxygen is pulled into the muscle tissue and the speed of nerve impulses to the muscle is increased. Both of these metabolic factors increase the work capacity—or *contractibility*—of the muscle, which improves the overall muscle performance.

The time required for a satisfactory warm-up routine varies from golfer to golfer and tends to increase with age. Generally speaking, a gradual, 7- to 12-minute warm-up routine is required to bring the body to a state of readiness prior to approaching the first tee-shot or practicing on the driving range. Like your exercise regimen, your warm-up routine should be specific for each individual athletic event in which you are involved. Your golf warm-up or pre-swing routine should be tailored to increase blood flow and flexibility to the specific muscles utilized in the golf swing (refer to Chapter 14). As a rule of thumb, you have achieved proper body and muscle temperature when you break into a mild sweat. If you are sweating lightly, your muscles are prepared to perform strenuous exercise.

> *Warm-up procedures prepare you physiologically and psychologically for physical performance.*

> *Your golf warm-up or pre-swing routine should be tailored to increase blood flow and flexibility to the specific muscles utilized in the golf swing.*

For the golfer, a formal warm-up includes 1) increasing heart rate, 2) stretching the golf muscles, and 3) briefly exercising them until they are ready to play (refer to Chapter 14). The extent of your warm-up will depend on your age and overall performance requirements, but every golfer's warm-up should be intense enough to produce a mild sweat without causing fatigue. And remember not to allow any significant lag period before teeing-off or heading to the driving range, because the effects of warming up wear off quickly. I recommend no more than 15 minutes between the completion of the warm-up routine and play. The shorter the time, the better, and it should be decreased on cooler days.

Begin your warm-up routine with general warm-up exercises—such as calisthenics, walking, or stair climbing—followed by flexibility maneuvers that improve the range of motion of your joints and increase your muscle length. Following the flexibility exercises, turn to your formal, golf-specific warm-up exercises.

The following benefits are generally associated with a proper warm-up routine:

1. Increased body and muscle temperature.
2. Increased blood flow to the active muscles.
3. Increased heart rate, which will improve cardiovascular function.
4. Increased metabolic rate, which will improve muscle function and endurance.
5. Increased body temperature, which will increase the speed at which nerve impulses travel, thereby improving muscle activity.
6. Decreased muscle tension.
7. Improved muscle and tendon extensibility.
8. Improved joint mobility.
9. Enhanced individual performance.

> *Every golfer's warm-up should be intense enough to produce a mild sweat without causing fatigue. And remember not to allow any significant lag period before teeing-off or heading to the driving range, because the effects of warming up wear off quickly.*

Perform your golf warm-up or pre-swing routine (refer to Chapter 14) immediately before every round. This is defined as a planned, deliberate, regular program of exercises that are done immediately before the round. The pre-swing routine is not designed to improve your overall flexibility, endurance, or strength, but it will provide improved flexibility of both muscles and joints during the round. This, in and of itself, will lower your score. I guarantee it!

Cooling Down

Following the round or after a driving-range session, there should be a cooling down period. The cool-down consists of a group of stretches and mild exercises performed immediately after play that provides the body a period of adjustment from exercise to rest. A cool-down routine also aids in improving flexibility. Your cool-down routine should be designed to diminish the work intensity gradually, which will allow for return of circulation and various body functions to pre-exercise levels. However, the main objectives with the cool-down routine are to increase muscle relaxation, to promote the removal of waste materials (lactic acid) from the muscles, and to reduce muscle soreness. The cool-down may not be as important following your golf round but may play a role following a strenuous session on the driving range.

I believe that golfers should stretch during the cool-down and perform mild, specific exercises involving the major muscle groups used during play so as to decrease muscle soreness and maintain flexibility. I recommend that your cool-down routine include the stretches and exercises of the pre-swing warm-up routine (refer to Chapter 14), only decreasing the time and intensity.

Intensity

Besides your genetic make-up, the intensity of your workout is the most important factor in obtaining maximum results from a strength-training program. To exercise effectively, you should apply the *overload principle* by constantly challenging your muscles with systematic increases in the workload they perform. Simply repeating your exercise routine without increasing the weight or resistance is of little value and will do nothing to increase your strength or improve your game. Instead, you should constantly upgrade your exercises to a higher level of achievement by progressively lifting, pulling, or pushing against a greater resistive force or by moving the force at an increased rate of speed—trying always to approach your maximum effort. This will improve your endurance, strength, and power of your muscles and will aid in improving muscle coordination. Utilizing the overload principle is as necessary in a golf exercise program as any other sport conditioning program. Use of the Golfercise System, by increasing the resistance and repetition speed, will greatly increase your endurance and strength.

In any strength-conditioning program, there is a level of intensity below which little or no improved strength occurs. The problem is in knowing what the minimum level of intensity is to produce an increase in muscle growth. For maximum response, the appropriate level of intensity during an exercise program should be 100 percent. Some trainers erroneously believe that 100 percent intensity can be achieved by increasing the number of sets or the number of exercises or the frequency of the workouts. Although at first glance this appears reasonable, I believe that this produces negative returns.

There is an inverse relationship between the length of the workout and the intensity of the workout. As the number of repetitions increases or the length

Besides your genetic make-up, the intensity of your workout is the most important factor in obtaining maximum results from a strength training program.

of the exercise activity increases, the intensity of the workout decreases. And as the intensity of the workout decreases, the maximum obtainable results from the workout also are decreased. Any golfer who has stayed too long on the driving range is familiar with this phenomenon. Continuing to hit balls down the driving range after your golf muscles have fatigued will fail to improve your conditioning and strength and often will result in negatively altering your swing.

Real intensity occurs over a short period of time. When you have exercised to the point of momentary muscular failure whereby the weight or resistive force can no longer be moved through further repetitions, then the exercise has stimulated the maximum number of muscle fibers for growth. Such intensity increases strength and power. This type of exercise occurs by continually fatiguing more muscle fibers during the exercise repetitions to the point where no further muscle fibers are available to generate enough force to complete the repetition. At the point of muscle failure, during the final repetition, the level of intensity is near maximal, or 100 percent, which stimulates growth of as many muscle fibers as possible to increase muscle strength.

So, to achieve maximum results in a strength-conditioning program, you should work the target muscle to fatigue or near fatigue by increasing the resistive force rather than by increasing the number of repetitions, the frequency of your workouts, or the number of exercises you perform. The same principle is true regardless of age or sex. Spending hours on the driving range will not bring you to 100 percent intensity. Specific golf muscles need to be strengthened by performing specific exercises that are strenuous enough to produce momentary muscular failure toward the end of the workout. This is what the Golfercise System is designed to do. Remember—in order to be successful with your physical conditioning and training program, you must give your best effort!

The simple fact that the results from any strength-conditioning program are directly related to the effort put in to the program should be of no surprise. Increasing strength and power requires hard work, just as honing the swing skills requires hours of practice. It is important to remember that a high level of intensity is a requirement for optimal gains in a strength-conditioning program.

In addition to the overload principle, there are other tenets to which you should adhere during your strength-conditioning program, whether the program utilizes exercise equipment, free weights, or resistive exercise tubing (as does the Golfercise System). By following these principles, you can maximize the return from your strength-training program and ensure a safe, efficient, productive, and comprehensive workout.

> *To achieve maximum results in a strength-conditioning program, work the target muscle to fatigue or near fatigue by increasing the resistive force rather than by increasing the number of exercises you perform.*

> *Specific golf muscles need to be strengthened by performing specific exercises that are strenuous enough to produce momentary muscular failure toward the end of the workout. This is what the Golfercise System is designed to do.*

Progression

Progression should be slow and steady so as not to cause injury to soft tissues.

As the overload principle implies, your strength-training program should be designed to progress in both weight and number of repetitions. Increase the resistance or number of repetitions if muscle fatigue is not accomplished during your workout. The progression should be slow and steady so as not to cause injury to soft tissues. I generally recommend 5 to 10 percent increments in a two-week period when utilizing free weights or exercise equipment.

Repetitions (Reps)

A good rule of thumb is 8 to 12 repetitions per exercise per set, with larger muscles requiring a few more repetitions.

Repetitions are the number of specific muscle exercises performed per set. Contrary to the opinions of some weight trainers, there is no conclusive evidence to indicate that few repetitions with high weight will produce increased muscle strength, bulk, and tone. An increase in strength, bulk, and tone is directly related to the exerciser's genetic makeup and to the overload principle. This being the case, what is a recommended number of repetitions per exercise? Research indicates that larger muscles need to be exercised for a longer time than small muscles in order to build muscle strength and power. The range is anywhere from 120 seconds for larger muscles to 40 seconds for smaller ones.

We can use this range to establish the number of repetitions per muscle group to better your golf swing. If a repetition takes approximately 5 to 6 seconds, then for the larger muscle groups, 15 to 20 reps are required, and 6 to 12 reps are required for the smaller muscle groups. A good rule of thumb is 8 to 12 repetitions per exercise per set, with larger muscles requiring a few more repetitions.

Sets

I generally recommend between one and three sets, with the last set reaching muscular fatigue.

A set is the group of repetitions for each exercise performed for a specific muscle before resting. The number of sets that should be performed with each exercise is somewhat controversial. Opinions range from one to five sets per exercise. Remember that if only one set of each exercise is used, *but maximum effort or muscle fatigue is reached,* you will achieve your goal of increased strength. I generally recommend between one and three sets, with the last set reaching muscular fatigue. If muscular fatigue is not reached on the third set, then the amount of the resistance should be increased.

Weight

The amount of weight necessary to increase strength and power is directly related to the weight necessary to produce muscular fatigue within a certain number of repetitions per exercise. If muscular fatigue occurs before the recommended 8 to 12 repetition range, the weight should be reduced. And vice versa: if the weight does not produce muscular fatigue at 8 to 12 repetitions, the weight should be increased. This is based on the recommended repetitions per size of the muscle group being exercised. It may take you a few exercise sessions to establish the weight appropriate for each of your exercises.

Form

Proper form is essential for increased strength and to reduce the potential for injury. The weight or resistance should be moved in a deliberate, slow, and controlled manner. This will ensure that your muscle, rather than momentum, does the work. Good form will also protect against injury. It is generally recommended that you raise the weight or resistive tubing more quickly than you lower it, but lowering the weight should not be neglected either. The same muscles that raised the weight are also used to lower it. By emphasizing and slowing the rate of lowering the weight or resistive tubing of the Golfercise System during each repetition, the exercise becomes more efficient, thereby increasing the rate of muscular fatigue or intensity. I recommend that you exercise throughout the full range of motion to ensure that flexibility is maintained and not decreased. This is particularly true for golfers, who require good flexibility of the hips and shoulders. By maintaining good flexibility of the joint, flexibility of the muscle is also improved.

> *By emphasizing and slowing the rate of lowering the weight or resistive tubing of the Golfercise System during each repetition, the exercise becomes more efficient, thereby increasing the rate of muscular fatigue or intensity.*

Duration

There is an inverse relationship between the intensity of a workout and the duration of the workout. As the length of the exercise program increases, the intensity decreases, thereby reducing your ability to reach the muscular fatigue necessary to improve strength and power. The time or duration of a workout depends upon many factors, including the type of equipment, the number of exercises, the time between each exercise set, etc. However, generally speaking, a 30- to 45-minute workout is considered more productive than an hour to an hour-and-a-half workout. Conceivably, you could perform a golf-specific exercise routine in as little as 20 to 30 minutes. This time frame can be achieved by

> *There is an inverse relationship between the intensity of a workout and the duration of the workout.*

using the Golfercise System. The time between each exercise will vary, depending on your level of conditioning and the type of equipment you are using. A general rule is to be able to "catch your breath" or feel that you are ready to enter the next exercise and reach the maximum level of effort or muscular fatigue. A good average appears to be approximately 1 to 3 minutes of recovery time between exercise sets. However, remember to proceed to the next exercise within a minimal amount of recovery time to ensure maximum return from the conditioning routine.

Volume

The golf-specific workout consists of approximately 10 to 20 exercises for both the upper and lower body.

The golf-specific workout consists of approximately 10 to 20 exercises for both the upper and lower body. For certain sports, fewer exercises are required; other sports require more. Because we use numerous muscle groups in performing the golf swing, the total number of exercises for a golfer will be more than for athletes who use fewer fine motor or smaller muscle groups in the performance of their activity. The number of exercises should be tailored for the specific sports event the athlete is performing. This book details specific exercises for the golf muscles required during the golf swing (refer to Chapters 11, 12, and 13).

Sequence

It is important to work from the larger muscles to the smaller muscles in any exercise routine.

It is important to work from the larger muscles to the smaller muscles in any exercise routine. The golfer, for example, should exercise the lower-extremity muscles—including the hips and legs—before moving to the trunk, shoulders, and arms. Never exercise your arms before exercising your upper trunk, and don't exercise your legs before exercising your buttocks. Remember the proper sequence if you hope to maintain maximum strength, improve your swing, and diminish the possibility of injury.

Frequency

Finally, the frequency with which you perform the exercises in your strength-training program is very important. If you exercise too frequently, the chance for injury is greatly increased, and if you exercise too infrequently, your ability to achieve maximum performance is diminished. It is recommended that strength training be performed a maximum of three times per week with a day off between exercising. The muscles require a 48- to 72-hour recovery period between workouts in order to improve their strength. It should be noted that a stretching or flexibility routine does not require a day off and that no more than four days should go by without returning to your exercise program. Any longer period will cause the muscles to become progressively weak. This is one reason why it is important to continue your physical conditioning and training program during the off season. I also recommend that you reduce the intensity of your workouts during the season.

In order for the dedicated golfer to achieve optimal performance on the course, physical conditioning and strength training are an absolute must. Physical conditioning should be thought of as a means to an end: improving performance and reducing the risk of injury. Think of the hours spent on the practice range and putting green trying to lower your scores. The time spent practicing will be more beneficial if you are in shape, particularly if your golf-specific muscles are toned-up, flexible, and strong. Practice and conditioning go hand-in-hand. You cannot achieve your own maximum level of performance without doing both. Golf, like other sports, demands good physical conditioning to be successful.

> *Remember that it is important to continue your physical conditioning and training program during the off season.*

> *Golf demands good physical conditioning to be successful.*

19

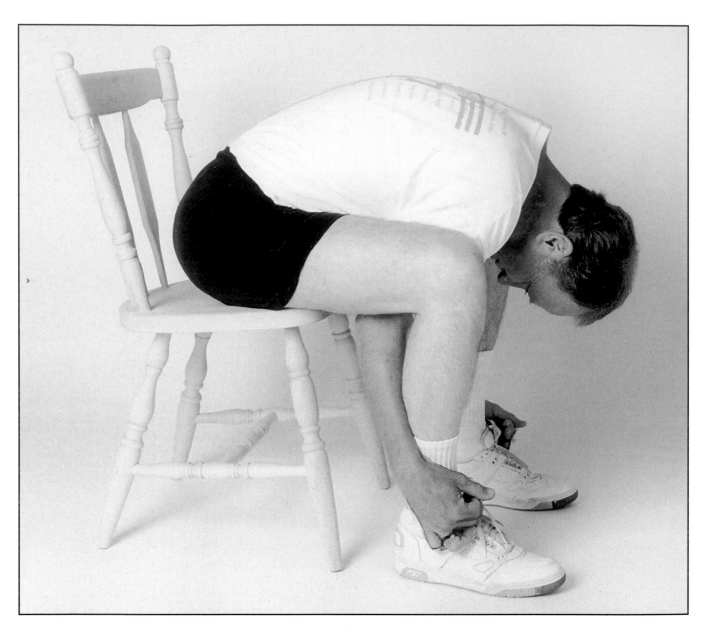

You will improve your performance by increasing your flexibility.

Basic Principles of Stretching

3

●●●●●●●●●●●●●●●●●●●●●●●●●●●●●●●● **Flexibility**

Stretching is an essential part of any physical-conditioning program. Stretching exercises increase joint and muscle flexibility. Flexibility is defined as the range of motion of a specific joint or group of joints which is dependent upon the integrity of the muscles, tendons, ligaments, bones, and other soft tissues that surround the joint. Increasing the flexibility or range of motion for the specific joints used in the golf swing will enhance your golf performance. Studies have also shown that by increasing the range of motion of any joint, you also decrease the extent and severity of injuries.

The range of motion (ROM) of any joint can be measured in linear units (inches or centimeters) or in angular units (degrees). Every joint in the body has a normal range of motion. That is to say that the amount or degree of ROM for each joint or set of joints may be dissimilar. Normal ROM of the hip does not ensure normal ROM of the shoulder. Similarly, normal ROM of the right hip does not ensure normal ROM of the left hip.

Good flexibility indicates that there are no adhesions or abnormalities of the soft tissue (muscles, ligaments, or tendons) in or around the joint and that there are no muscular limitations (tight, stiff, or shortened). Good flexibility allows the joint to move freely and easily through the full ROM in any direction without restriction.

In golf, as in other sports, good flexibility is important for good play. Good flexibility also increases your ability to avoid injuries. If you have poor shoulder movement or decreased trunk and hip rotation, you will be significantly limited in your ability to swing the club properly. I believe that flexibility is just as important for optimal performance as either endurance or strength. The "tight" or inflexible golfer is unable to compete with the more flexible golfer, regardless of his or her overall endurance or strength.

Flexibility is defined as the ability to perform movements over a wide range of motion. Flexibility has two components: joint mobility and stretchability. Joint mobility refers to the degree a joint is able to move through its normal range of motion. Stretchability refers to the ability of muscles, tendons, and ligaments (as well as the joint capsules) to achieve normal range of motion. ROM is dependent upon joint motion or freedom within the joint; the stretchability of the muscles, tendons, and ligaments; and the strength of the muscles that move the joint.

Flexibility is influenced by numerous external factors. Increasing age decreases joint mobility and stretchability due to chemical and structural changes in the muscles, tendons, and joints. The aging process also leads to a decrease in the elasticity of all physiological structures. Although there is conflicting evidence on the relationship between age and flexibility, consensus is that flexibility tends to level off during adolescence. Research shows that maximum flexibility and stretchability occur between the ages of 7 and 11. By the age of 15, flexibility begins to decrease gradually over time. Flexibility *can be* increased at any age, given the appropriate training, but the rate of improvement will not be the same at every age, nor will the potential for improvement. By age 50, there is a significant drop in joint mobility and stretchability.

Research also reveals that a stretching program becomes increasingly important for all athletes beginning in their early twenties and continuing throughout life. If a young athlete begins a strict stretching program in early adolescence and maintains it throughout his or her life, the natural tendency toward decreased flexibility and mobility of the joints and muscles over time will be significantly altered. It is important, therefore, to continue to stretch throughout your life and for younger golfers to maintain a strict stretching routine to ensure continued flexibility.

It is never too late to begin a stretching routine to increase your flexibility. Evidence suggests that even senior golfers can achieve tremendous gains in flexibility and can improve joint ROM and muscle stretchability by engaging in a daily stretching program. However, the longer you wait to start some type of stretching program, the more difficult it will be to improve or maintain your flexibility. The goal of a flexibility training program is not solely to improve range of motion and muscle stretchability, but also to help prevent loss of ROM or muscle stretchability as you age.

To obtain the maximum benefits from a stretching program, you must know and understand the specific muscles involved in the golf swing and the specific joints that interplay with proper golf biomechanics. Once you have a working knowledge of the primary joints and muscles used in the swing, you

> *It is never too late to begin a stretching routine to increase your flexibility. However, the longer you wait to start some type of stretching program, the more difficult it will be to improve or maintain your flexibility.*

> *To obtain maximum benefits from a stretching program, you must know and understand the specific muscles involved in the golf swing and the specific joints that interplay with proper golf biomechanics.*

can develop your own golf-specific stretching program. A stretching program is defined as a planned, deliberate, and regular program of stretching exercises that can permanently and progressively increase the range of motion of a joint or set of joints over time. A golf-specific stretching program is discussed in Chapters 11 and 12.

Stretching techniques have evolved over the years. Most stretching routines include one of the following basic stretching maneuvers with special stretching exercises and drills: 1) ballistic stretching, 2) static stretching, and 3) proprioceptive neuromuscular facilitation (PNF), or stretch-contract-relax stretching maneuvers.

Ballistic Stretching

Ballistic stretching techniques use repetitive bouncing, bobbing, rebounding, and/or rhythmic motion. This form of stretching is an outdated method that may even be dangerous, because you may easily exceed the extensible limits of your muscles when bouncing or bobbing. Ballistic stretching should certainly be avoided in sedentary individuals. However, in the *highly trained* athlete, ballistic stretching will conceivably improve and develop dynamic flexibility, which is important to the golf swing.

It is reasonable to argue that ballistic stretching should be discontinued due to its potential for causing tissue damage. It potentially stretches the athlete's muscles too rapidly, which gets in the way of developing long-term flexibility. Research shows that permanent lengthening or flexibility occurs during lower-force, longer-duration stretching, which cannot be achieved by ballistic maneuvers. In addition, ballistic stretching on occasion has been shown to strain or rupture muscles, tendons, and ligaments. Each of these injuries will result in pain and decreased ROM, rather than increasing flexibility, which is what your stretching routine should do for you.

Another reason why I feel ballistic stretching should be avoided is that it generates uncontrollably large amounts of angular momentum. When a stretch is performed rapidly, the tendon and joint reach their limit or end range suddenly, with the angular momentum often exceeding the absorption capacity of the muscle and tendon being stretched. This, too, may cause injury. This kind of tendon-ligament damage occurs when you place the club behind both of your arms and rapidly rotate your torso. This is the kind of ballistic stretching often seen with amateur golfers prior to teeing off. I believe that this particular stretching maneuver should be discontinued so as not to injure the chest and stomach muscles, tendons, ligaments, or the shoulder joint capsule. This maneuver also will aggravate a golfer's low-back problems.

I recommend that the amateur golfer avoid all forms of ballistic stretching. The possibility of injury is just too great. Passive static or stretch-contract-relax (PNF) techniques are much less hazardous and produce greater benefits.

Another concern is that a muscle that is suddenly stretched initiates a reflex action that produces a muscle contraction. As a result of this muscle contraction, the stretch capability of the exercise is decreased greatly. In short, the rapidity of the stretching defeats the purpose of improving flexibility by causing involuntary muscle contraction. Optimal stretching cannot be achieved unless the muscle is totally relaxed.

I recommend that the amateur golfer avoid *all* forms of ballistic stretching. The possibility of injury is just too great. Passive static or stretch-contract-relax (PNF) techniques are much less hazardous and produce greater benefits.

Passive Static Stretching

This is the more popular form of stretching due to its greater effectiveness and decreased risk of producing injury. I recommend passive static stretching because 1) it requires less energy expenditure than ballistic stretching, 2) it appears to decrease muscle soreness, and 3) it is believed to provide greater flexibility over time.

Passive static stretching involves passively stretching a given muscle by placing it in the maximum stretch position and holding it there for a specific period of time. I recommend holding the stretch anywhere from 3 seconds to as long as 60 seconds, depending on the flexibility and size of the muscle being stretched. Although the data appears inconclusive, there is a consensus that holding most stretches for approximately 20 seconds is optimal. The passive static stretch should be repeated three to four times for approximately 20 seconds to optimize the stretching effect on the muscle and joint.

In order to obtain optimal benefit from passive static stretching techniques, you should adhere to the following principles:

1. Static stretching should be performed only after a "general" warm-up and before engaging in any vigorous exercise activity.
2. Use static stretching techniques following any vigorous activity during the cooling-down routine.
3. Begin with "easy-stretch" holding for approximately 5 to 20 seconds, which produces mild muscle tension and relaxation.
4. During the stretch, *focus* on the muscle being stretched.
5. Follow the easy stretch with a more progressive stretch, holding for approximately 20 to 30 seconds. This depends on the size of the muscle. The larger the muscle, the longer the stretch should be held.
6. Continue to breathe in a slow, relaxed, and rhythmic manner while stretching.

> *Passive static stretching requires less energy than ballistic stretching, it appears to decrease muscle soreness, and it is believed to provide greater flexibility over time.*

7. At all costs, *avoid pain* during the stretching period; any pain is an indicator that you are overdoing the maneuver and injuring the tissues.
8. Perform each static stretching routine a minimum of 1 to 3 times every other day for maximum benefit. If you are experiencing a significant restriction of ROM, you may stretch on a daily basis until normal or near-normal ROM has been attained. Remember that stretching with pain will not only decrease the rate of increased motion, but may actually decrease your flexibility due to injury.

> *Avoid pain during the stretching period. Pain indicates that you are overdoing the maneuver and are injuring the tissues.*

Stretch-Contract-Relax (PNF) Stretching

The third type of stretching technique is called proprioceptive neuromuscular facilitation (PNF), or stretch-contract-relax technique. Stretch-contract-relax techniques are the most efficient and the preferred method utilized in a stretching program designed to improve flexibility. Stretch-contract-relax maneuvers involve alternating muscle contractions with static stretching of both the muscle being stretched (agonist) and the muscle that counteracts the action of the stretching muscle (antagonist). If the biceps muscle is being stretched (agonist), for instance, the triceps muscle is the counteracting muscle (antagonist).

The benefits of PNF include the largest gains produced in muscle flexibility, increased strength, increased muscle balance, and stability of the joint. Like many physicians and trainers, I believe that stretch-contract-relax maneuvers improve endurance, increase blood circulation, enhance coordination, and allow superior relaxation of the muscle being stretched. Following a PNF stretching session, there is a greater ease of passive motion. When employed properly, PNF will certainly improve your flexibility, especially the dynamic flexibility of the muscles used in your golf swing.

This technique is not, however, without some disadvantages. In some individuals, this technique may be uncomfortable or even painful. If not performed properly, or if overdone, PNF may injure the muscles, causing increased muscle soreness and decreased flexibility. However, the likelihood of this is remote if you use correct techniques. Patients with high blood pressure should consult their physicians prior to performing stretch-contract-relax exercises.

Stretch-contract-relax stretching techniques involve a combination of isometric, isotonic, and static-stretch techniques. Numerous combinations are often used in performing PNF stretching techniques. All PNF combinations alter the contraction and relaxation of the agonist and antagonist muscles. PNF stretching exercises rely upon a 5- to 10-second stretch, followed by a 5- to 10-second pushing phase (contraction), which, in turn, is followed by a 5- to 10-

> *When employed properly, the stretch-contract-relax technique will improve your flexibility, especially the dynamic flexibility of the muscles used in your golf swing.*

second relaxation phase. Each of these techniques requires some form of assistance—either a partner, a stationary object, or exercise tubing like that used in the Golfercise System. The following are a few of the more beneficial stretch-contract-relax techniques.

Contract-relax techniques are used to improve flexibility but should be used with caution.

1. **Contract-relax technique.** This technique involves a maximum isotonic contraction of the muscle to be stretched (antagonist) followed by a 5- to 10-second period of relaxation. Next, the muscle is passively stretched to its limitations. This process is then repeated. Contract-relax techniques are used to improve flexibility (range of motion), but should be used with caution, because there is a chance of injury due to the gradual increase of tension within the muscle.

2. **Hold-relax technique.** This technique involves an isometric contraction of the involved muscle followed by a 5-second period of relaxation. The muscle is then moved against minimal resistance through the newly gained range to a new point of limitation. This technique is effective when ROM has decreased because of muscle tightness on one side of a joint or muscle imbalance.

3. **Stretch-contract-relax technique.** This technique involves stretching the involved muscle to limit without pain, holding for 5 to 10 seconds, followed by an isometric (static) muscle contraction of 5 to 10 seconds with a 5-second period of relaxation. This process is then repeated. I recommend this technique, because it produces maximum gains in flexibility. The Golfercise System is designed to enable you to perform this technique alone; otherwise you will need a partner. For specific stretch-contract-relax stretch exercises, see Chapters 11 and 12.

Stretch-contract-relax techniques produce a greater increase in range of motion than other methods.

All three stretching techniques (ballistic, static, and stretch-contract-relax), if performed correctly, will improve muscle and joint flexibility. I have found that stretch-contract-relax techniques produce a greater increase in ROM than the other methods. Even during one stretching session, dramatic increases in flexibility may occur. PNF is unique in that, by using this method during play, you can make minor improvements in your flexibility and decrease your stiffness.

Studies have shown that PNF stretching is capable of producing greater improvement and flexibility over an extended training period than either ballistic or static techniques. Today, PNF is considered the stretching technique of choice by most athletic trainers in order to achieve maximum joint mobility and muscle flexibility.

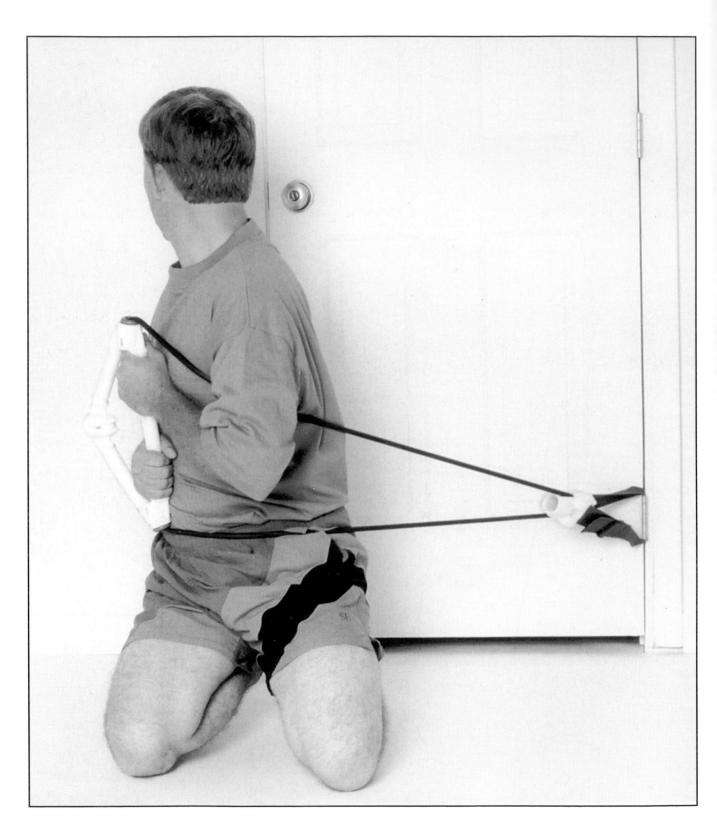

Strengthening the golf muscles can only be done with exercise.

Principles of Exercise

4

S winging a golf club accurately, aggressively, and consistently for 18 holes is very demanding and requires the golf muscles to be well conditioned. Some players pretend that hitting a bucket of balls on the driving range prior to playing a round is all that is needed for golf fitness. *This is simply not the case.* When you strike the golf ball correctly, you generate distance through the power of the major muscle groups of, primarily, the legs, the hips, and the trunk. Hitting hundreds of golf balls on the driving range will not provide the optimal power and strength of specific muscles required for good play. Strengthening the golf-specific muscles requires working out or exercising those muscles through a specific physical-conditioning and training program.

To maintain proper swing mechanics through your entire round, you also need to develop endurance, not only of the leg and hip muscles, but of the trunk, the shoulder, and the arm muscles as well. Endurance cannot be maximally achieved just by play or by practicing on the range! You must make a concerted effort to improve the stamina and strength of your golf-specific muscles by actively engaging in a well-designed exercise program. By utilizing the golf-specific strengthening and endurance conditioning exercises described in Chapters 11, 12, and 13, you will lower your handicap, enjoy the game more, and, as an added bonus, improve your overall physical condition and health.

Conditioning Principles

Prior to beginning any golf endurance and strength-conditioning program, it is important to understand the basic principles of conditioning and exercise. The musculoskeletal system is basically a lever system made of bones, joints, and muscles. Movement of the joints is produced by contraction of the muscles, each of which comprises several thousand muscle fibers. You have more than 600 muscles in your body that work to move your joints and extremities, including 19 separate muscles in your forearms alone. In fact, the muscles of the body account for 40 to 50 percent of your total body weight, making them collectively, by far, the largest organ in your body. The muscles, of course, play a vital role in determining performance for any sport. This is particularly true for golf, although not until recently has this been generally recognized and accepted.

The muscle contains a muscle "belly," with adjoining tendons at each end that anchor in the bone. The muscle is made up of numerous muscle fibers composed of contractile elements. It is through these contractile elements— called sarcomeres—that the muscle lengthening and shortening occurs which develops muscle force and strength. It is well known that by increasing the muscle diameter through exercise, the overall strength and endurance of the muscle will be increased. An increase in muscle girth or diameter occurs by an increase in both the size of the muscle fibers and the number of blood vessels in the muscle. This is accomplished only through strength conditioning and training. Proper biomechanics of the golf swing require agility, endurance, strength, and power, none of which can be gained without conditioning and training the golf-specific muscles that produce the smooth, rhythmic swing.

Muscles have basically two types of muscle fibers: the slow-twitch fiber (fiber type I or red fibers) and the fast-twitch fiber (fiber type II or white fibers). The slow-twitch fibers have a slow rate of contraction. These fibers, which use oxygen and glucose for their metabolism, are characterized as "aerobic" fibers. Slow-twitch fibers have high resistance to fatigue and are more prevalent in athletes who perform in endurance events such as cycling, long-distance running, and cross-country skiing. Fast-twitch fibers have a high rate of contraction and use fats rather than oxygen for their energy source. These fibers are characterized as "anaerobic" fibers. Fast-twitch fibers have low resistance to fatigue and are more prevalent in athletes who participate in events that require strength, explosive movements, and rapid changes of direction. These are generally considered ball-sport activities. The golfer utilizes both types of fibers (aerobic and anaerobic) during play.

The golfer can increase either of the slow- or fast-twitch fibers within his or her muscles by choosing the correct training program. A low-intensity conditioning program will develop slow-twitch fibers but will not adequately develop strength or recruit fast-twitch fibers. It is important to remember that the more specific the conditioning program, the more specific the type of muscle-fiber development the athlete will accomplish. The golfer utilizes both types of fibers but requires a larger preponderance of fast-twitch fibers for power and strength during the downswing and acceleration swing phases.

Some players pretend that hitting a bucket of balls on the driving range prior to playing a round is all that is needed for golf fitness. This is simply not the case. Strengthening the golf-specific muscles requires working out or exercising those muscles through a specific physical-conditioning and training program.

By using the golf-specific exercises described in Chapters 11, 12, and 13, you will lower your handicap, enjoy the game more, and improve your overall physical condition.

Although it is important to maintain development of slow-twitch muscle fibers for endurance, a golf-specific conditioning program certainly should incorporate specific exercises that develop the fast-twitch muscle fibers necessary for power and speed.

Muscle strength is necessary for agility (the ability to make rapid and coordinated movements) and for power (the ability of a muscle to contract with speed and strength). Agility is essential to proper swing biomechanics, and power plays an important role in the acceleration swing phase, when large amounts of force are generated quickly. If you are unable to generate power during the acceleration swing phase, you will have less distance off the tee and have greater difficulty with shots out of the rough and sand traps.

Depending on the type of force and duration of the training program you use, you can develop three types of strength: maximal strength, rapid strength, and endurance strength. Maximal strength is the greatest possible force that can be voluntarily opposed to a resistance, or, in other words, the maximum strength of the muscle. This strength is dependent upon the diameter of the muscle and the intramuscular coordination. The greater the diameter and the coordination, the higher the maximal strength. Muscle diameter, or its cross-section, is determined by the number and thickness of the muscle fibers. Intramuscular coordination is dependent on the nerves, which "talk" to the muscle, and it has a strong genetic basis. The maximal strength of a muscle is achieved when *all* of the individual muscle fibers within the muscle contract simultaneously.

Rapid strength refers to the ability to produce force at a given time instantaneously and to maintain this force through the range of motion. It is obvious that this type of muscle contraction is vital for proper golf biomechanics. Rapid strength is highly dependent upon intramuscular coordination.

Endurance strength refers to the fatigue factor of a muscle during long-lasting or repetitive contractions. Endurance strength is dependent upon maximal strength and aerobic conditioning. By choosing the right type of strength-training program, you can improve your maximal strength or rapid strength or endurance, or a combination thereof.

Methods of strength training are divided into dynamic and static programs. Dynamic strength training involves muscle contraction with joint movement. Static strength training involves muscle contraction without joint movement or contraction against a nonmovable object. Dynamic strength training, the most common method, can be divided into rapid-strength and slow-strength training. Dynamic rapid-strength training includes individual repetitions of the specific exercise performed with high to maximal use of strength. This type of training improves all types of strength: maximal strength, rapid strength, and endurance strength. The number of repetitions and the weight or resistance used should vary according to the desired effect.

Rapid strength is highly dependent upon intramuscular coordination. Endurance strength is dependent upon maximal strength and aerobic conditioning. By choosing the right type of strength-training program, you can improve your maximal strength or rapid strength or endurance, or a combination thereof.

For improving *maximal strength* utilizing dynamic rapid-strength training principles, I recommend between 8 and 10 repetitions during the second set (Level II) and from 8 to 12 repetitions during the third set (Level III) using 70 to 85 percent of your maximal load. For improving *maximal endurance* utilizing dynamic stretch-training principles, I recommend between 10 and 25 repetitions during the second set and from 25 to 50 repetitions during the third set using 30 to 50 percent of your maximum load or resistance.

Dynamic slow-strength training involves movements that are applied slowly and evenly throughout the range of motion. This training method is often called isokinetic strength training. Dynamic slow-strength training is suitable for increasing muscle girth (cross-section) and endurance but not for improving rapid strength. Therefore, this is not the preferred method for the golfer, who also requires rapid-strength training for maximum muscle contraction during the acceleration swing phase.

Static-strength training incorporates force against a fixed resistance to improve strength. This type of training improves endurance strength and, to some degree, maximal strength. Static-strength training is generally not recognized as beneficial in most types of sports because it does not improve or promote either muscle coordination or rapid strength. However, this training method may be beneficial for the senior player who is out of shape or for any player coming out of an injury. For these groups, I often recommend beginning with a static-strengthening routine that progresses to a dynamic routine. This conditioning method helps the senior player reduce the risk of injury and protects against reinjury in the player who is rehabbing an existing injury. This type of exercise is also beneficial in developing tone of the trunk musculature.

Because golf requires power, explosive muscle contraction during the acceleration swing phase, and endurance strength to maintain proper swing biomechanics, *dynamic rapid-strength* training methods are recommended over dynamic slow and static-strength training.

Strengthening programs may incorporate different types of muscle contraction exercises. Essentially there are three types: isometric, isotonic, and isokinetic.

Isometric exercise is performed by forcefully contracting the muscle in a static position. A static position is where the muscle is contracted without any change in its length or in the angle of the joint in which the contraction takes place. Attempting to lift or push an immovable object is a typical method of isometric or static exercise and incorporates the static-strength training principles. Isometric exercises are most effective when the contraction is maximally held for at least six seconds and repeated up to ten times daily. Improved strength can be accomplished through an isometric program but is specific to

> *Because golf requires power, explosive muscle contraction during the acceleration swing phase, and endurance strength to maintain proper swing biomechanics, dynamic rapid-strength training methods are recommended over dynamic slow and static-strength training.*

the joint angle at which the contraction takes place. Therefore, it is advisable to exercise the joint through the range of motion in multiple positions, holding the isometric contractions at variable degrees for a proper workout. This type of exercise is ideally suited for increasing strength and endurance of specific muscles of the senior player or in the beginning of rehabilitation following an injury. The businessperson can also easily employ these exercises on a daily routine while at the office.

Isotonic exercises occur by lengthening or shortening the muscle with the joint moving through the full range of motion. Isotonic exercises involve moving a resistive force, such as a dumbbell, or by working out with the Golfercise System, through a full range of motion. This is described as a *dynamic* contraction. A major benefit in performing isotonic exercises is the maintenance of normal range of motion for the joint, an optimal method for improving endurance. To perform an isotonic exercise properly, the muscle should be placed in the stretched position, with the body part fully extended and the weight or resistive exercise tubing pulled toward the flexed position. To ensure maximum efficiency during isotonic exercise, move the resistance as smoothly and quickly as possible, and return it at a much slower rate. In other words, push the resistance off smoothly and quickly, and allow it to return slowly.

Isotonic exercise, where the muscle works through its full range of motion against an increasing resistance, is known as progressive resistance exercise and was first introduced by De Lormen Watkins in 1951. This type of exercise has been shown to be superior to isometric exercise in developing strength and endurance. The fundamental principles of an isotonic exercise conditioning program include the following:

1. Precede all isotonic exercises with a warm-up routine (refer to Chapters 2 and 14).
2. Begin the isotonic contraction in the stretch or extended position of the joint.
3. Perform the movements in a slow and deliberate fashion.
4. Use two or three sets of 8 to 12 repetitions, performing the first set at half your maximum resistance, the second set at three-quarters maximum, and the final set at full maximum resistance.
5. Apply the overload principle by improving the resistance and number of repetitions, progressing to maximum contraction toward the end of the workout.
6. When utilizing weights or machines, the low-handicap golfer should confine heavy workout to the off season or pre-season!

A light to medium isotonic program should be maintained during the regular season. Work with weights on an on-day/off-day schedule, exercising a maximum of

> *It is advisable to exercise the joint through the range of motion in multiple positions, holding the isometric contractions at variable degrees for a proper workout.*

> *Isotonic exercises involve moving a resistive force, such as a dumbbell, or by working out with the Golfercise System, through a full range of motion. This is described as a dynamic contraction.*

four days per week. The resistance or weight should be lifted rapidly, with the weight moving against gravity at maximum speed and force. Conversely, when you lower the weight, the contraction should be relatively slow and gradual. Observe proper breathing procedures during lifting to assist in fixing and stabilizing the muscles of the trunk. This is performed by exhaling while lifting the weight and deeply inhaling while lowering it. Workouts of three to four times weekly with eight to ten repetitions for each of three sets produce the greatest strength gains. When you are able to complete the series (three sets) successfully without achieving maximal output, apply a weight increment or increase the resistance utilizing the overload principle (*refer to* Chapter 2).

Various machines and devices utilize isotonic exercise methods. These include free weights, barbells, resistive stretch tubing such as that used with the Golfercise System, and machines such as Universal and Nautilus. Free weights have both advantages and disadvantages. The disadvantages of free weights and machines are the expense and safety factors involved.

Isokinetic exercise is a third method of strength training in which the length of the muscle changes while the contraction is performed at a constant velocity. Theoretically, this ensures that maximum resistance is provided throughout the entire range of motion of the exercise, since the resistance will move only at some pre-set speed, regardless of the force applied. The key to isokinetic exercise is not the resistance but the speed at which the resistance can be moved. This exercise can be performed only with specific isokinetic exercise machines such as Cybex, Orthotron, Biodex, Lido, and many others. Such exercise equipment is generally used in rehabilitation facilities to rehabilitate athletes after surgery and in the training rooms of major college and professional teams. When isokinetic training is done properly, it is felt to be the most beneficial way to maximize strength gains. However, few golfers have access to this type of expensive equipment.

For all but the most advanced golfer, I believe that progressive variable resistance exercise tubing can provide maximum strength and endurance conditioning for the golf-specific muscles. I have, therefore, designed the Golfercise System for the physical-conditioning program and strength-training program described in this book. The Golfercise System uses resistive stretch tubing in performing specifically designed exercises to strengthen and improve the endurance of the specific muscles used in the golf swing. Please refer to Chapters 11, 12, and 13.

> *The key to isokinetic exercise is not the resistance but the speed at which the resistance can be moved.*

> *The Golfercise System uses resistive stretch tubing in performing specifically designed exercises to strengthen and improve the endurance of the specific muscles used in the golf swing.*

Section III

Golf Swing Biomechanics

Tight or weak shoulder muscles will prevent a smooth, rhythmic swing.

Upper-Body Biomechanics

Understanding
Biomechanics
of the Golf Swing
in the Four
Swing Phases

5

A comprehensive, golf-specific conditioning program should include specific flexibility and stretching exercises, endurance training, and strength-conditioning exercises. The first step in establishing an effective golf-specific program is to understand the biomechanics of the golf swing of the upper body throughout the four swing phases: 1) the takeaway phase, 2) the forward phase, 3) the acceleration phase, and 4) the follow-through phase. Understanding which joints and muscles are active during these phases will enable you to participate in a flexibility, endurance, and strength-conditioning program that will maximize your performance and decrease your chance of injury.

For optimal performance, the upper-body muscles used during the swing must be loose, conditioned, and strengthened for a smooth, rhythmic swing. Your performance will be affected by the following:

- Muscle imbalance or weakness in any of the major muscle groups that are required for a technically correct golf swing
- Muscle shortening or tightness of the upper-body muscles used during the golf swing
- Muscle weakness due to lack of stamina or endurance
- Decreased range of motion of specific joints of the upper torso

All of these factors play a significant role in your ability to get the most of your game.

The Upper-Body Golf Muscles

For optimal performance, the upper-body muscles used during the swing must be loose, conditioned, and strengthened for a smooth, rhythmic swing.

The primary upper-body muscles that are most active during your swing are: 1) the shoulder rotator cuff muscles, which include the shoulder abductor, the external shoulder rotator, and the internal shoulder rotator, 2) the chest muscles, 3) the upper-back muscles, 4) the anterior shoulder muscle, and 5) the forearm muscles, which include the wrist and finger flexors, extensors, radial deviator, ulnar deviator, supinator, and pronators.

The upper body also has secondary muscles that help to stabilize and support the primary active muscles during the golf swing. These muscles include the shoulder muscles, the shoulder girdle muscles, the arm flexor (biceps), the arm extensor (triceps), and the neck and upper-back muscles. If any of these stabilizer muscles are weak, shortened, or imbalanced, your golf swing will be affected, causing not only a decrease in your performance, but also an increase in the potential for injuries.

UPPER-BODY PRIMARY MUSCLES	
Muscles of the Shoulders, Upper Trunk, and Arms	**Action**
A. Shoulder Rotator Cuff Muscles 　1. Supraspinatus 　2. Infraspinatus 　3. Subscapularis	Arm Movement 　Shoulder abduction — raises arm 　External shoulder rotation 　Internal shoulder rotation
B. Chest Muscle 　1. Pectoralis muscle	Arm Movement 　Forward flexion 　Adduction of raised arm — pulls down 　Internally rotates arm
C. Upper Back Muscles 　1. Latissimus Dorsi	Arm Movement 　Adduction of raised arm 　Internally rotates arm
D. Shoulder Muscle 　1. Anterior Deltoid	Shoulder Turn and Arm Movement 　Abduction of shoulder
E. Forearm and Wrist Muscles 　1. Flexors 　2. Extensors 　3. Radial Deviation 　4. Ulnar Deviation 　5. Supination 　6. Pronation	Wrist Action 　Flexes the wrist 　Flexes the fingers (required for strong grip) 　Extends the wrist and fingers 　"Cocks" the wrist 　"Uncocks" the wrist 　Rolls wrist and forearm outward (Left wrist at impact) 　Rolls wrist and forearm inward (Right wrist at impact)

Pictorial Diagram of Upper-Body Primary and Stabilizing Muscles
Anterior View

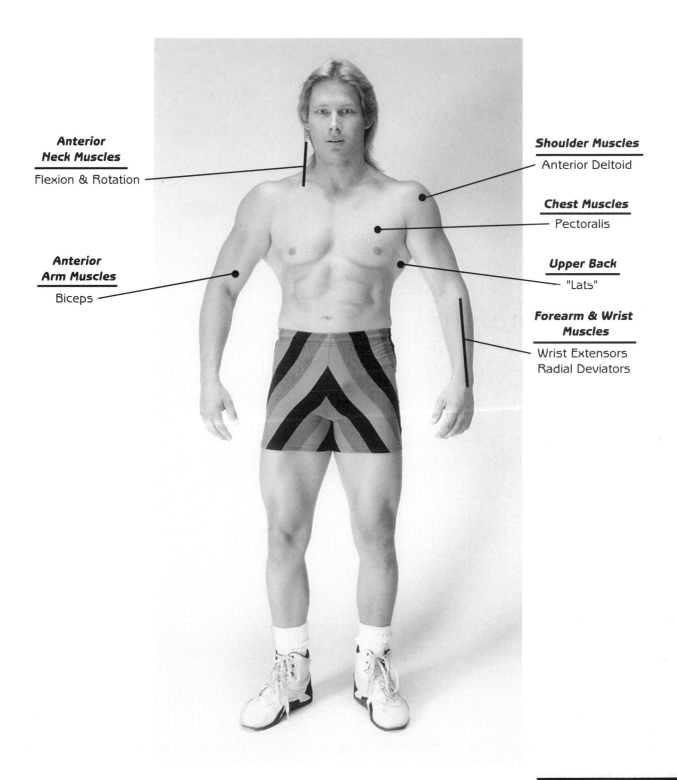

**Anterior
Neck Muscles**
Flexion & Rotation

**Anterior
Arm Muscles**
Biceps

Shoulder Muscles
Anterior Deltoid

Chest Muscles
Pectoralis

Upper Back
"Lats"

**Forearm & Wrist
Muscles**
Wrist Extensors
Radial Deviators

Pictorial Diagram of Upper-Body Primary and Stabilizing Muscles
Posterior View

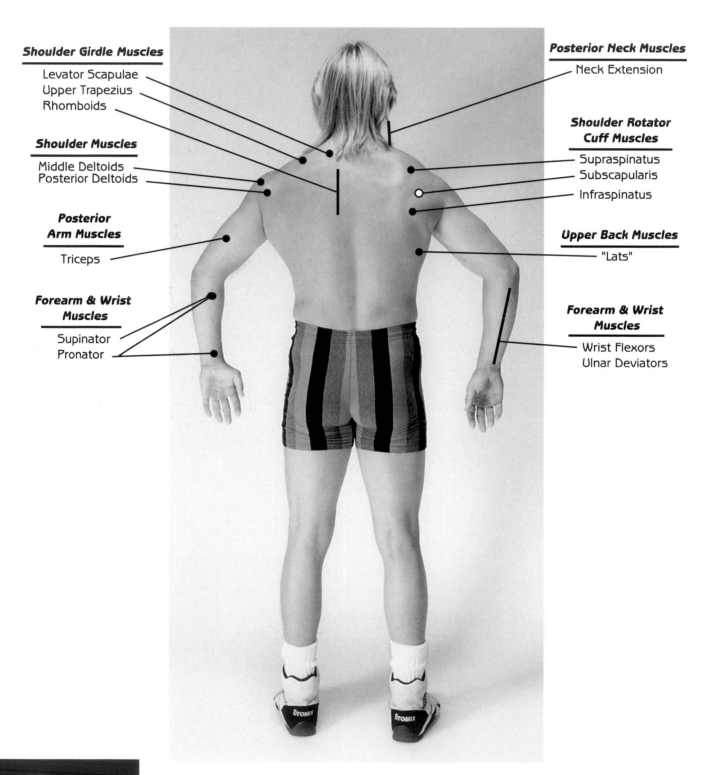

Shoulder Girdle Muscles
Levator Scapulae
Upper Trapezius
Rhomboids

Shoulder Muscles
Middle Deltoids
Posterior Deltoids

Posterior Arm Muscles
Triceps

Forearm & Wrist Muscles
Supinator
Pronator

Posterior Neck Muscles
Neck Extension

Shoulder Rotator Cuff Muscles
Supraspinatus
Subscapularis
Infraspinatus

Upper Back Muscles
"Lats"

Forearm & Wrist Muscles
Wrist Flexors
Ulnar Deviators

UPPER-BODY STABILIZING MUSCLES	
Stabilizers of the Upper Body	**Action**
A. Neck Muscles	Head rotation Head and neck flexion (Forward movement) Head and neck extension (Backward movement)

B. Shoulder Muscles
  1. Middle Deltoid
  2. Posterior Deltoid
	
	Raises arm (shoulder abduction)
	Raises arm (shoulder abduction)

C. Front of the Arm (Anterior) 1. Biceps	 Flexion of elbow (Bends elbow)
D. Back of the Arm (Posterior) 1. Triceps	 Extension of elbow (Straightens elbow)

E. Shoulder Girdle Muscles
  1. Levator Scapulae
 	
  2. Upper Trapezius
  3. Rhomboids
	
	Raises the shoulder girdle
	(Elevation of shoulder blade)
	Stabilization of shoulder blade
	Pulls shoulder blade toward spine

F. Accessory Shoulder Muscle 1. Serratus Anterior	 Stabilization of shoulder blade

The Upper-Body Joints

These upper-body joints allow for a technically correct golf swing: 1) neck and spine, 2) shoulder, 3) elbow, and 4) wrist. If the range of motion of any of these joints is greatly decreased due to arthritis, shortened or tightened muscles, or injury, the biomechanics of your swing will be altered, affecting your performance capability.

Self-Evaluation of Joints and Muscles

All golfers, but especially the amateur golfer, will experience various problems involving the upper-body muscles and joints. Tight or stiff shoulder muscles, weak or deconditioned upper-body muscles, muscle imbalance, or decreased range of motion of the neck, shoulders, or arms will hinder the smooth, rhythmic motion of the swing that is so vital to maximizing your performance. Try my simple self-evaluation (below) to detect any problems you may have with joint movement and flexibility. Once you have identified problem areas, you can work on correcting each of them with specific stretches and exercises.

Evaluating Range of Motion of the Upper-Body Joints

It is important for you to understand the normal range of motion of the major joints of the upper body so that you can determine any restrictions in their movement that may be affecting your swing. The four major joints of the upper body that enable you to perform a smooth, rhythmic golf swing are the neck and upper back, the shoulder joint, the elbow, and the wrist.

The four major joints of the upper body that enable you to perform a smooth, rhythmic golf swing are the neck and upper back, the shoulder joint, the elbow, and the wrist.

Neck and Upper Back

The biomechanics of the swing can be slightly affected by decreased range of motion of the spine, including the neck and mid- and upper back. The neck is made up of seven cervical vertebrae. These vertebrae and their accompanying joints determine the range of motion of your head and neck. The head and neck are capable of performing six motions in any combination. These include flexion (looking down), extension (looking up), left lateral bending, right lateral bending, left rotation, and right rotation. In the golf swing, the body rotates around the head, so the head and neck must be able to rotate to allow proper circular motion of the torso. If there is a decrease in cervical rotation, you may need to alter your swing biomechanics by increasing your upper-body (torso) rotation.

If there is a decrease in cervical rotation, you may need to alter your swing biomechanics by increasing your upper-body rotation.

Rotation of the head and neck in a young adult is approximately 90°. Unfortunately, as the natural aging process occurs, and occasionally from trauma, rotation of the head and neck is decreased. Should this occur, your head and neck may be forced to rotate away from the ball at the end of the backswing during the takeaway phase. This will affect shoulder turn and decrease your ability to maintain eye contact with the ball. If you suffer significant loss in neck flexion (looking down), this may alter your stance, which will cause an abnormal amount of bending at the waist or at the hips. This posture has a tendency to cause an outside-in swing, producing the dreaded slice. Fortunately, there must be at least a 20° reduction in neck rotation and flexion to cause this effect. Because the biomechanics of the swing are affected only by neck and head rotation and flexion, restriction in the other neck movements does not appear to play a major role in the golf swing.

You can make a quick self-evaluation of your neck by performing the following active range-of-motion maneuvers:

Neck and Head Rotation

To evaluate neck and head rotation: While looking forward, rotate your head in both directions by looking over your shoulders. Your head should rotate approximately 80° to 90° in each direction. This may be greatly reduced with age.

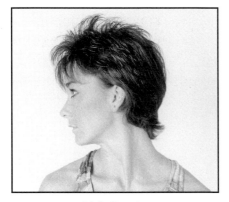

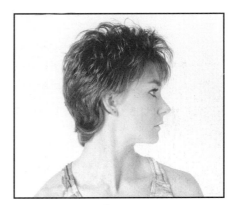

Right Rotation   *Neutral Position*   *Left Rotation*

Neck and Head Flexion

To evaluate neck and head flexion: While looking forward, try to put your chin on your chest. Your chin should move about 40° or within approximately two finger widths of your chest.

Neck and Head Extension

To evaluate neck and head extension: While looking forward, bend your head backward as far as possible. Your head should move approximately 40° so that you can look straight up at the ceiling.

Neck and Head Lateral Bending

To evaluate your neck and head lateral bending: While looking forward, bend your head sideways, moving your ear toward your shoulder. Your head should move approximately 40°.

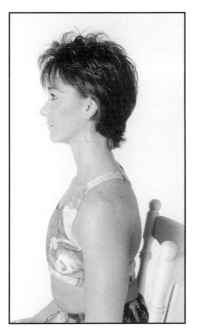
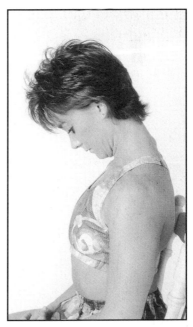

Neutral Lateral Position   *Neck and Head Flexion*

> *By self-evaluating the active range of motion and determining any limitations of the joints of your upper body, you will be able to address and correct your specific problem areas.*

Upper Torso or Back

The active range of motion of the mid- and upper back includes forward bending, backward bending, lateral bending, and rotation. Except for extreme limitations in movement of the upper thoracic spine, the biomechanics of the golf swing should not be affected. Golfers with a thoracic scoliosis may need to compensate in the shoulder turn or hip turn at the end of the backswing and follow-through in order to achieve proper trunk rotation. Otherwise, it is extremely rare for a problem with range of motion in upper-back movement to affect golf-swing biomechanics.

By self-evaluating the active range of motion and determining any limitations of the joints of your upper body, you will be able to address—and correct—your specific problem areas. You can achieve optimal swing biomechanics by improving the range of motion of the joints of your upper body. Often, this can easily be achieved by improving the flexibility of your upper-body muscles.

Shoulder

The shoulder joint has more impact on the golf swing than any other joint of the upper body. There are essentially six movements of the shoulder joint. These are internal rotation, external rotation, abduction, adduction, flexion, and extension. Significant restriction in any of these movements may alter and adversely affect your golf swing.

You can make a quick self-evaluation of the shoulder by performing the following active range-of-motion maneuvers with your shoulder.

External Rotation

To evaluate your shoulder range of motion or external rotation: Hold your arms away from your body (shoulder at 90° with the body) with your elbows at 90° so that your palms face down (see top photo, page 45). Raise your forearms by rotating at the shoulder until your palms face forward. The arm should externally rotate approximately 90°, as shown in the middle photo on page 45.

Internal Rotation

To evaluate your shoulder range of motion or internal rotation: Hold your arms in the same position as shown in the middle photograph on page 45. Lower your forearms by rotating at the shoulder until your palms face backward. The arm should internally rotate approximately 90° (see bottom photo, page 45).

Shoulder Abduction (Shoulder Elevation)

To evaluate shoulder abduction: Hold your arms down to the side of your body, palms facing forward. Move your arms in an arc away from your body until they are above your head. The shoulder should rotate approximately 180°.

Shoulder Adduction

To evaluate shoulder adduction: Hold your arms down to the side of your body, palms facing forward. Move your hand across your body toward midline. Shoulder adduction should approximate 50°.

Shoulder Flexion

To evaluate shoulder flexion: Hold your arms down to the side of your body, palms facing backward. Move your arm forward toward the ceiling until your palm faces forward. Shoulder flexion should approximate 180°.

Shoulder Extension

To evaluate shoulder extension: Hold your arms down to the side of your body, palms facing backward. Move your arms straight back. Shoulder extension should approximate 50°.

The important shoulder movements for the golf swing are external rotation, adduction, internal rotation, and abduction. Flexion and extension shoulder movements are less important. If the right shoulder has decreased external rotation, right-handed golfers will have a tendency to swing from the outside in, producing a fade or slice.

Elbow

The range of motion of the elbow has less impact on your swing, and so the effect that limitations have on motion will be negligible. Active range of motion of the elbow includes flexion, extension, supination, and pronation. During the takeaway phase, the forward swing, and the acceleration phase, the left arm should be almost fully extended for proper golf-swing biomechanics.

Shoulder: External rotation

Shoulder: Neutral Position

Shoulder: Internal Rotation

The opposite is true for a left-handed golfer. The flexion of the right elbow comes into play at the end of the backswing or takeaway phase and at the end of the follow-through phase. Restriction in flexion may have a mild effect on the biomechanics of your backswing. Should you have restriction in active wrist and forearm supination and/or pronation during the so-called "rolling of the wrist" during the acceleration phase, your swing will be hindered, producing decreased length and accuracy.

The left wrist must be able to supinate at impact. This means that you must have essentially normal left-elbow supination. The same holds true for pronation of the right elbow. However, this is not as critical as it seems, for you are moving the wrist and forearms toward the normal position at impact. The key is to ensure that the forearm and wrist supinator and pronator muscles are not tight or stiff so as to allow for a smooth, rhythmic "rolling of the wrists" at impact.

You can make a quick self-evaluation of your elbow motion by performing the following active range-of-motion maneuvers:

Elbow Flexion

To evaluate elbow flexion: While in a seated position, have your elbow bent at 90° with your palms facing upward. Then move your forearm and palm toward your shoulder. This should place your elbow in the full flexed position or approximately 40° from the starting position.

Elbow Extension

To evaluate elbow extension: While in a seated position, keep your elbows bent at 90° with your palms facing upward. Then move your arm down so that your palm faces forward. This should place your elbow in the full extended position or approximately 80° to 90° from the starting position.

Elbow and Forearm Supination and Pronation

To evaluate elbow supination and pronation: In a seated position, have your elbow bent at 90° with your thumbs pointing upward. Then rotate your thumbs outward in supination. Your thumbs should be horizontal or should achieve 90° of movement. Likewise, rotate your thumbs inward in pronation; they should be horizontal or should achieve 90° of movement (see photos on page 47).

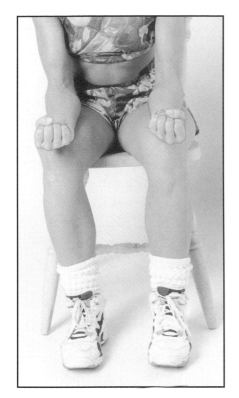

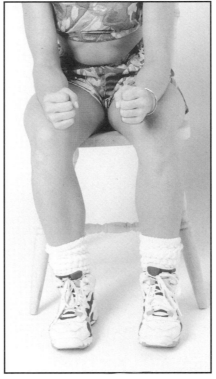

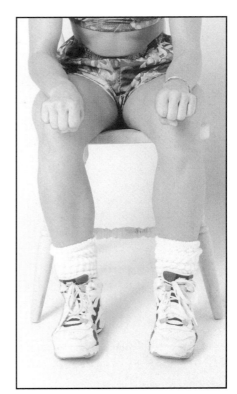

Forearm: Supination   *Forearm: Neutral Position*   *Forearm: Pronation*

Wrist

Active range of motion of the wrist includes flexion, extension, outward (radial) deviation, and inward (ulnar) deviation. Of these four motions, outward movement or radial deviation and right-wrist extension play important roles in the mechanics of the swing. The "cocking" of the wrist is performed by outward movement or radial deviation of the wrist during the takeaway phase of the golf swing. Decreased radial movement of the wrists will significantly reduce the power and acceleration of your club in the forward and acceleration swing phases. Fortunately, this is a very rare condition in the general population.

Diminished active range of motion of wrist flexion, wrist extension, and inward deviation of the wrist does not appear to have an impact on the mechanics of the swing because the wrists should be maintained in a fairly neutral position throughout the four swing phases. For right-handed golfers, there is slight right-wrist extension at the end of the takeaway swing phase. If your wrist extensor muscles are tight, stiff, or weak, your ability to "cock" the wrist properly will be affected. This can easily be corrected with the specific stretching maneuvers and exercises described in Chapters 11 and 13.

Hip and thigh
lateral rotation initiates
the forward swing.

Lower-Body Biomechanics

6

••••••••••••••••••••••••••••••••••

Understanding Biomechanics of the Golf Swing in the Four Swing Phases

Even though the lower-body muscles of the legs, hips, and trunk play a vital role in a technically correct golf swing, they are the least understood.

The lower-body muscles are responsible for the leg, hip, and trunk turn, as well as for weight transfer. The hip turn and weight transfer from right side to left side are critical movements in a right-handed golfer's swing. For proper lower-body biomechanics, the muscles of the legs, hip, and trunk must contract in a synchronous, smooth, and finely timed sequence. The lower-body muscle action produces a majority of the power at impact and is critical for accurate shots. To a lesser degree, the joints of the low back, hip, knees, and ankles also play a role in proper swing biomechanics.

A comprehensive, golf-specific conditioning and training program must focus on specific flexibility and strengthening exercises of the golf-specific muscles of the lower body to ensure technically correct swing biomechanics. Muscle imbalance or weakness in any of the major muscle groups of the legs, hips, or trunk will have a detrimental effect, as will muscle shortening or stiffness and decreased stamina of the specific muscles. Experiencing any of these problems will make it almost impossible for a technically correct golf swing to occur.

The larger muscles that provide power and distance in the golf swing are located in the legs and hips. The muscles of the legs, hips, and trunk produce the hip turn that is necessary for a technically correct golf swing. However, extremes in trunk and hip joint range of motion are not required for an adequate hip turn. Therefore, the range of motion of the lower back and hip joints is not as critical for a technically correct swing as is the flexibility of the lower-body muscles.

However, the strength of the legs, hips, and trunk muscles provides the power generated at impact that is so necessary for distance from the tee, for being able to blast out of the rough and bunkers, and for longer iron shots. I cannot stress enough the need for strong leg, hip, and trunk muscles, for these muscles are vital for distance and for achieving a smooth, synchronous, coordinated swing.

The Lower-Body Golf Muscles

The primary lower-body muscles that are required for a technically correct swing are the lateral trunk muscles, the abdominal muscles (primarily the internal and external obliques), the medial hip rotators, the lateral hip rotators, the hip extensor, the medial thigh adductor, the outer thigh abductor, the foot invertor (which rolls the ankle outward), and the foot evertor (which rolls the ankle inward).

Technically correct trunk and hip rotation is critical for correct swing biomechanics. Trunk rotation is produced by contraction of the internal and external abdominal oblique muscles and, to a lesser degree, the lateral trunk muscles. These muscles also aid in proper shoulder turn. The abdominal oblique muscles (internal and external obliques) contract together to produce trunk rotation.

These stomach muscles require strengthening and conditioning to ensure correct swing biomechanics as it relates to hip and shoulder turn. It is these muscles, rather than the range of movement of the spine and hips, which produce the technically correct trunk rotation in the takeaway and follow-through portions of the swing. They also contribute to power and distance by their strong contraction during the acceleration swing phase.

Hip turn is produced by contraction of the left lateral hip rotator (piriformis and accessory muscles) and right medial hip rotator. Proper hip turn of approximately 40° to 60° cannot be reached if the posterior hip muscles are weak or tight. I have found that these muscles are often very weak in the amateur player. When this is the case, the player generally compensates by using too much shoulder and arm action. These muscles also produce thigh rotation and are the key muscles that correctly "point" the knees at the ball during the takeaway and acceleration swing phases. The left medial hip rotator "points" the left knee at the ball during the takeaway. The right medial hip rotator "points" the right knee to the ball during the acceleration swing phase.

The lower body and trunk also have stabilizing muscles that support the primary active muscles during the four swing phases. These muscles include the stomach muscles, the knee extensor muscle, the knee flexor muscle (hamstring), and the calf muscles, which aid in proper front-to-back weight distribution. If any of these muscles are weak, shortened, or imbalanced, proper golf swing biomechanics will be affected.

The strength of the legs, hips, and trunk muscles provides the power generated at impact that is so necessary for distance from the tee, for being able to blast out of the rough and bunkers, and for longer iron shots.

A comprehensive, golf-specific conditioning and training program must focus on specific flexibility and strengthening exercises of the golf-specific muscles of the lower body to ensure technically correct swing biomechanics.

LOWER-BODY PRIMARY MUSCLES	
Muscles of the Trunk, Hips, and Legs	**Action**

A. Abdominal Oblique Muscles
   1. Internal Obliques
   2. External Obliques
	Trunk Turn
	   Rotates trunk to same side
	   Rotates trunk to opposite side

B. Lateral Trunk Muscles
   1. Quadratus Lumborum
	Trunk Lateral Bend ("C" Posture)
	   Bends trunk to same side, raises hips

C. Posterior Hip Muscles (Buttock)
   1. Gluteus Maximus
   2. Gluteus Minimus
   3. Piriformis and accessory muscles
	Hip Turn
	   Extends the hip
	   Rotates hip and thigh medially or "in"
	   Rotates hip and thigh laterally or "out"

D. Medial Thigh Muscles
   1. Adductor Muscles
	Lateral Weight Shift
	   Pulls thigh and hip inward (adduction)

E. Outer Thigh Muscles
   1. Tensor Fascia Lata (TFL)
   2. Gluteus Medius
	Lateral Weight Shift
	   Pulls thigh and hip outward (abduction)
	   Pulls thigh and hip outward (abduction)

F. Anterior Lower Leg Muscles
   1. Anterior Tibialis
   2. Peroneus Longus and Brevis
   3. Extensor Digitorum Longus and Brevis
	Lateral Weight Shift
	   Rolls the ankle outward (foot inversion)
	   Rolls the ankle inward (foot eversion)
	   Raises the foot (foot dorsiflexion)

Pictorial Diagram of Lower-Body Primary and Stabilizing Muscles
Anterior View

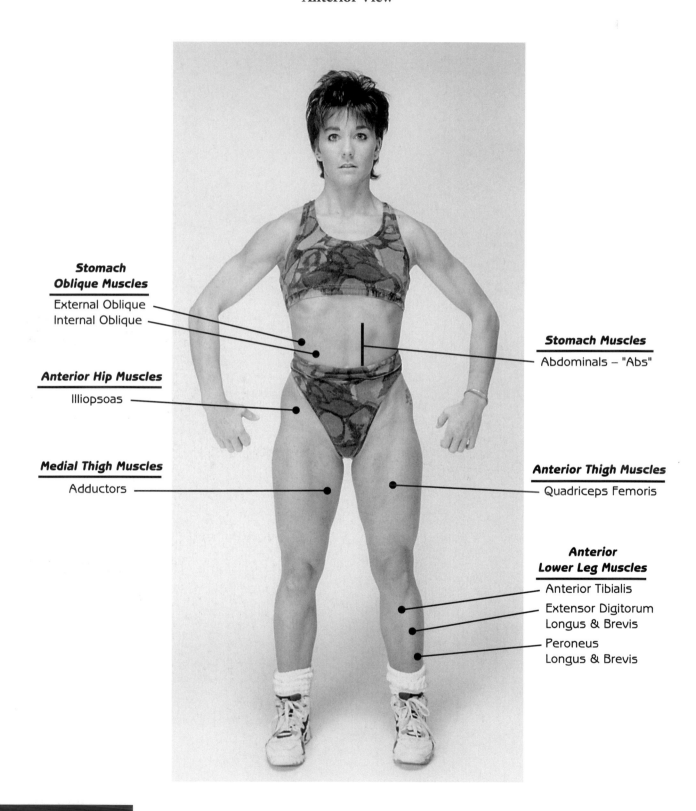

Stomach
Oblique Muscles
External Oblique
Internal Oblique

Anterior Hip Muscles
Illiopsoas

Medial Thigh Muscles
Adductors

Stomach Muscles
Abdominals – "Abs"

Anterior Thigh Muscles
Quadriceps Femoris

Anterior
Lower Leg Muscles
Anterior Tibialis
Extensor Digitorum
Longus & Brevis
Peroneus
Longus & Brevis

Pictorial Diagram of Lower-Body Primary and Stabilizing Muscles
Posterior View

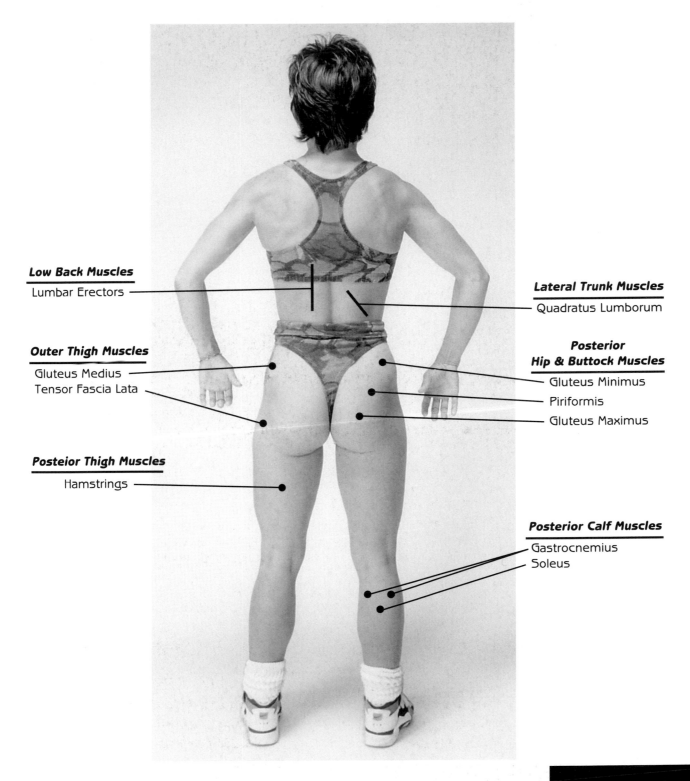

Low Back Muscles
Lumbar Erectors

Lateral Trunk Muscles
Quadratus Lumborum

Outer Thigh Muscles
Gluteus Medius
Tensor Fascia Lata

**Posterior
Hip & Buttock Muscles**
Gluteus Minimus
Piriformis
Gluteus Maximus

Posteior Thigh Muscles
Hamstrings

Posterior Calf Muscles
Gastrocnemius
Soleus

LOWER-BODY STABILIZING MUSCLES	
Muscles of the Trunk, Hip, and Leg	**Action**
A. Abdominal Muscles 1. Erectus Abdominous	Bends trunk forward

B. Back Muscles
   1. Erector spinae of lumbar and
      thoracic spine
	Raises the back (extension)
	Bends spine to side
	Stabilizes spine

C. Anterior Hip Muscles 1. Iliopsoas muscle	Flexion of hip and lower spine stabilizers
D. Anterior Thigh Muscles 1. Quadriceps Femoris	Knee extension, hip flexion
E. Posterior Thigh Muscles 1. Hamstring	Knee flexion, hip extension
F. Posterior Calf Muscles 1. Gastrocnemius and Soleus muscles	Lowering the foot (plantar flexion)

The Lower-Body Joints

A decrease in the overall flexibility of the joints of the trunk and lower body will have an impact on the smooth, rhythmic motion required for a technically correct golf swing.

The joints of the trunk and lower body that are involved during the four swing phases include the lumbar spine, the hip, the knee joints, and the ankle joints. As stated previously, the maximum end range of these joints is not required for proper hip rotation or movement of the trunk and lower body during the four swing phases. Therefore, unless there is significant decrease in motion of these joints due to arthritis, any painful condition, or significantly shortened or tightened muscles, the biomechanics of the golf swing will not be affected.

However, a decrease in the overall flexibility of these joints will have an impact on the smooth, rhythmic motion required for a technically correct golf swing. A simple self-evaluation of these joints will help detect problems that arise from decreased flexibility or range of motion. Any significant limitation in the range of motion may be corrected—if due to decreased flexibility—by simply utilizing proper stretching techniques. Often, it is tight or shortened muscles that decrease normal range of motion. Tight or shortened muscles can generally be stretched out by utilizing proper stretching techniques that will increase the range of motion of a joint as well as improve the flexibility of the muscle.

Evaluating Range of Motion of the Lower-Body Joints

As mentioned previously, the major joint complexes involved in the golf swing of the trunk and lower body are the lumbar spine, the hip, the knee, and the ankle. It is helpful to understand the role of these joints in the golf swing so that any existing problems may be addressed.

Lumbar Spine

The lumbar spine is mildly flexed or bent forward at address and stays in this posture throughout the forward and acceleration swing phases. At the end of the follow-through phase, the lumbar spine becomes mildly extended. The forward bend or flexed posture of the trunk during the first three phases of the swing is produced primarily by hip flexion rather than by flexion of the lumbar spine. The lumbar spine should remain fairly straight at address with forward trunk flexion coming primarily from hip flexion.

There are six basic movements of the lumbar spine. These include flexion (forward bending), extension (backward bending), lateral trunk bending (right and left), and trunk rotation (right and left). Unless you have an injury or arthritic condition that significantly limits the motion of the lumbar spine, limitations of any of these motions will not likely have an adverse effect on the biomechanics of your golf swing.

Most of the trunk rotation comes from the mid- to upper spine rather than from the lower lumbar spine, which normally rotates only a few degrees. Hip rotation or turn is not affected by decreased rotational movement of the lumbar spine. Hip rotation is affected primarily by shortening or tightening of the medial and lateral hip-rotator musculature and to some degree by tightened lumbar and thoracic musculature. However, due to the small amount of normal rotation of the lumbar spine, any low-back condition may be aggravated from the natural hip and trunk rotation that is required during the takeaway and follow-through swing phases.

Extension of the lumbar spine (bending backwards) at the end of the follow-through may also place stress on your low back, and this may occasionally aggravate an existing low-back condition. I do not believe, however, that performing a technically correct, i.e., smooth, coordinated golf swing, in and of itself causes low-back problems. Rather, weakened or tight trunk and hip muscles, along with a pre-existing condition, often aggravate the low back during play. I have found that, by properly strengthening the trunk muscles, a major-

The forward bend or flexed posture of the trunk during the first three phases of the swing is produced primarily by hip flexion rather than by flexion of the lumbar spine. The lumbar spine should remain fairly straight at address.

Any low-back condition may be aggravated from the natural hip and trunk rotation that is required during the takeaway and follow-through swing phases.

ity of golfers with occasional low-back pain can continue to play with minimal or no discomfort. Golfers who have chronic low-back pain should participate in an aggressive stretching and conditioning program.

You can make a quick self-evaluation of your lumbar spine ranges of motion by performing the following tests:

Lumbar Extension

To evaluate lumbar extension: While in a standing position with your hands on your hips, lean backward as far as you can. The lumbar spine should extend backward approximately 25°.

Lumbar Spine Flexion

To evaluate lumbar flexion: While in a standing position with your arms to the side, bend forward as far as you can (as in touching your toes), keeping your knees straight. The lumbar spine should bend forward or flex approximately 80° to 90°.

Lumbar Spine Lateral Bending

To evaluate lateral bending of your back: While in the standing position with your arms to the side, laterally flex or bend your trunk to the side to the limit of motion. You should be able to bend to the side approximately 40°. Ensure that both sides are measured to determine symmetry. Should you bend farther to one side than to the other, you may have shortened or tight low-back muscles. This problem needs to be corrected to ensure proper swing biomechanics. Refer to Chapter 12 for stretching exercises of lateral trunk, hip, and thigh muscles.

Lumbar Spine Rotation (Trunk)

To evaluate lumbar rotation: While in a sitting position with your hands held to your side, rotate your torso to the right and to the left to the limit of motion. You should be able to rotate approximately 30°. Again, measure both sides to evaluate for symmetry. Should there be a decrease in the limit of motion from one side to the other, you

> *By properly strengthening the trunk muscles, a majority of golfers with occasional low-back pain can continue to play with minimal or no discomfort.*

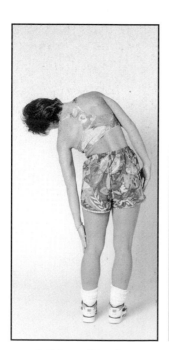

Left Lateral Bending

Neutral Position

Right Lateral Bending

may have a possible shortening or tightening of your trunk rotator muscles (abdominal obliques). This finding will affect proper swing biomechanics, particularly in the takeaway and follow-through swing phases. A problem in this area can generally be corrected by stretching your low-back and stomach muscles. Refer to Chapter 12 for stretching exercises of the low-back muscles.

The important thing to remember in lumbar-spine movement is that maximum limits are not required for a technically correct golf swing. Therefore, unless the restriction of any of these movements is significant or you experience pain at the end range, you should be able to perform a technically correct swing even if you have some limitations in your range of motion.

Hip

Although the range of motion of the hip does not play a crucial role during the golf swing, it is important that there be adequate motion of this joint for proper swing biomechanics. Active range of motion of the hip includes flexion, extension, abduction, adduction, medial rotation, and lateral rotation.

At address and throughout the takeaway, forward, and acceleration swing phases, the hips are bent forward (mildly flexed). This allows you to lean forward to address the ball. At the end of the follow-through phase, the hips become extended. In the takeaway swing phase, there is mild adduction and medial rotation of the left hip. This motion "points" the left knee to the ball. In the forward and acceleration swing phases, there is mild adduction and medial rotation of the right hip, which "point" the right knee to the ball. In order for these motions to affect your swing, you must have no significant restriction in hip motion. Fortunately, such restriction is rare. However, if you experience pain or a "catch" in your hips during any of the four swing phases, this will have a detrimental effect on proper biomechanics of your swing.

You can make a quick self-evaluation of your hip motion by performing the following active range-of-motion maneuvers:

Hip Extension (Bends Leg Backward)
To evaluate hip extension: While in a standing position, hold on to the back of a chair for support and raise one foot off the ground. Extend or move your leg backward to the limit of motion. The leg or thigh should move backward approximately 30°. Check the extension of both hips.

Hip Flexion (Bends Leg Forward)
To evaluate hip flexion: While in a standing position, hold on to the back of a chair for support and flex or raise one thigh as high as possible. The thigh should rise approximately 120°. Check flexion of your other hip.

> The important thing to remember in lumbar-spine movement is that maximum limits are not required for a technically correct golf swing.

> Although the range of motion of the hip does not play a crucial role during the golf swing, it is important that there be adequate motion of this joint for proper swing biomechanics.

Hip Adduction (Moves Leg Inward)

To evaluate hip adduction: While in a standing position, hold on to the back of a chair for support, raise one leg, and move it inward across the front of the leg on which you are standing. The leg should move inward to the limit of motion at approximately 30°.

Hip Abduction (Moves Leg Outward)

To evaluate hip abduction: While in a standing position, hold on to the back of a chair for support and move your leg outward to its maximum limit of motion. The leg should move approximately 45° outward.

Medial Hip Rotation (Rotates Hip and Thigh Inward)

To evaluate medial hip rotation: While in a seated position, with your legs off the floor and your knee secure, raise your foot outward. This motion produces medial rotation of the hip. Raise your foot keeping your knee stable. The calf and foot should move outward approximately 40°. Check both hips.

Lateral Hip Rotation (Rotates Hip and Thigh Outward)

To evaluate lateral hip rotation: While in a seated position, with your legs off the floor and your knee secured, move your calf and foot inward to the limit of motion. This motion produces lateral rotation of the hip. The calf and foot should move inward approximately 40°. Check both hips.

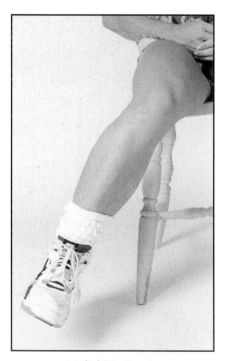
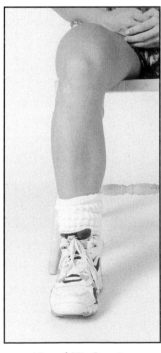

Medial Hip Rotation   *Neutral Hip Rotation*   *Lateral Hip Rotation*

Active range of motion of the hips is important for a technically correct swing. Your hips should be able to rotate approximately 25° to 35°. Hip medial and lateral rotation is required for proper hip turn. Hip turn occurs throughout all four swing phases and is particularly important at the top of the backswing or end of the takeaway swing phase and at the end of the follow-through swing phase. Decreased range of motion of your hips may keep you from reaching a full hip turn in the takeaway or from completing a full and high follow-through. This problem is often found in golfers with arthritic hips. If you have no "bony" or structural problems with your hip joints and still have decreased hip motion, it is most likely from tight or shortened hip muscles. This problem can generally be corrected by using the golf-specific stretching techniques described in Chapters 3 and 12. Therefore, unless you have significant limits in hip-joint movement or recent hip injury that causes pain with movement, a mild decrease in hip movement will have little bearing on achieving a technically correct golf swing.

Hip turn occurs throughout all four swing phases and is particularly important at the top of the backswing or end of the takeaway swing phase and at the end of the follow-through swing phase.

Knee

The knees are slightly bent (flexed) throughout most of the golf swing, except at the end of the follow-through when the left knee becomes almost straight (extended). Maximum movement of the knees is not required for a technically correct golf swing. However, instability of the ligaments from a pre-existing condition may have a negative effect on the smooth, rhythmic motion that is so important for your swing.

Golfers who have injured their knee ligaments or who have unstable knees must strengthen the knee muscles in order to perform at their optimal level. This is done by aggressively strengthening the quadriceps femoris (front of the thigh) and hamstring (back of the thigh) muscles. Any golfer who has knee soreness following a round should exercise the knee extensor and flexor muscles. This will strengthen the knee, decreasing the stress on the knee ligaments and improving knee stability during play.

There are four active ranges of motion of the knee. The knee is able to flex (bend backward), extend (straighten), rotate internally, and rotate externally. For proper swing biomechanics, you must be able to rotate your knee internally and externally approximately 5° to 10°. This is particularly true at the end of the takeaway phase or top of the backswing, in which the left knee is maximally rotated internally. Knee rotation is also important at the end of the acceleration phase (at impact), in which the right knee is rotated internally and the left knee is slightly rotated externally. If your knee ligaments or cartilage are unstable, these positions may cause some discomfort or even pain. Again, this can be overcome to a certain degree by strengthening your thigh muscles.

You can make a quick self-evaluation of your knee motion by performing the following active range-of-motion maneuvers:

Any golfer who has knee soreness following a round should exercise the knee extensor and flexor muscles. This will strengthen the knee, decreasing the stress on the knee ligaments and improving knee stability during play.

Knee Extension

To evaluate knee extension: If you are able to lock your knees straight when in a standing position, you are able to accomplish full or normal knee extension. Check both knees. If there is a slight backward bend of the knee, this is called hyperextension and may be normal in individuals up to 10°. Hyperextension of greater than 10° indicates ligament instability. You may wish to check with your doctor regarding this finding, particularly if you have knee pain during play.

Knee Flexion

To evaluate knee flexion: While lying in a face-down position (prone), raise your foot toward your buttock by bending your knee, keeping your thigh flat on the surface. The angle of your thigh with your lower leg should approximate 120° to 130°. Check both knees. For a technically correct golf swing, knee flexion of only approximately 30° is required.

Internal Knee Rotation

To evaluate internal knee rotation: While in a seated position, with your legs off the ground, rotate your ankle inward. The limit of motion should be approximately 25°. Check both knees.

External Knee Rotation

To evaluate external knee rotation: While in a seated position, with your feet off the floor, rotate your ankle outward. The limit of motion should approximate 25°. Check both knees.

Ankle

All that is required is for your ankles to move approximately 50% of the normal range of motion. I have found that ankle motion is very rarely decreased enough to alter the swing.

Some ankle movement is required for correct lower-body swing biomechanics. In right-handed golfers, the right ankle "rolls out" and the left ankle "rolls in" during the takeaway swing phase. This action reverses during the forward and acceleration swing phases. At the end of the follow-through, the right ankle is pointed downward (plantar flexed), and the left ankle is maximally "rolled out" with the weight on the outside of the foot.

There are four active movements of the ankle. The ankle rises upward (dorsiflexion), points downward (plantar flexion), rolls inward (eversion), and rolls outward (inversion). For correct swing biomechanics, your ankles must be able to perform these four movements. As with the other lower-body joints, however, you do not need to be able to move your ankle to the maximum limit or range of motion. All that is required is for your ankles to move approximately 50% of the normal range of motion. I have found that ankle motion is very rarely decreased enough to alter the swing.

You can make a quick self-evaluation of ankle motion by performing the following active range-of-motion maneuvers:

Ankle and Foot Dorsiflexion (Raises Foot)

To evaluate ankle and foot dorsiflexion: While in a seated position, with your feet off the floor, raise your foot upward by bending at the ankle. The limit of motion should approximate 20°. Check both ankles.

Ankle and Foot Plantar Flexion (Lowers Foot)

To evaluate ankle and foot plantar flexion: While in a seated position, with your feet off the floor, point your foot downward by bending at the ankle. The limit of motion should approximate 50°. Check both ankles.

Ankle and Foot Inversion (Rolls Ankle Outward)

To evaluate ankle inversion: While in a seated position, with your feet off the floor, roll your ankle outward. The limit of motion should approximate 30°. Check both ankles.

Ankle and Foot Eversion (Rolls Ankle Inward)

To evaluate ankle eversion: While in a seated position, with your feet off the floor, roll your ankle inward. The limit of motion should approximate 20°. Check both ankles.

  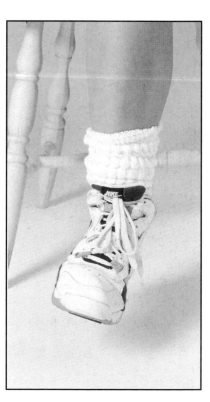

| *Ankle and Foot Inversion* | *Neutral Position* | *Ankle and Foot Eversion* |

By analyzing the active range of motion of your lumbar spine, hip, knee, and ankle, you can identify any significant joint-motion limitations. However, do not be discouraged if you find some limits in the range of motion of these joints. Remember that, in order to perform a technically correct golf swing from beginning of address to the end of the follow-through phase, the active ranges of motion required of the lumbar spine, hip, knee, and ankle are a great deal less than the normal ranges of motion for these joints. Unless you have a pre-existing condition of these joints from arthritis, ligamentous instability, or pain due to the natural stresses put on these joints during the golf swing, the range of motion should not have a significant effect on your swing biomechanics or on your performance.

If you find motion restrictions of these joints after your self-evaluation, correction or improvement will most likely occur following proper stretching. By properly stretching the muscles that move these joints, you will most likely be able to increase their active ranges of motion. Generally, mild limitations of joint motion occur from shortening or tightening of the muscles that move the joint. Correction is a simple process of lengthening the muscles by engaging in the muscle-specific flexibility and stretch training program described in this book. However, if you have decreased range of motion in any of these joints due to arthritis or other "bony" (structural) problems, adjusting your swing by increasing your shoulder turn can often overcome these problems. Always consult your teaching professional when adjusting your swing.

In the following chapters on the biomechanics of the four swing phases, I will discuss the golf-specific muscles of the legs, hips, and trunk that are active during your swing and that produce a technically correct swing. I also will describe a golf-specific flexibility and strength physical-conditioning and training program. This system is designed to increase the flexibility, endurance, and strength of the primary and stabilizing muscles of the trunk and lower body. This golf-specific exercise system will ensure proper golf biomechanics, timing, and synchrony of your swing in order to lower your score. But most important, by strengthening the golf-specific muscles of your lower body, you will increase your distance by improving your power.

Section IV

Four Swing Phases

The stomach oblique muscles are prime initiators of the takeaway swing phase.

Takeaway Swing Phase

7

● ●

Golf-Specific Muscle and Joint Involvement of the Upper and Lower Body

The takeaway phase of the golf swing begins when you address the ball and ends at the top of your backswing. Jack Nicklaus and other top touring professionals believe that the first 18 inches of the takeaway swing phase are the most important segment of the golf swing. This is because the takeaway sets the pattern—including muscle memory, tempo, and rhythm—for the entire swing. An essential key for a proper takeaway is to bring the club back correctly, with the club gliding away from the ball, staying as close to the ground as possible for as long as possible to form a wide arc. By developing a wide-arc takeaway, you will set up the rest of the swing to deliver maximum force and power upon impact.

Proper swing tempo and rhythm during the takeaway phase of the golf swing cannot occur without proper muscle and joint flexibility and good muscle tone. You must *swing* the club back very slowly from address. Never move it in a quick, jerky motion. In order to *swing* the club back correctly, you must have good muscle and joint flexibility, and you must be in shape. All amateur golfers have experienced a breakdown of the "feel" of the swing as they get tired toward the end of the round. In other words, you must be in good physical condition to bring the club back properly 70 to 100 or more times a round. If you push the club back too quickly in a jerky motion, you will inevitably overcompensate (or decompensate) at impact, the results of which are most aggravating. This is a common finding in golfers whose "golf muscles" are out of shape, but it can be overcome easily by engaging in a golf-specific physical conditioning and training program.

Upper-Body Muscle and Joint Involvement

In each phase of the golf swing, specific upper-body muscles come into play. In the takeaway swing phase, specific shoulder muscles of the rotator cuff play an active role. Any of the shoulder rotator cuff muscles that are out of shape (weak), stiff, or tight will interfere with your ability to swing the club back in a slow, smooth, rhythmic motion. Specifically, if your shoulder motion is decreased, your shoulder turn will be decreased.

The same is true if your shoulder muscles are tight. Tight shoulder muscles will hinder left arm movement by interfering with the reach across your body during the takeaway. Tight shoulder muscles will hinder right-arm movement by decreasing your ability to rotate your shoulder externally. Such shoulder joint and muscle problems may be corrected through the specific stretches and exercises discussed in Chapters 11 and 13.

The shoulder rotator cuff muscles include the internal rotator muscle, the external rotator muscle, and the arm-shoulder abductor, which elevates the arm. If any of these muscles are weak or tight, it is difficult to maintain a smooth, rhythmic takeaway. A rhythmic, non-jerky takeaway requires smooth contraction of the right external shoulder rotator muscle and right-arm abductor muscle. In a right-handed golfer, the right arm is rotated externally and is raised (abducted) slightly at the end of the backswing. This movement is produced by active contraction of the right external rotator and the right shoulder abductor. The right deltoid muscles, which cover the shoulder, play a minor role in this action. If you wish to achieve repetitive external rotation of your right shoulder, your right external shoulder rotator must be in shape, and if you want to achieve repetitive right arm elevation, your right shoulder abductor muscle must be in shape. These muscles must contract in concert for a smooth, rhythmic takeaway. If they are weak or tight, you will have problems during this swing segment.

The other muscles of the right shoulder that play a stabilizing role are the subscapularis of the rotator cuff, the pectoralis muscle, the latissimus dorsi, and the deltoids. Although important, these stabilizing muscles play a less active role during this swing phase.

The left internal rotator muscle of the shoulder rotator cuff muscles is the most active left shoulder muscle during the takeaway phase. The anterior chest adductor muscle (pectoralis major) also plays an active role during the takeaway. The other muscles of the left shoulder, including the infraspinatus, supraspinatus, and deltoids, although necessary, play a more stabilizing role and are less active during this swing phase.

A golf-specific exercise conditioning and training program designed to improve the takeaway segment of the golf swing must therefore include flexibility and strengthening exercises of the left-shoulder internal rotator muscle, the left-shoulder adductor and flexor muscle (pectoralis major), the right-shoulder abductor muscle, and the right-shoulder external rotator muscle. These muscles must be flexible and in good shape. If any of these muscles are tight, your shoulder turn will be decreased. Any skilled player knows that poor shoulder biomechanics, whether it be tight shoulder muscles decreasing the shoulder turn or out-of-shape muscles that lose "muscle memory" in the latter holes, is a major source of erratic play. In short, decreased shoulder turn can be devastating.

Because of the importance of the takeaway phase, the specific muscles necessary to achieve a smooth and rhythmic backswing must not be neglected in any golf-specific physical conditioning and training program. If those muscles are weak or inflexible (tight or stiff), they will fatigue rapidly through 18 holes, affecting the overall quality of your play. Remember—once any muscle becomes fatigued, it will fail to perform as needed.

The forearm muscles are also important for a biomechanically correct takeaway. The active muscles of the forearms in the takeaway phase include the wrist extensor and flexor muscles. The wrist extensor muscles produce the "wrist cock" during the takeaway swing phase. If these muscles are weak, you will find it difficult to "cock" your wrist properly. This problem will greatly affect both the accuracy and the distance of your shots.

The grip is achieved by contracting the finger flexor musculature, which is part of the wrist flexor muscles. These muscles must be well conditioned for a strong grip. Many golfers experience forearm pain following a round. This condition, commonly called "tennis elbow" (lateral epicondylitis), is due to deconditioned or weakened forearm extensor muscles. The golfer may also experience pain in the medial elbow. This condition is commonly called "golfer's elbow" (medial epicondylitis) and results from an injury to the forearm flexor muscles. The forearm extensor and flexor muscles require optimum conditioning and strength to provide the endurance necessary for a smooth, rhythmic takeaway and to prevent injury.

The takeaway phase also requires unrestricted, fluid motion of the shoulder joints. Near-to-normal external rotation (90°) of the right shoulder is necessary to achieve optimal shoulder turn at the end of the backswing. Near-normal adduction (40°) of the left shoulder is also helpful in achieving proper club and arm position at the end of the backswing. If either the right-shoulder external rotation or the left-shoulder adduction is restricted significantly, the right-handed golfer may need to compensate with excessive trunk rotation in order to achieve proper positioning at the end of the backswing. Abnormal shoulder turn reduces power at impact and tends to produce an outside-in swing, which is one cause of the dreaded slice.

> *Because of the importance of the takeaway phase, the specific muscles necessary to achieve a smooth and rhythmic backswing must not be neglected in any golf-specific physical conditioning and training program. If those muscles are weak or inflexible, they will fatigue rapidly through 18 holes, affecting the overall quality of your play.*

By properly stretching the right-shoulder external rotator muscle, you may be able to increase your right-shoulder external rotation.

The shoulder rotator cuff muscles are the primary muscles that allow you to turn your shoulders. This movement is vital for proper takeaway swing biomechanics, particularly so that you can reach the top of your backswing. If you have problems reaching close to an 80° to 100° shoulder turn at the top of your backswing, stretching the following muscles will be helpful. By properly stretching the right-shoulder external rotator muscle, you may be able to increase your right-shoulder external rotation. I recommend using the stretch-contract-relax method or PNF as described in Chapter 3 if you find that this muscle is tight or shortened.

The same holds true for correcting tight or shortened left-shoulder muscles (i.e., pectoralis, left-shoulder abductor, left rhomboid, and levator scapula). The left rhomboid and levator scapula muscles help to stabilize the left shoulder during the swing and will decrease shoulder turn if they are shortened, tight, or stiff. By stretching these muscles, you should have an increased shoulder turn, resulting in a higher elevated backswing. Again, the stretching method of choice is the stretch-contract-relax or PNF method if these muscles are tight or shortened.

The following muscles are the primary active muscles of the upper body used during the takeaway swing phase. To ensure optimal swing biomechanics, endurance, strength, and flexibility in the takeaway phase, these specific muscles should be conditioned.

TAKEAWAY SWING PHASE	
Primary Upper-Body Muscles	**Action**
A. Shoulder Rotator Cuff Muscles	
1. Infraspinatus (right)	Externally rotates arm
2. Supraspinatus (right)	Abduction of arm
3. Subscapularis (left)	Adduction and internal rotation of arm
B. Chest Muscles	
1. Pectoralis (left)	Adduction of arm, internally rotates arm
C. Forearm and Wrist Muscles	
1. Flexors	Flexes forearm and wrist, necessary for strong grip
2. Extensors and Radial Deviator	"Cocks" wrist

The stabilizing muscles active during the takeaway swing phase include the remaining shoulder rotator cuff muscles, the shoulder girdle muscles (rhomboid, levator scapula, upper trapezius), the deltoids, the biceps, the triceps, and the upper-back muscles (latissimus dorsi). These muscles also should be stretched and conditioned for optimal swing performance.

Lower-Body Muscle and Joint Involvement

Just as in the upper body, weak trunk and lower-body muscles that are stiff and tight will interfere with your ability to take the club back in a slow, rhythmic, one-piece motion. The specific muscles of the trunk and lower extremities that are involved in a technically correct, slow, rhythmic takeaway include the stomach muscles or the abdominal obliques, the buttock muscles (including the medial and lateral hip rotators), the left hip and thigh adductor muscles, and the left-foot evertor muscles, which roll the ankle inward. Other muscles that play a stabilizing or accessory role include the lower-back muscles, the stomach muscles, the knee flexors, the knee extensors (hamstrings), and the muscles of the calves.

Proper hip turn or rotation requires active contraction of the stomach oblique muscles and the hip rotator muscles. You should strive to achieve approximately 50° to 65° of hip turn at the end of the takeaway. The left external abdominal oblique and the right internal abdominal oblique muscles rotate the trunk. The left-hip medial rotator is the muscle that is primarily responsible for the hip turn during the takeaway. If the left-hip medial rotator is weak or there is tightening of the left-hip lateral rotator, your hip turn will be limited. Shortening or stiffness of the muscles that rotate the hips will significantly limit your ability to achieve the degree of hip rotation necessary for proper body turn at the top of the backswing. If you have difficulty reaching a hip turn of approximately 60°, stretching your hip muscles will be very helpful. This is a common problem in golfers above the age of 35 and it gradually worsens as you grow older. If you find yourself with diminished hip turn and you have no history of hip arthritis or joint problems, you can increase your rotation by simply stretching the left-hip lateral rotator. This will allow the left medial hip rotator to contract maximally without hindrance from the shortened lateral rotator muscles. I recommend stretching both hips to maintain muscle balance.

By increasing your hip turn, you will naturally be able to increase your shoulder turn. The shoulder turn recommended by teaching professionals should be approximately 90°. The hip turn should approximate 60°. These are considered "standards" and vary considerably among the professional ranks. However, neither the correct shoulder nor hip turn is possible without flexible shoulder and hip muscles. It is very important for the shoulder turn to be far enough to force a stretch of the trunk and hip muscles. The power in the swing comes from "coiling" the trunk and hip muscles during the takeaway. The more flexible the shoulder, trunk, and hip muscles, the greater the coiling, which makes for a more powerful turn.

The left leg is moved slightly inward (adducted) by activity of the left hip and thigh adductors. This muscle action "points" the left knee toward the ball

Just as in the upper body, weak trunk and lower-body muscles that are stiff and tight will interfere with your ability to take the club back in a slow, rhythmic, one-piece motion.

If you have difficulty reaching a hip turn of approximately 60°, stretching your hip muscles will be very helpful. This is a common problem in golfers above the age of 35 and it gradually worsens as you grow older.

at the top of the backswing. Proper weight distribution is maintained at the top of the backswing by the right-foot evertors, which must contract to keep the weight evenly distributed in the heel and inside of the right foot by slightly rolling the ankle inward. This muscle action keeps your weight from shifting to the outside of the foot, which causes sway at the top of the backswing. You must make a deliberate effort to strengthen these muscles as they progressively weaken with age. As this occurs, stability at the top of your backswing will be affected.

The following are the primary active muscles of the lower body used during the takeaway swing phase:

TAKEAWAY SWING PHASE	
Primary Lower-Body Muscles	**Action**
A. Abdominal Oblique Muscles 　1. Internal Oblique 　2. External Oblique	Rotates trunk to same side Rotates trunk to opposite side
B. Posterior Hip Muscles (Buttock) 　1. Gluteus Minimis (left)	Medial hip and thigh rotation
C. Medial Thigh Muscles 　1. Adductor Muscles (left)	Pulls thigh and hip inward (adduction)
D. Anterior Lower-Leg Muscles 　1. Peroneal Muscles (primarily right)	Rolls ankle and foot inward (eversion)

Muscles that help to stabilize the trunk, hips, and legs during the takeaway swing phase include the low-back muscles that stabilize the trunk during rotation, the left-hip abductor muscles, the left-knee extensor, the gluteus maximus or buttock musculature, the right-hip lateral rotator, and the right-hip abductor.

The joints of the trunk and lower body that are involved in the takeaway include the lumbar spine, the hip, and the knee. The range of these joints during the takeaway is minimal. Therefore, unless there is significant arthritis or other joint problems that severely decrease the range of motion of these joints, they will have minimal impact on a technically correct takeaway. The lumbar spine should be flexed slightly, which produces the slight bend at the waist throughout the takeaway swing phase. Golfers with a low-back injury or chronic low-back pain often find that this position aggravates their back conditions. If you find this to be affecting your game, I recommend that you decrease the forward-bend position by bending more at the hips. This will take the strain off of your lower back during your swing.

If you have knee problems, particularly unstable knee ligaments, you may experience discomfort with proper knee position at the top of the backswing, in which the left knee is rotated inward and the right knee is in its maximum weight-bearing position. The internal rotation of the left knee required during the end of the takeaway can put stress on the knee ligaments. If the natural position of the left knee at the end of the takeaway phase causes you pain, you may need to compensate your swing by rotating your torso farther, using less left-knee internal rotation and less bend of your left knee. This will help reduce the strain on the ligaments. For a majority of golfers, the required range of motion of the trunk and lower extremities is generally so minimal as to have little effect on the takeaway phase of the golf swing.

As is evident, a lot of muscle activity is required to produce a slow, coordinated, rhythmic takeaway of the club. If performed properly, this muscle activity establishes the tempo for the entire swing and ensures proper biomechanics throughout the other swing phases. These golf-specific muscles must be flexible and well conditioned to ensure optimal shoulder and hip turn. By actively engaging in a physical-conditioning and training program to increase flexibility and endurance of the specific muscles used during the takeaway swing phase, you can dramatically improve your game. Remember—the swing movement or biomechanics of the takeaway dictate how perfect the rest of your swing will be.

> *Remember:*
> *The swing movement or biomechanics of the takeaway dictate how perfect the rest of your swing will be.*

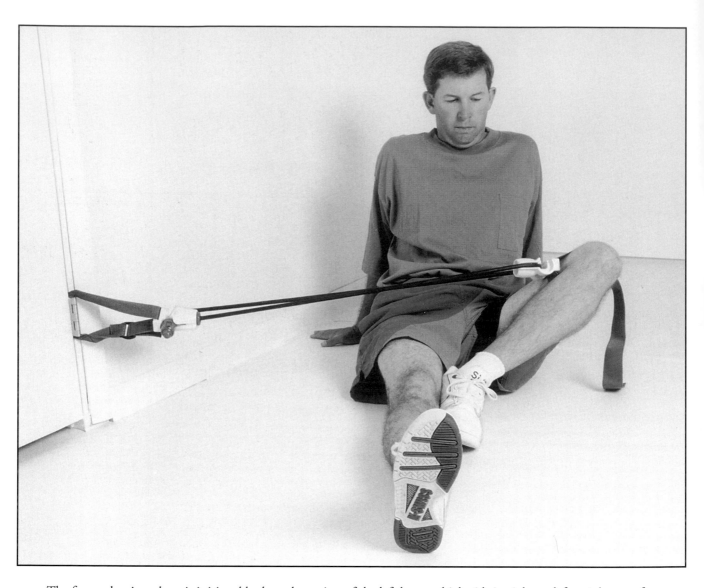

The forward swing phase is initiated by lateral rotation of the left knee, which aids in right-to-left weight transfer.

Forward Swing Phase

8

Golf-Specific
Muscle and
Joint Involvement
of the
Upper and
Lower Body

T
he forward swing phase begins at the initiation of the downswing (end of the backswing) and continues until the club shaft is horizontal. Teaching professionals will often tell you that, after the takeaway phase, the transition from the end of the backswing to the beginning of the downswing is the most critical move in golf.

For the right-handed golfer, the forward swing phase is initiated by transferring your weight from the right side of your body laterally to the left side by pushing off the inside of your right foot, making a lateral body shift toward the hole, and initiating hip turn. The right-to-left weight shift during the forward swing is aided by lateral rotation of your left hip, which moves your left knee out toward the target line. This action is performed by contracting the left-hip lateral rotator muscles (including the piriformis and accessory muscles of the posterior hip). The left-hip lateral rotator and the right-hip medial rotator, along with the right-foot evertor, are active at the same time. These biomechanical movements produce the synchronous weight shift from the right side to the left side, which initiates the forward swing.

Laterally rotating the left hip and knee toward the target causes an "uncoiling" effect that releases power at impact. This weight shift actually begins prior to the shoulders and hands reaching the top of the backswing. Just prior to the upper body finishing the takeaway phase, the feet, legs, and hips begin their turn, shifting the weight from the right leg to the left leg toward the target.

By simply rotating your left hip and knee outward at the beginning of the downswing, your weight is automatically transferred from your right foot to your left foot. This action, along with turning your right hip inward (medial rotation) and rolling your right ankle inward (eversion), guarantees correct right-to-left weight shift. Practice this motion at home in front of a mirror and on the driving range so that you can develop smooth, synchronous muscle contraction. You can feel this motion easily when you use the Golfercise System, because it helps you to feel the resistance in your buttocks as your hips and knees are laterally rotated at the beginning of the forward swing phase.

Once the lower-body muscles have come into play to initiate the forward swing, the upper-body muscles are activated. Jack Nicklaus describes the beginning of the forward swing phase as feeling the left shoulder move up as the right shoulder moves down. This feeling should occur as a consequence of the lower-body weight shift from right to left. The wrists remain fully "cocked" throughout the forward swing phase. The shoulders, arms, and hands should feel as though they are being pulled along by the lateral weight shift to the left side. During the weight shift that initiates the forward swing, the shoulder, arm, and hand muscles should be quiet. If they are active, you have developed the bad habit of hitting from the top. This occurs when the forearm and shoulder muscles initiate the forward swing before the hips move. In order to play your best golf, you must overcome this tendency.

As the body "uncoils" during the forward swing phase, the hands and wrists remain in the same position relative to the forearms. The wrists remain "cocked" throughout the forward swing. In order to keep from "uncocking" your wrists prematurely and hitting from the top, let your hip turn dictate upper-body shoulder and arm position. If you concentrate on maintaining a firm left side while your left elbow remains only slightly bent, you will achieve the correct swing arc. This swing arc of the upper body moves in concert with, albeit slightly behind, the lower-body weight shift and hip turn. If your left arm bends, the swing arc will come over the ball, weakening the club leverage and, more often than not, slicing the ball. The amateur golfer also has a natural tendency to rush the shoulder and arm turn during the forward swing phase, which tends to cause weak slices.

The power in the swing is developed by the "uncoiling" of the hip, back, and shoulder muscles. This "uncoiling" action is produced by transferring the muscle action from the feet to the legs through the hips and upper trunk into the shoulders, arms, and hands. The muscle action must occur in a smooth, synchronous manner, beginning in the lower body and moving up through the trunk to the shoulders and eventually to the wrists and hands. The "uncoiling" muscle action produces tremendous centrifugal force in the club head at the point of impact. Club-head speed begins during the latter part of the forward swing phase and increases during the acceleration swing phase, reaching maximum speed just after impact.

If any of the muscle groups that are required for a smooth, synchronous forward swing are weak or fatigued, this portion of the swing will suffer, resulting

Teaching professionals will often tell you that, after the takeaway phase, the transition from the end of the backswing to the beginning of the downswing is the most critical move in golf.

Jack Nicklaus describes the beginning of the forward swing phase as feeling the left shoulder move up as the right shoulder moves down.

in less power off the tee and shorter fairway shots. Technically correct movement of the "golf-specific" upper- and lower-body muscles activated during the downward swing phase requires flexibility and good conditioning.

Upper-Body Muscle and Joint Involvement

Although the forward swing is initiated by the lower body, muscles of the upper body do play an important role in providing proper biomechanics. Initially, at the top of the backswing, the upper-back muscles pull the arms downward. This downward motion initiates the upper-body forward swing. Toward the end of the forward swing phase, the shoulder internal rotator muscle begins to contract actively. This activity continues during the acceleration phase and throughout the rest of the swing.

The contraction of the left-shoulder internal rotator muscle is critical for a technically correct swing, because this contraction acts as the lever that firms up the left upper body. I believe that you cannot become a highly skilled golfer without developing a strong left-shoulder internal rotator that actively contracts during the forward swing phase.

The right-chest muscle, or pectoralis, is also active during the forward swing and brings the right arm inward (right shoulder and arm adduction). The left-chest muscle, although active, plays a less important role in the forward swing.

The following upper-body muscles are the most active during the forward swing phase. They must be in good condition to ensure proper biomechanics for a technically correct forward swing.

During the weight shift that initiates the forward swing, the shoulder, arm, and hand muscles should be quiet. If they are active, you have developed the bad habit of hitting from the top. This occurs when the forearm and shoulder muscles initiate the forward swing before the hips move. In order to play your best golf, you must overcome this tendency.

FORWARD SWING PHASE	
Primary Upper-Body Muscles	**Action**
A. Shoulder Rotator Cuff Muscles 1. Subscapularis (both sides active)	Internally rotates and adducts the arm
B. Chest Muscles 1. Pectoralis (primarily right)	Internally rotates arm Adduction of raised arm — pulls down
C. Upper-Back Muscles 1. Latissimus Dorsi (both sides active)	Internally rotates arm Adduction of raised arm — pulls down

The upper-body stabilizing muscles active during the forward swing phase are the shoulder rotator cuff muscles, including infraspinatus and supraspinatus, biceps, triceps, forearm muscles (wrist flexors and extensors), forearm radial deviators that keep the wrists "cocked," and wrist pronators and supinators.

The muscles of the upper body involved in the forward swing phase require stamina rather than strength. Stamina is of major importance in maintaining a smooth, rhythmic downward motion. This is particularly helpful toward the end of the round when these muscles begin to fatigue.

Flexibility does not play a major role in the middle or end of this swing phase but is important at the beginning or top of the backswing. Flexibility and range of motion of the shoulders were addressed in the previous chapter on the takeaway swing phase. It is enough to remember that upper-body strength is less critical than stamina during this phase of the swing. Upper-body muscle strength comes more into play during the acceleration phase, particularly through the "impact zone." This will be discussed in the next chapter.

However, endurance and conditioning cannot be stressed enough for proper forward swing biomechanics. If the upper-body musculature begins to fatigue from being out of shape, your swing will lose the smooth, rhythmic motion so necessary for a technically correct swing. Any alteration of the swing in the forward phase due to weak or tight upper-body muscles will significantly affect performance by altering the tracking of the club during this most critical portion of the golf swing.

> *The muscles of the upper body involved in the forward swing phase require stamina rather than strength. Stamina is of major importance in maintaining a smooth, rhythmic downward motion.*

Lower-Body Muscle and Joint Involvement

Anyone who has played much golf realizes that the transition from the backswing to the beginning of the forward swing is the most difficult phase of the golf swing to master because it requires considerable coordination, which generally comes only with natural athletic ability. The slightest biomechanical flaw that may occur during this transition will be a primary cause for errant shots and high scores. Without a technically correct transition from the end of the takeaway to the beginning of the forward swing, it is next to impossible to lower your score.

You should begin the forward swing with your lower body before your upper body has completed the takeaway swing phase. This is done by initiating the forward hip turn as your shoulder turn completes the backswing. The forward swing begins by a right-to-left weight shift and hip rotation. This critical action sets the rest of the swing for proper sequencing. During the left lateral hip turn, your weight is *automatically* transferred from the right foot to the left foot. This should be done without conscious effort. Correct hip turn also

> *The transition from the backswing to the beginning of the forward swing is the most difficult phase of the golf swing to master because it requires considerable coordination.*

rotates your left hip out of the way, allowing for proper shoulder and arm movement through the ball at impact. But most importantly, it is the hip turn at the beginning of the forward phase which begins to unleash the force and power so necessary for distance. This motion places you in a powerful hitting position with the large muscles of the legs, buttock, and trunk able to perform optimally at impact.

The initial hip movement is produced by the left-hip lateral rotator muscle group, which is located deep in the left buttock. Left-hip rotation must occur in concert with contraction of the right medial hip rotator. By synchronizing contraction of the left lateral hip rotator with right medial hip rotation, you will achieve a smooth hip turn. These muscles become stretched or "coiled" at the end of the takeaway phase, allowing for maximum contraction as you begin the forward swing. If these hip muscles are weak or tight (shortened), your hip turn, beginning at the top of the backswing, will be hindered. The hip rotation or turn is also aided by the trunk turn, produced by contraction of the stomach oblique muscles. Decreased hip turn will produce less speed and force at impact, resulting in shorter shots. It is therefore necessary not only to strengthen these muscles but to stretch them for proper hip rotation to ensure maximum power at impact. Specific hip-muscle exercises are described in Chapters 12 and 13.

Hip rotation initiates the sequence of the forward swing—not the hands, arms, or shoulders, which is so often the case in the poorer player. If you do not initiate proper hip turn or rotation, your swing plane will be from the outside-in, producing a slice, fade, or pull because the club is forced to cut across the ball. All players, from the amateur to the professional, must initiate the downswing with the hips and make a conscious effort to keep the hands and shoulders from interfering with this action. If hip turn is initiated correctly, the hands and shoulders will automatically follow, coming into play at the proper time.

Strong hip rotators are critical for proper hip turn or rotation, but these muscles are often weak or shortened in the amateur golfer. This weakness produces many an errant shot and cannot be overcome by instruction alone. In addition to the hip turn, the lateral weight shift is also aided by the left-hip abductor muscles. Contraction of these muscles aids in the weight shift from the right to the left side. This weight shift also is enhanced by contraction of the right medial thigh muscles or adductors. Specific thigh-muscle exercises are described in Chapters 12 and 13. You must stretch and condition this crucial muscle group.

The correct swing sequence for the forward swing phase begins with lateral movement of the left hip and knee, produced by contracting the left lateral hip rotator muscles. At the same time as this is occurring, the right knee begins to

> *You should begin the forward swing with your lower body before your upper body has completed the takeaway phase. This is done by initiating the forward hip turn as your shoulder turn completes the backswing.*

> *Strong hip rotators are critical for proper hip turn or rotation, but these muscles are often weak or shortened in the amateur golfer. This weakness produces many an errant shot and cannot be overcome by instruction alone.*

drive toward the hole. This motion is produced by contraction of the right medial hip rotator muscles and the right medial thigh muscles (thigh adductors).

During the hip turn, there is right-ankle eversion or rolling of the right ankle inward. This movement is achieved by contraction of the anterior leg muscles. If this muscle group, located in the lateral part of the anterior leg, is weak, the ankle will not roll inward, and this will decrease your ability to push off your right medial foot at impact. Weakness of the right ankle and foot eversion muscles will also affect weight transfer from the right to the left side, with the weight having a tendency to remain on the outside of the right foot at the top of the backswing. This occurs because the ankle is rolled outward due to poor swing mechanics and weak anterior leg muscles. The weight should be distributed evenly on the heel and ball of your right foot at the top of the backswing. This weight distribution is difficult to accomplish without slightly rolling your right ankle "inward" by contracting your ankle eversion muscles.

The ankle roll is followed by your left arm being pulled downward by contraction of your upper-back muscles and chest muscles along with strong contraction of your left-shoulder internal rotator muscle, which internally rotates your left shoulder and pulls your left arm into the hitting zone. The internal rotation of your left shoulder at impact rotates your forearm toward the target for straight shots. This action also produces tremendous firmness and power of your left arm at impact. As your left knee begins to rotate externally, due to the left hip turn, there is simultaneous contraction of your abdominal oblique muscles, your right abdominal external oblique, and your left abdominal internal oblique. Contraction of your abdominal oblique muscles produces the trunk rotation that accompanies the hip turn.

The primary muscles that are active during the forward swing phase include the left lateral hip rotator, which causes the left knee and hip to rotate laterally, initiating left hip turn. This is aided by contraction of the left lateral thigh and hip abductor muscles. As your left hip begins to turn, contraction of your right medial hip rotator muscle aids in initiating proper hip turn and lateral weight shifting from your right foot to your left foot. This weight shift is enhanced by contraction of the right medial thigh and hip adductor muscle and the right-foot evertor muscle. Once the hip turn is initiated, contraction of your stomach oblique muscles comes into play, producing rotation of the trunk. By first contracting your hip and trunk muscles in this fashion, you will force your shoulders to follow the hip turn, ensuring a technically correct forward swing.

The following are the primary hip and trunk muscles that are active during the forward swing phase. These muscles must not be neglected in your golf-specific strength and conditioning program.

The correct swing sequence for the forward swing phase begins with lateral movement of the left hip and knee. At the same time, the right knee begins to drive toward the hole.

FORWARD SWING PHASE

Primary Lower-Body Muscles	Action

A   Stomach Oblique Muscles
    1. Internal Oblique
    2. External Oblique
	Trunk Turn
	   Rotates trunk to same side
	   Rotates trunk to opposite side

B. Posterior Hip Muscles (Buttock)
    1. Lateral Hip Rotator — Piriformis (left)
    2. Medial Hip Rotator (right)
	Hip Turn
	   Rotates hip and knee laterally
	   Rotates hip and knee medially

C. Medial Thigh Muscles
    1. Adductor Muscle (right)
	Lateral Weight Shift
	   Pulls thigh and hip inward (adduction)

D. Outer Thigh Muscles
    1. Tensor Fascia Lata (left)
    2. Gluteus Medius (left)
	Lateral Weight Shift
	   Pulls thigh and hip outward (abduction)
	   Pulls thigh and hip outward (abduction)

E. Anterior Lower-Leg Muscles
    1. Foot and Ankle Eversion (right)
        Peroneal Muscles
	Lateral Weight Shift
	   Rolls ankle and foot inward (eversion)

The stabilizing or accessory muscles that aid the primary muscles of the trunk and lower body include the low-back muscles, the hip extensors, the posterior thigh muscles (hamstring), the anterior thigh muscles, and the calf muscles. Supportive action of these muscles will allow the primary muscles to perform optimally during the forward swing phase.

In performing a golf-specific flexibility, endurance, and strengthening program, all the primary muscles involved in the forward swing must be stretched and strengthened for proper swing biomechanics as described in Chapters 11, 12, and 13. By selectively conditioning these specific muscles, a smooth, rhythmic transition from the end of the takeaway to the beginning of the forward swing phase becomes possible. The specific muscles of the shoulder, trunk, and hips require optimal conditioning for proper swing biomechanics. These muscles should be selectively stretched and strengthened for a complete golf physical-conditioning and training program.

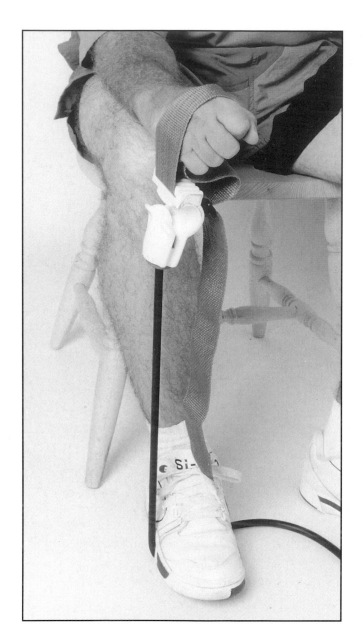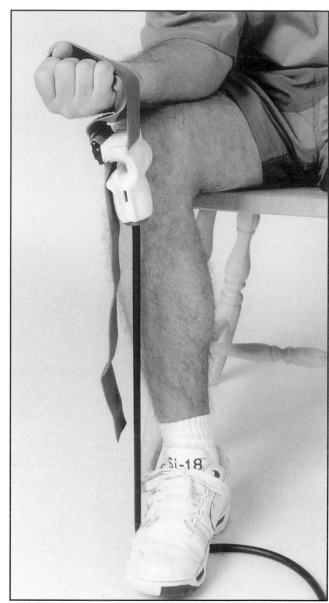

The forearm muscles play a pivotal role in squaring the club face on impact.

Acceleration Swing Phase

9

Golf-Specific
Muscle and
Joint Involvement
of the
Upper and
Lower Body

T he acceleration swing phase begins at the end of the forward swing phase with the club shaft horizontal and continues through impact with the ball. At the beginning of the acceleration swing phase, the wrists are fully "cocked," with the arms and hands relaxed so as to allow the natural tendency of the club to move as your body uncoils. At this early point in the acceleration phase, try not to accelerate or decelerate the club head consciously. Allow your arms to work automatically with your legs and hips.

At the end of the acceleration swing phase, when the club enters the impact zone—the point where maximum centrifugal club-head speed is achieved—the wrists should automatically "uncock" from the force. The right arm should be bent slightly with the elbow facing downward and close to the body at impact. Many teaching professionals refer to this action as similar to the arm biomechanics of a softball pitcher. Just prior to impact, the wrists "uncock" as the right arm starts to straighten, producing a whipping sensation of the club head toward the ball. This "uncocking" or release of the wrists will produce maximum speed and power at impact.

Many amateur players tend to hurry the club head by "uncocking" the wrists too early. This tendency is alleviated by allowing the natural centrifugal force to build up in the wrists to the point where they "uncock" naturally by allowing the hips and trunk to pull the arms into the ball rather than hitting from the "top." Keeping the right elbow behind the right hip prior to impact is important in aiding this motion. If your shoulders and arms move ahead of the hip turn during the acceleration swing phase, the club will move across the target line on an outside-to-inside motion. This club path produces inaccurate shots, decreases power at impact, and significantly affects performance. The preferred club path is for the club to move through the target line from an inside-to-outside path.

Jack Nicklaus discusses four movements to strive for as the club head impacts the ball: 1) keeping the head steady and behind the ball; 2) swinging the club head through the ball, not at the ball; 3) maintaining a straight left arm moving toward the target; and 4) resisting any twisting of the club with the hands or wrists. These movements, if perfected, will increase your power at impact by aligning the club down the target, squaring the club face with the ball, and increasing club-head speed. This will also greatly increase your distance by maximizing your power.

Unfortunately, power or distance is often confused with the size or strength of the golfer. Being "muscle bound" does not equate with power or distance. Nor does overpowering the ball down the fairway by trying to "kill it" produce distance. *Distance comes from timing your swing and applying technically correct swing biomechanics. Timing is produced by a smooth, rhythmic swing with the muscles working in concert.* This action cannot be achieved by trying to "muscle" or "force" your shot. The keys to a smooth, rhythmic swing are to practice developing a technically correct swing and to condition your muscles so that they respond the same way over and over again in the same synchronous manner. If your golf muscles are out of shape or tight, I do not believe that you can achieve a technically correct swing on a consistent basis.

There are some fundamental biomechanical movements that all successful players are able to accomplish just prior to impact. At the beginning of the acceleration phase, a right-handed golfer's body weight is shifted to the left side as the hips turn. Hip turn is then followed by the shoulder turn, with the arms pulling down the target line. Finally, the hands "uncock" as the club face turns square with the ball during the "unhinging" motion of the wrists. The left elbow or wrist must not collapse or bend at impact. These biomechanical movements must be performed unconsciously in a smooth, synchronous manner, which cannot be achieved consistently unless the muscles that produce this motion are in shape.

During the acceleration phase, stamina and strength play key roles in your performance, particularly for a consistently smooth and rhythmic swing and during the latter holes of play when you begin to tire. Joint and muscle flexibility play a less important role than endurance and strength. The primary muscles that are active during this portion of the swing must be conditioned and strengthened for maximum performance. Descriptions of these specific exercises are in Chapters 11, 12, and 13.

Upper-Body Muscle and Joint Involvement

In the acceleration swing phase, both upper- and lower-body muscles play a vital role in achieving a technically correct swing that ensures accuracy and

---

Many amateur players tend to hurry the club head by "uncocking" the wrists too early. This tendency is alleviated by allowing the natural centrifugal force to build up in the wrists to the point where they "uncock" naturally by allowing the hips and trunk to pull the arms into the ball rather than hitting from the "top."

Distance comes from timing your swing and applying technically correct swing biomechanics. Timing is produced by a smooth, rhythmic swing with the muscles working in concert.

---

distance. The shoulder muscles, both front (chest) and back (rotator cuff muscles), are quite active during the acceleration swing phase. The power generated by the upper body during acceleration is produced by the lateral upper-back muscles (lats) and the chest muscles. These muscles produce maximum velocity or centrifugal force of the club head just prior to impact. The left latissimus dorsi pulls the left shoulder downward during the forward swing and in early acceleration and brings the arms and hands into the hitting zone just prior to "uncocking" the wrists. The right latissimus dorsi pulls the right shoulder and arm downward and under during this swing phase.

The chest muscles are also very active throughout the acceleration swing phase, as they bring the arms in close to the body (arm adduction) and aid in internal rotation of the shoulders. Research has shown that the chest muscles are the most active of the upper-body muscles during the acceleration swing phase, producing a major portion of the power that the upper body generates at impact. The chest muscles contract along with the lateral upper-back muscles (lats) and shoulder rotator cuff muscles in a synchronous manner. The muscles on *both* sides of the body work in concert to produce this power. Because the lats and chest muscles generate the power at impact, strengthening these muscles is vital for distance and accuracy and should not be neglected in any golf-specific conditioning program.

The rotator cuff muscles of the shoulders also are very active during the acceleration swing phase. Contraction of the right-shoulder internal rotator muscle, part of the rotator cuff muscle group, internally rotates the right arm and shoulder during the forward swing phase and continues through the acceleration-impact swing phase. This action brings the club into the hitting zone as the wrists unhinge or "uncock" prior to impact and is necessary for proper club alignment through the hitting zone. Should the shoulder internal rotator muscle be weak, tight, or stiff, it is very difficult to maintain a smooth, rhythmic swing. Contraction of the left-shoulder internal rotator of the rotator cuff muscle keeps the left shoulder and arm medially rotated at impact. If you roll your left shoulder or arm outward (lateral rotation) at impact, you will have a tendency to come "across" the ball, closing the club head. This will produce a wide variety of aberrant shots. Internal rotation of the left shoulder at impact ensures a firm left upper body. This muscle action is required for accuracy and distance.

Your left wrist, forearm, and elbow should face down the target line at impact. This arm position is produced by correctly rotating your left shoulder internally by contraction of the left subscapularis during the acceleration phase. The subscapularis muscles on both sides of the body need to be stretched and strengthened to ensure proper forearm alignment throughout the acceleration swing phase and through the hitting zone. Contrary to current teaching concepts, research now shows that the left-shoulder muscles do *not* give any more power

Because the lats and chest muscles generate the power at impact, strengthening these muscles is vital for distance and accuracy and should not be neglected in any golf-specific conditioning program.

Your left wrist, forearm, and elbow should face down the target line at impact. This arm position is produced by correctly rotating your left shoulder internally by contraction of the left subscapularis during the acceleration phase.

or "drive" through the acceleration swing phase than the right-side muscles. Therefore, exercising the upper-body muscles must be done equally and *bilaterally* to achieve maximum results. You should focus your conditioning program on bilaterally exercising your chest muscles, your upper-back muscles, and your shoulder internal rotator cuff muscle.

The forearm muscles are also very active during the acceleration swing phase. Just prior to impact, active contraction of the wrist flexor muscles "uncocks" the wrists (ulnar deviation). The contraction of these muscles aids in releasing centrifugal force at impact. These forearm muscles must be conditioned and strengthened for endurance and power. In addition, the forearm wrist extensors, particularly the left-forearm extensors, must be strong enough to maintain a flat or straightened left wrist upon impact. If your wrists "break" or "slap" at the ball at impact, you are sure to have many errant shots. Strong forearm muscles will help you to avoid this incorrect wrist motion. In addition, the forearm muscles are also responsible for wrist supination/pronation just prior to impact. This action occurs as the wrists "uncock." If either the forearm extensor or flexor muscles are weak, stiff, or tight, the unhinging or "uncocking" of the wrist at impact will be affected. A common result of weak forearm muscles is a fade, push, or slice due to the club head's being open at impact. This occurs because the wrists are not "squared" with the ball.

The following muscles are the primary active muscles of the upper body used during the acceleration swing phase.

ACCELERATION SWING PHASE

Primary Upper-Body Muscles	Action
A. Shoulder Rotator Cuff Muscles 1. Subscapularis	Adduction and internal rotation of arm
B. Chest Muscles 1. Pectoralis Major	Adduction of raised arm — pulls downward Internally rotates arm
C. Upper-Back Muscles 1. Latissimus Dorsi (lats)	Adduction of raised arm — pulls downward Internally rotates arm
D. Forearm and Wrist Muscles 1. Flexors 2. Extensors 3. Ulnar Deviation 4. Pronation/Supination	Flexes the wrist Extends the wrists "Uncocks" the wrists Rolls the wrists into the hitting zone

Other muscles of the shoulders and arms that play a stabilizing role in ensuring a smooth and rhythmic acceleration swing phase motion include the biceps, the triceps, the deltoids, the neck muscles, and the shoulder-girdle muscles.

It is important to stretch and strengthen these golf-specific upper-body muscles, especially the chest muscles, lats, internal shoulder rotator muscles, and forearm muscles, to ensure maximum power and distance at impact. Chapters 11 and 13 outline a specific conditioning and training program for these muscles that will improve your performance during the acceleration swing phase.

Lower-Body Muscle and Joint Involvement

During the acceleration swing phase, the legs and hips provide the primary motivating force that produces the club-head speed. The skilled amateur and the professional have developed the strong leg and hip action necessary for distance off the tee. The strong contraction or firing of the leg and hip muscles during the acceleration swing phase produces most of the acceleration and power at impact. The coupling of the lower-body, leg, and hip muscles with the upper-body muscles unleashes tremendous centrifugal force at impact. The less skilled amateur often uncouples this action by overutilizing the shoulders and arms during the forward and acceleration swing phases. Swinging from the "top," rather than initiating the lower-body hip turn, greatly reduces acceleration, power, and accuracy.

During the acceleration swing phase, your legs should laterally thrust down the target line as your hips and trunk rotate into the hitting plane. It is recommended by some to shift the hips laterally toward the target prior to the actual hip turn. The weight shift from the right leg to the left leg requires active contraction of the left lateral thigh abductor muscles. These muscles should feel firm or tight just prior to impact. The weight transfer also requires active contraction of the right medial thigh adductor muscles. These muscles, located in the medial thigh of the right leg, shift the weight to your left side and aid in medially rotating the right knee toward the ball.

You can develop the "feel" for what these muscles are doing as you shift your weight from the right side to the left by practicing with the Golfercise System. Use the resistive tubing to hold back your swing while you swing through the end of the acceleration swing phase. Attach the resistive tubing to the handle and secure the other end of the support strap to a door; then pull down on the club handle in the mid-forward swing phase position. By shifting your weight with proper hip turn and lateral movement, you should be able to feel contraction of the outside muscles of your left thigh and the inside muscles

During the acceleration swing phase, the legs and hips provide the primary motivating force that produces the club-head speed.

Swinging from the "top," rather than initiating the lower-body hip turn, greatly reduces acceleration, power, and accuracy.

of your right thigh, as well as firmness of your buttock muscles. These muscles must contract in synchrony for weight transfer from the right to the left side in the acceleration swing phase. If these muscles are weak, tight, or stiff, a smooth, rhythmic weight transfer and lateral body shift toward the ball will be difficult. Problems with smooth lateral body shift will tend to interfere with the alignment of the club head at impact, making square contact with the ball almost impossible.

Toward the middle of the acceleration swing phase, the hips actively rotate or turn toward the target line by contracting the medial and lateral hip muscles. This action produces the hip turn that is so critical for a technically correct swing. The hip turn occurs with the right hip pushing toward the target and the left hip pulled out of the way, allowing for a clear path of the forearms through the ball. The right hip thrust into the ball produces the correct knee turn with the right knee pointing toward the ball at impact. This action occurs as the hips begin to turn prior to impact. By controlling the amount of hip turn, you will be able to produce an "educated" fade or draw.

There is a tendency to fade the ball with an earlier hip turn and to draw with a delayed hip turn. This action is controlled by the timing of the contraction of the hip rotator muscles.

There is a tendency to fade the ball with an earlier hip turn and to draw with a delayed hip turn. This action is controlled by the timing of the contraction of the hip rotator muscles. As the hips begin to turn prior to impact, there should be a strong feeling of muscle tightness or firmness of the left side of the leg due to strong contraction of the left lateral leg muscles, which are producing the left lateral weight shift as well as aiding in the hip rotation. In addition, there should be a feeling of muscle tightness or firmness in the left buttock region, which is due to contraction of the lateral hip rotator muscle that produces the left hip turn.

Throughout this swing phase, your knees should remain slightly bent or flexed. The medial and lateral leg muscles and posterior hip muscles must contract in a smooth, synchronous manner throughout impact in order for the club head to be accelerating at impact. When these muscles work in a synchronous fashion, you will "feel" the shot at the exact time of impact. Remember that when you initiate the hip turn too quickly, you will tend to produce a fade or slice. By strengthening the medial and lateral leg muscles and the posterior hip muscles, you should be able to develop a smooth, synchronous lateral weight shift accompanied by a correct hip turn.

The leg and hip muscles must be strengthened and stretched to provide maximum hip turn at impact. If they are weak, you will again tend to hit from the "top" by using your arms to initiate the downward swing.

The leg and hip muscles must be strengthened and stretched to provide maximum hip turn at impact. If they are weak, you will again tend to hit from the "top" by using your arms to initiate the downward swing. It has been my experience in evaluating golfers that these muscles are often weak, tightened, or shortened, prohibiting a proper hip turn. I am continually recommending to amateur golfers that they pay particular attention to stretching and strengthening the posterior hip muscles, because they are vital for a technically correct swing and produce tremendous club-head force at impact.

It is surprising to me how often the posterior hip muscles are overlooked in physical-conditioning programs. These muscles are so important to golf that they should be near or at the top of the list of muscles to be stretched and exercised if you want to perfect your game. I have known many amateur golfers who lowered their scores significantly just by focusing on improving the flexibility and condition of these posterior hip muscles.

The muscles that produce the weight transfer with subsequent lateral thrust of the lower body toward the target and the muscles that cause the hip and trunk rotation just prior to impact are not generally considered strong muscles. In addition, the muscles that produce this action have a tendency to shorten and weaken with age. Although the strong knee and hip flexors and extensors aid in the acceleration swing phase, they are not the primary active muscles. I have found that the primary lower-body muscles active during the acceleration swing phase are weak or shortened on most amateur golfers. Because of this common condition, the amateur golfer has a built-in handicap from the beginning. It is important to isolate these muscles specifically in order to determine any shortening or weakness. These muscles must be stretched and strengthened for a technically correct swing and are vital during the acceleration swing phase. Of all the muscles utilized during the golf swing, it is my opinion that the hip rotators, the thigh abductor, and the thigh adductor are the most important and must be exercised to improve the quality of your game. Refer to Chapters 12 and 13 for specific recommendations on how to stretch and exercise these critical golf muscles.

In addition to the hips, the trunk also turns down the target line during the acceleration swing phase. This occurs by the action of the internal and external abdominal oblique muscles. Contraction of the right abdominal external oblique muscle and the left abdominal internal oblique muscle rotates the trunk to the left. These oblique muscles must act in concert for strong trunk rotation. As you age, these muscles weaken, decreasing the amount of strength available for trunk turn at impact. Without proper hip and trunk turn, distance is greatly affected. Synchronous contraction of the right external oblique and left internal oblique produces rotation of the trunk into the ball. If you have weakened stomach muscles, your trunk turn will be affected. Weak stomach muscles cause you to swing more with your arms, which decreases acceleration at impact. This produces decreased distance and forces you to swing from the outside-in, causing slices or fades. The well-conditioned golfer is able to rotate the trunk by strong contraction of the abdominal muscles as the club meets the ball. This action, coupled with the contraction of the leg and hip muscles, produces tremendous power at impact.

The lateral trunk muscles of the back allow for lateral flexion of the spine just prior to impact. This action occurs simultaneously with trunk turn. If this

> *It is surprising how often the posterior hip muscles are overlooked in physical-conditioning programs. These muscles are so important to golf that they should be near or at the top of the list of muscles to be stretched and exercised if you want to perfect your game.*

Some touring professionals prefer to have the weight distributed evenly on the sole and slightly on the inside of the left foot at impact, with the ankle beginning to roll outward after impact.

muscle is weak, you will be prone to developing back pain or exacerbating an existing back condition during play. The quadratus lumborum muscle, which laterally bends the spine, should be strengthened on both sides for proper muscle balance.

Right-ankle eversion, or rolling the ankle inward, also plays an important role during the acceleration swing phase. The muscles that roll the ankle inward allow you to push off with the inside of your right foot just prior to impact. These muscles are also often weak and shortened in the amateur golfer. As the club enters the hitting zone at the end of the acceleration swing phase, the left ankle rolls outward slightly. This movement must occur slowly as the weight moves from the inside of the left foot toward the outside. Some touring professionals prefer to have the weight distributed evenly on the sole and heel and slightly on the inside of the left foot at impact, with the ankle beginning to roll outward after impact. This action helps to maintain a firm left side at impact.

ACCELERATION SWING PHASE	
Primary Lower-Body Muscles	**Action**

A. Abdominal Oblique Muscles
    1. Internal Oblique
    2. External Oblique
	Trunk Rotation
	    Rotates trunk to same side
	    Rotates trunk to opposite side

B. Lateral Trunk Muscles
    1. Quadratus Lumborum (right)
	Lateral Trunk Bending
	    Bends trunk to same side;
	    raises hip of same side

C. Posterior Hip Muscles (Buttock)
    1. Gluteus Minimis (right)
    2. Piriformis and accessory muscles
       (left)
	Hip Turn
	    Medial hip and thigh rotation
	    Lateral hip and thigh rotation

D. Medial Thigh Muscles
    1. Adductor Muscles (right)
	Lateral Weight Shift
	    Pulls thigh and hip inward (adduction)

E. Outer Thigh Muscles
    1. Tensor Fascia Lata (left)
    2. Gluteus Medius (left)
	Lateral Weight Shift
	    Pulls thigh and hip outward (abduction)
	    Pulls thigh and hip outward (abduction)

F. Anterior Lower-Leg Muscles
    1. Anterior Tibialis (left)
    2. Peroneal Muscles (right)
	Lateral Weight Shift
	    Rolls ankle and foot outward (inversion)
	    Rolls ankle and foot inward (eversion)

The ankle muscles that produce rolling of the ankle must be strong or you will experience a breakdown in correct swing biomechanics as the club enters the hitting zone. The muscles that roll the ankle inward and outward are located in the anterior leg. The ankle eversion muscles roll the ankle and foot inward. Active contraction of these muscles of the right foot allows you to drive off the inside of your right foot at impact. If you tend to sprain your ankle frequently, strengthening these muscles is a must. The ankle inversion muscles roll the ankle and foot outward. Just after impact, the left ankle rolls outward during the follow-through swing phase. In addition, ankle inversion and eversion muscles support the arch of your foot and therefore need to be exercised to protect against "fallen arches," which can be a source of discomfort for the golfer who walks the course carrying clubs. You can use the Golfercise System to get the feel for how these muscles work during the acceleration swing phase.

The muscles listed in the previous chart are the primary active lower-body muscles used during the acceleration swing phase. To ensure proper swing biomechanics during acceleration through impact, these lower-body muscles must be strengthened and exercised for maximum performance.

In addition to the primary muscles, numerous stabilizing muscles must be in good condition for proper swing biomechanics during the acceleration swing phase: the hip extensor musculature, the knee extensor, the knee flexor (hamstring muscles), and the calf muscles. A complete golf-specific exercise conditioning program should include stretching and strengthening of these muscles, as well as of the primary ones.

The primary muscles of the upper and lower body that actively contract during the acceleration swing phase provide the maximum centrifugal force at impact, which generates your power. Common sense follows that these muscles need to be conditioned and strengthened for maximum power and distance. However, I have found that many "generic" weight-conditioning programs limit or ignore exercise routines for these important muscles. This is particularly true of the hip rotator muscles, the thigh abductors, the anterior leg muscles (which roll the ankle inward and outward), the lateral trunk muscles (which bend the spine to the side), and the rotator cuff muscles of the shoulders. When I ask a golfer which muscles he routinely exercises in the gym, these muscles are usually not mentioned. You cannot ignore these muscle groups if you desire to improve your game and lower your score. Conditioning them is as important as practicing on the range.

A systematic conditioning and training program designed to exercise these muscles is described in Chapters 11, 12, and 13. I guarantee that if you follow these golf-specific conditioning exercises, your distance will improve and you will decrease your chance of injury. Remember—conditioning must accompany time on the practice range for best results.

The ankle muscles that produce rolling of the ankle must be strong or you will experience a breakdown in correct swing biomechanics as the club enters the hitting zone.

Remember: Conditioning must accompany time on the practice range for best results.

Strong lateral trunk muscles (outer lower back) stabilize the trunk for a complete and balanced follow-through.

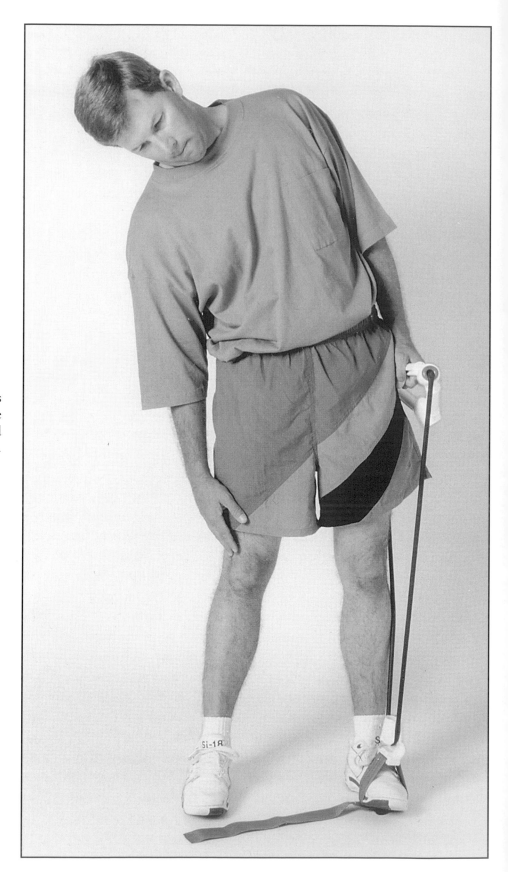

Follow-Through Swing Phase

Golf-Specific
Muscle and
Joint Involvement
of the
Upper and
Lower Body

10

The follow-through swing phase begins after impact with the ball and ends with your hands and the club at the top of the finish of the swing. This phase of the golf swing is important because a technically correct follow-through forces you to swing through the ball at impact rather than "at" it. Many amateurs tend to chop or hit at the ball, with the club slowing down at impact. This swing flaw decreases your power and makes hitting the ball squarely almost impossible. It can be alleviated by a proper follow-through.

The speed developed during the acceleration phase and through impact produces the high follow-through. You should think consciously about a full follow-through, because thinking about hitting the ball, as most amateurs do, tends to slow the club down before impact. A conscious follow-through, in contrast, will help you accelerate through the ball. Remember that, in a technically correct swing, the club head does not reach maximum speed until just beyond impact with the ball.

The speed that is developed in the impact zone produces the momentum that carries the club up and over the shoulders with the hips rotating down the target line. At the end of the follow-through, the hips should be facing the target line with the shoulders rotating past the target line. Some teaching professionals even go so far as to suggest that the hips may turn even further down the target line. This action can be done only with a full follow-through. For maximum club-head speed to occur just past impact, imagine hitting a second ball about a foot beyond your actual ball. Greg Norman recommends this mental picture to accelerate the club rather than slowing it down at impact. When performed properly, the follow-through ensures that your club head is

Many amateurs tend to chop or hit at the ball, with the club slowing down at impact. This swing flaw decreases your power and makes hitting the ball squarely almost impossible.

still accelerating well past impact and throughout the hitting zone. Always keep in mind that once you have hit the ball, nothing you say or do will affect its flight path.

At the point just beyond impact in the early stage of the follow-through, most of your weight should be on your left foot. Some professionals recommend that the weight be on the inside of the left foot with the weight rolling to the outside of the foot as the club reaches horizontal and finishes at the top. By keeping your weight on the inside of your left foot through impact, you maintain a firm, strong left side of the body, which provides maximum power. As the club elevates after impact, the weight is then transferred to the outside of your left foot and remains there through the end of the follow-through. In the early stage of the follow-through, the weight on your right foot is on the inside, predominantly in the forefoot region. Your right heel begins to leave the ground and continues to rise until the sole of your shoe faces backward at the end of the follow-through. This action is done unconsciously and is produced by the rotation of your hips down the target line.

By keeping your weight on the inside of your left foot through impact, you maintain a firm, strong left side of the body, which provides maximum power.

With your drives and long iron shots, your upper body, including the shoulders, arms, wrists, and hands, are pulled along by the momentum of the acceleration through the ball and the rotation of the hips down the target line during the full follow-through. Just past impact, the back of your left wrist and arm should face down the target line. As you complete your follow-through, your arms should swing out toward the target line, ending up and out. This ensures a full, high finish, with your hands held over your shoulders. Just past impact, the shoulder turn is dictated by the momentum of the club. In the early follow-through phase, your left shoulder is moving upward and your right shoulder is moving downward. This shoulder turn continues until, at the end of the follow-through, your right shoulder has been rotated underneath your chin and your left shoulder is behind your head.

Through the impact zone, keep your head "down" on the shot until your shoulders begin to pull your chin upward toward the end of the follow-through. This action generally occurs when your hands are about parallel with the ground. It is important that you don't sneak a peek during the early stage of the follow-through, because it will affect the impact of the club on the ball. Many an errant shot has occurred because of this simple swing flaw.

Upper-Body Muscle and Joint Involvement

Although the joints of the upper body, including the shoulders, the neck, and the wrists, are pulled through the shot by the momentum developed during the acceleration swing phase, there is some upper-body muscle activity during the follow-through swing phase. As discussed in the previous chapter, the anterior chest muscles and upper-back muscles (lats)—the primary upper-body muscles responsible for the power generated at impact—gradually decrease their level of activity throughout the follow-through. However, they are still very active during this swing phase.

The left-shoulder internal rotator muscle is also active during the acceleration phase and continues to be so throughout the follow-through. Of the primary active upper-body muscles, including the shoulder rotator cuff muscles, the chest, and the upper back, the right side is more active than the left, except for the left-shoulder internal rotator. Strengthening and conditioning the chest muscles, the upper-back muscles, and the shoulder rotator cuff muscles will help to develop the muscle tone and strength for a full and high follow-through. A description of these specific muscles is found in Chapters 11 and 13.

The following primary upper-body muscles are active for a smooth, rhythmic follow-through swing.

> *It is important that you don't sneak a peek during the early stage of the follow-through, because it will affect the impact of the club on the ball.*

FOLLOW-THROUGH SWING PHASE	
Primary Upper-Body Muscles	**Action**
A. Chest Muscles 1. Pectoralis Major	Internally rotates and adducts the arm (early stage)
B. Upper-Back Muscles 1. Latissimus Dorsi	Adducts and internally rotates the arm (early stage)
C. Shoulder Rotator Cuff Muscles 1. Subscapularis	Internally rotates and adducts the arm (early and late stage)
2. Infraspinatus (primarily left)	Externally rotates the arm (late stage)

Upper-body muscles that play a stabilizing role during the follow-through swing phase include the forearm muscles, which produce supination of the left wrist and pronation of the right wrist. This muscle action allows the wrists to roll up and out at the top of the backswing. Any student of the game will readily recognize that this rolling of the wrist is missing at the end of Arnold Palmer's backswing, because he is not allowing the wrist to roll completely at the top. Other stabilizing muscles include the shoulder rotator cuff muscles of the left shoulder, which are active during the late stage of the follow-through to elevate the left arm. If your shoulder rotator cuff muscles are weak, tight, or shortened, you will have difficulty achieving a high follow-through.

> *Throughout this guidebook, the importance of the shoulder rotator cuff muscles in all four phases of the golf swing is stressed.*
> *It is next to impossible to have a smooth, rhythmic, technically correct golf swing if these muscles are tight or shortened.*

Throughout this guidebook, the importance of the shoulder rotator cuff muscles in all four phases of the golf swing is stressed. It is next to impossible to have a smooth, rhythmic, technically correct golf swing if these muscles are tight or shortened. I recommend that during your golf-specific exercise conditioning and training program you pay particular attention to stretching and strengthening the rotator cuff muscles, which include the supraspinatus, the infraspinatus, and the subscapularis. The same holds true for the anterior chest muscles (pectoralis) and upper-back muscles (latissimus dorsi). By improving the flexibility and strength of these muscles, you will immediately begin to notice that your follow-through is higher, more rhythmic, and smooth. This, in and of itself, will greatly enhance your ability to hit <u>through</u> the ball rather than <u>at</u> it. As in the other phases of the golf swing, it is important to condition and strengthen the upper-body muscles utilized in the follow-through. A golf-specific physical conditioning and training program for these muscles is described in Chapters 11 and 13.

Lower-Body Muscle and Joint Involvement

The centrifugal force released at the time of impact from the angular momentum generated by the legs and hips is the force that carries the club through to a high follow-through. In the early stage of the follow-through, the right-handed golfer's weight has almost entirely shifted to the left foot, with the weight on the inside of the foot until the club is well past the hitting zone. As the club elevates, the left ankle rolls outward, shifting the weight to the outside of the foot. To keep your weight distributed properly on the inside of the left foot through the hitting zone, the left-foot eversion muscles must be active.

> *Keep your weight on the inside of your left foot at impact and shortly thereafter, because it will help you to maintain a firm left side through the hitting zone.*

Keep your weight on the inside of your left foot at impact and shortly thereafter, because it will help you to maintain a firm left side through the hitting zone. This left-side firmness is produced from active contraction of the left-foot eversion muscles, the left-leg abductor muscles, and the left lateral hip rotators, as well as the upper-body muscles. Synchronous, active contraction of these muscles helps maintain a fairly straight and firm left arm and leg at impact and during the early stage of the follow-through. This muscle action is critical for long, straight shots. The left side softens as the club starts to pull the left shoulder upward. The weight is transferred to the outside of the left foot, causing the ankle to roll outward. The outward rolling of the left ankle is aided by contraction of the anterior tibialis musculature, which is located in the anterior part of the leg.

As your weight is being transferred to the outside of your left foot, your hip and trunk rotators are contracting to provide maximum turn down the target line. The hip and trunk turn is produced by action of the left lateral hip rotators, the right medial hip rotators, and the abdominal oblique muscles, including the left internal oblique and right external oblique. The action of the hip and stomach rotator muscles produces the body turn so that the hips face down the target line at the end of the follow-through. Hip and trunk turn is accompanied by side bending of the trunk, which produces the "C" curve of your back at the end of the backswing. This posture is produced by contraction of the lateral trunk muscle, which comes into play during the acceleration swing phase and continues to be active in forcing the upper body into a "C" shape position at the end of the follow-through. It is important to strengthen both sides of your lateral trunk muscles in your low back in order to stabilize your spine during the swing. This helps prevent injuries or exacerbation of an existing low-back condition. The lower body and trunk are erect at the end of the follow-through. This posture is produced by contraction of the long strap muscles of the back and the hip extensor muscles.

The following primary lower-body muscles are active in a technically correct follow-through.

> *It is important to strengthen both sides of your lateral trunk muscles in your low back in order to stabilize your spine during the swing.*

FOLLOW-THROUGH SWING PHASE	
Primary Lower-Body Muscles	**Action**

A. Abdominal Oblique Muscles
  1. Internal Oblique
  2. External Oblique
	Trunk Rotation
	  Rotates trunk to same side
	  Rotates trunk to opposite side

B. Lateral Trunk Muscles
  1. Quadratus Lumborum (right)
	Lateral Trunk Bending
	  Bends trunk to same side;
	  raises hip of same side

C. Posterior Hip Muscles (Buttock)
  1. Gluteus Minimis (right)
  2. Piriformis and accessory muscles
  (left)
	Hip Turn
	  Medial hip and thigh rotation
	  Lateral hip and thigh rotation

D. Anterior Lower-Leg Muscles
  1. Anterior Tibialis (left)
  2. Peroneal Muscles (right)
	Lateral Weight Shift
	  Rolls ankle and foot outward (inversion)
	  Rolls ankle and foot inward (eversion)

If you have weak, tight, or shortened hip rotator muscles, you will have problems reaching the full hip or trunk turn that is so necessary for a full follow-through.

The stabilizing muscles of the lower body that aid the primary active muscles include the long strap muscles of the low back that straighten the trunk at the end of the follow-through, the hip extensor muscles, the knee extensors, and the knee flexors (hamstrings), which stabilize the knees for a smooth, rhythmic follow-through.

If you have weak, tight, or shortened hip rotator muscles, you will have problems reaching the full hip or trunk turn that is so necessary for a full follow-through. Stretching and strengthening the hip rotator muscles allows for correct swing biomechanics of the follow-through swing phase.

The other primary muscles of the lower body that should be strengthened to improve your follow-through include the abdominal oblique muscles (internal, external); the ankle inversion and eversion muscles, which roll the ankles from in-to-out as the club moves toward the top of the backswing; and the right lateral trunk muscle, which bends the spine to the right, allowing for a proper "C" position at the top of the follow-through and for a down-and-through action of the club rather than an over-and-around movement during the acceleration swing phase. The long strap muscles of the low back and the hip extensor muscles aid in bringing the hips and trunk erect for a complete follow-through. I recommend that these specific muscles be stretched and conditioned in order to ensure proper swing biomechanics of the follow-through swing phase. Turn to Chapters 11, 12, and 13 for the golf-specific stretch and strengthening physical conditioning and training routine to improve your follow-through.

Section V

Exercise
Routines

The shoulder rotator cuff muscles play a vital role in proper swing biomechanics.

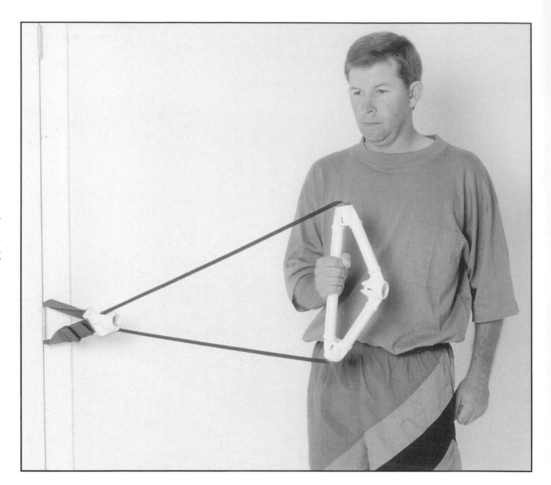

NOTE: The Golfercise System exercises described in this chapter use the unique patented design exercise equipment. This computer-designed and engineered equipment has four pieces and incorporates the revolutionary *progressive variable resistance tubing*. The equipment includes:

1. **Progressive variable resistance exercise tube**
2. **Exercise handle with exercise tube connectors at:**
   position(s) A — ends of handle and
   position B — apex of handle
3. **Exercise tube anchor with adjustable strap lock**
4. **Door hinge anchor**

Upper-Body Exercises

● ●

The following systematic, golf-specific stretches and exercises are designed to improve flexibility, endurance, and strength in every muscle group of the upper body that is required for a technically correct golf swing. Stretching and strengthening exercises of the primary and stabilizing muscle groups that are active during any of the four swing phases are shown, and the anatomy, function, and swing phase in which the muscle is most active are described for better comprehension. Stretching and exercising the specific muscles (with and without the aid of the Golfercise System equipment) is described so that you can understand the biomechanical action involved in conditioning each muscle. Finally, additional information is provided about medical precautions for some of the more demanding exercises.

These exercises are designed specifically to improve your game by stretching and by increasing the endurance and strength of the golf muscles. To achieve maximum benefit, perform the exercises every other day. Always remember to stretch before you exercise any muscle, using the principles of physical conditioning discussed in Chapters 2-4.

The exercise routines in this chapter begin with the primary muscles of the upper body that are vital for a technically correct swing. These are followed by exercises for the stabilizing muscles, which aid the primary muscles and give support to the spine and joints during your swing.

By performing all of the exercises or by identifying the areas of weakness in your swing, you can use these exercises successfully to 1) increase the flexibility of your muscles, which will improve joint motion, 2) increase your body tone or condition by improving your overall endurance, which will decrease the potential for fatigue during the latter holes, and 3) increase your strength and power for longer drives and more accuracy out of the rough.

Primary Active Upper-Body Muscles

ROTATOR CUFF SHOULDER MUSCLES
External Shoulder Rotator • *Infraspinatus*

SWING PHASE: Active in Takeaway and Follow-through swing phases
FUNCTION: Externally rotates the arm

Upper Body

STRETCH-OUT

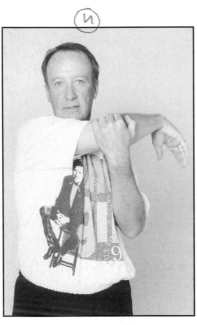

Self Stretch:

1. In a seated or standing position, reach across the front of your body with your involved arm while grasping your elbow with your uninvolved hand. Pull the involved arm toward the opposite shoulder. Hold for 5 to 10 seconds. Repeat the stretch for the opposite side.
   Note: This stretch is recommended for golfers with previous shoulder injuries, because it will not place undue stress on the shoulder. This maneuver also stretches the supraspinatus of the rotator cuff muscles.
2. In a standing position, place your involved hand against your side with your palm facing outward. With your involved elbow at about 90°, rotate your elbow forward. Grasp above your elbow with your uninvolved hand and pull across and downward. Hold the stretch for 5 to 10 seconds. Repeat the stretch for the opposite side.
   Caution: You should not experience any pain.

Golfercise System Stretch:

Position: Standing
Set-up: Connect one end of the exercise tube to position A of the exercise handle.
Action: Reach down and behind your back with your involved forearm and grasp the exercise handle. Then grasp the other end of the exercise tube with your opposite hand held overhead and pull upward. Hold for 5 to 10 seconds. Repeat the stretch for the opposite side.
Caution: You should not experience any pain.
Note: This stretch can also be performed using the golf-club shaft.

Stretch-contract-relax (PNF): At the end of the stretch described above, strongly contract the muscle pulling against the resistive tubing for 5 seconds. Then relax for 5 seconds and repeat the sequence 1 to 3 times, beginning with the stretch.

ROTATOR CUFF SHOULDER MUSCLES
External Shoulder Rotator • *Infraspinatus*

STRENGTHENING EXERCISE

Free-Weight Exercise:

In a side-lying position with your uninvolved side down, hold your involved arm at your side with your elbow bent at 90°. While holding the weight against your trunk, raise your forearm upward as far as tolerable while keeping your elbow fixed against your side. Hold for 5 seconds and lower slowly. Repeat the exercise for the opposite side.

Golfercise System Exercise:

Position:	Standing
Set-up:	Connect both ends of the exercise tube to the A positions of the exercise handle.
	Secure the door hinge anchor around the middle hinge.
	Secure the exercise tube within the track of the door hinge anchor.
Action:	Grasp the exercise handle with your involved hand and move away until the tubing is taut. Your involved arm should be across the front of your body and your uninvolved side should be facing the door. Pull the exercise handle out and away from your body, with your palm facing toward the door and your elbow bent at 90° and fixed to your side. Hold for 5 seconds and return slowly. Repeat the exercise for the opposite side.
Note:	This same maneuver can be performed by grasping the exercise handle connected to the exercise tube, palm facing down, and using a correct golf grip.

Upper Body

ROTATOR CUFF SHOULDER MUSCLES
Internal Shoulder Rotator • *Subscapularis*

SWING PHASE: Active in all phases, particularly Forward and Acceleration phases
FUNCTION: Internally rotates and adducts the arm

STRETCH-OUT

Self Stretch:

1. In a standing position, reach up and behind your back with the involved forearm, palm toward your back. Reach toward your opposite shoulder blade. For maximum stretch, grasp the elbow of your involved arm with your opposite hand and pull backward. Hold the stretch for 5 to 10 seconds. Repeat the stretch for the opposite side.
2. In a standing position, reach across the front of your chest with the involved side while grasping just above your elbow with your other hand. Pull the involved arm across your body with the uninvolved hand. Hold the stretch for 5 to 10 seconds. Repeat the stretch for the opposite side.
   Note: This is the preferred method for seniors or anyone with previous shoulder injuries. This maneuver also stretches the posterior shoulder capsule ligament.

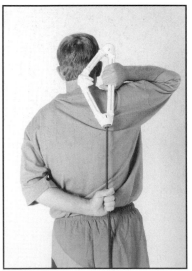

Golfercise System Stretch:

Position:	Standing
Set-up:	Connect one end of the exercise tube to position A of the exercise handle.
Action:	Reach up and behind your back with the involved arm and grasp the exercise handle. With your uninvolved arm, reach down and behind your back, grasp the exercise tube, and pull down gently. Hold for 5 to 10 seconds. Repeat the stretch for the opposite side.
Caution:	You should not experience any pain.
Note:	This stretch can also be performed using the golf-club shaft.

Stretch-contract-relax (PNF): At the end of the stretch described above, strongly contract the muscle by pulling against the resistive tubing for 5 seconds. Then relax for 5 seconds and repeat the sequence 1 to 3 times, beginning with the stretch.

ROTATOR CUFF SHOULDER MUSCLES
Internal Shoulder Rotator • *Subscapularis*

STRENGTHENING EXERCISE

Free-Weight Exercise:

In a side-lying position with your involved side down, hold your arm against your side with your elbow bent at 90°. While keeping your elbow fixed against your side, lower your forearm to the floor while grasping the weight. Do not lower your arm any further than tolerable. Then raise your forearm to your trunk across your stomach. Hold for 5 seconds and lower slowly. Repeat the exercise for the opposite side.

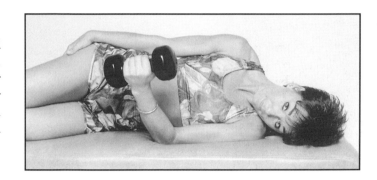

Golfercise System Exercise:

Position:	Standing
Set-up:	Connect both ends of the exercise tube to the A positions of the exercise handle.
	Secure the door hinge anchor around the middle hinge.
	Secure the exercise tube within the track of the door hinge anchor.
Action:	Grasp the handle with your involved side, moving away until the tubing is taut, with your involved side facing the door. Pull the handle toward your stomach, with your palm facing inward and your elbow bent at 90° and fixed to your side. Hold for 5 seconds and return slowly. Repeat the exercise for the opposite side.
Note:	This same maneuver can be performed by grasping the exercise handle connected to the exercise tube, palm facing upward.

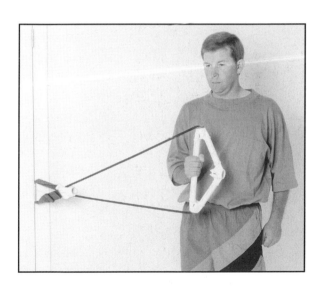

Upper Body

ROTATOR CUFF SHOULDER MUSCLES
Shoulder Abductor • *Supraspinatus*

SWING PHASE: Active in Takeaway and Follow-through swing phases
FUNCTION: Raises the arm upward, away from the body (arm abduction)

STRETCH-OUT

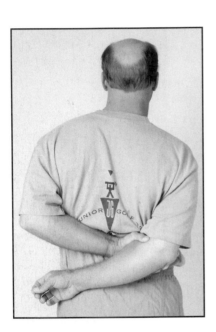

Self Stretch:

1. In a seated or standing position, reach down and behind your back with your involved forearm, palm facing outward. Raise your forearm toward the opposite shoulder blade as high as tolerable. To increase the stretch, reach behind your back with your opposite arm grasping just above your elbow, pulling the involved arm toward the middle of your back. Hold the stretch for 5 to 10 seconds. Repeat the stretch for the opposite side.
2. In a standing position, reach across the front of your chest with the involved side while grasping just above your elbow with your other hand. Pull the involved arm across your body with the uninvolved hand. Hold the stretch for 5 to 10 seconds. Repeat the stretch for the opposite side.
    Note: This is the preferred method for seniors or anyone with previous shoulder injuries. This maneuver also stretches the posterior shoulder capsule ligament.

Golfercise System Stretch:

Position: Standing
Set-up: Connect one end of the exercise tube to position A of the exercise handle.
Action: Reach down and behind your back with your involved forearm and grasp the exercise handle. Then grasp the other end of the exercise tube with your opposite hand held overhead and pull upward. Hold for 5 to 10 seconds. Repeat the stretch for the opposite side.
Caution: You should not experience any pain.
Note: This stretch can be performed using the golf-club shaft.

Stretch-contract-relax (PNF): At the end of the stretch described above, strongly contract the muscle by pulling against the resistive tubing for 5 seconds. Then relax for 5 seconds and repeat the sequence 1 to 3 times, beginning with the stretch.

ROTATOR CUFF SHOULDER MUSCLES
Shoulder Abductor • *Supraspinatus*

STRENGTHENING EXERCISE

Free-Weight Exercise:

In a standing position, hold the weight with your involved arm, and raise your arm to just below shoulder height while keeping your elbow straight and your thumb pointing downward. Hold for 5 seconds and lower slowly. Repeat the exercise for the opposite side.
Note: Do not raise the weight above shoulder height, because this may cause muscle/tendon injury.

Golfercise System Exercise:

Position:	Standing
Set-up:	Connect one end of the exercise tube to position A and the other end to position B of the exercise handle.
	Secure the door hinge anchor around the lower hinge.
	Secure the exercise tube within the track of the door hinge anchor.
Action:	Grasp the exercise handle and move away until the resistive tubing is taut, with your uninvolved side toward the door. With your arm in the center of your body, raise your arm to just below shoulder level while keeping your elbow straight and your thumb down. Hold for 5 seconds and lower slowly. Repeat the exercise for the opposite side.
Caution:	Do not raise your arm above shoulder height, because this may cause muscle/tendon injury.

Upper Body

ANTERIOR CHEST MUSCLES
Pectoralis

SWING PHASE: Active in Forward, Acceleration, and Follow-through phases
FUNCTION: Internally rotates the arm and adducts the raised arm

STRETCH-OUT

Self Stretch:

1. In a standing position, reach backward holding onto a fence or both sides of a door jamb. Keep your arms as close to shoulder height as possible. Lean forward, straightening your arms. Hold 5 to 10 seconds.
2. In a standing position, raise one arm against a fence or door jamb and turn away with your body by rotating your shoulder. Bring your opposite arm behind your back and grab the fence to help you rotate your torso and shoulders. Hold 5 to 10 seconds. Repeat the stretch for the opposite side.
3. In a standing position, facing a corner of a room, raise your arms and put your palms against the opposite walls. Slowly bend toward the corner with your chest, keeping your feet stationary. Hold 5 to 10 seconds.
4. In a standing position, interlace your hands behind your back, straighten your elbows, and slowly raise your arms. Perform to tolerance. Hold 5 to 10 seconds.

Golfercise System Stretch:

Position: Standing
Set-up: Connect both ends of the exercise tube to the A positions of the exercise handle.
Secure the door hinge anchor around the top hinge.
Secure the exercise tube within the track of the door hinge anchor.
Action: Face away from the door. Grasp the handle with both hands behind you at the small of your back, palms facing downward. Move away from the door or support until the exercise tube is taut, pulling on the anterior chest muscles. Your arms should be straight, extending backward. Stretch for 15 to 20 seconds and relax.

Stretch-contract-relax (PNF): At the end of the stretch described above, strongly contract the muscle by pulling against the resistive tubing for 5 seconds. Then relax for 5 seconds and repeat the sequence 1 to 3 times, beginning with the stretch.

ANTERIOR CHEST MUSCLES
Pectoralis

STRENGTHENING EXERCISE

Free-Weight Exercise:

1. In a lying-down, face-up position (supine), grasp the weights with both hands and press the weight straight upward. Hold for 10 seconds and return slowly.
2. In a lying-down, face-up position (supine), with the weight in each hand and your elbows bent, push the weight up so that the weights touch. Hold for 5 seconds and lower slowly.

Golfercise System Exercise:

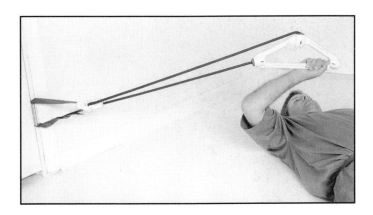

Position:	Lying face-up
Set-up:	Connect one end of the exercise tube to position A and the other end to position B of the exercise handle.
	Secure the door hinge anchor around the lower hinge.
	Secure the exercise tube within the track of the door hinge anchor.
Action:	Lying face-up with the involved side toward the door, grasp the handle. Pull the handle in front and across your body. Hold for 5 seconds and return slowly. Repeat the exercise for the opposite side.

Upper Body

UPPER-BACK MUSCLES
Latissimus Dorsi — "LATS"

SWING PHASE: Active in Forward, Acceleration, and early Follow-through phases
FUNCTION: Pulls the arm downward and assists in internal rotation of the arm

STRETCH-OUT

Self Stretch:

In a standing position, cross one leg over the other, and raise your arms above your head with your fingers interlaced, palms facing upward. Slowly bend your trunk to the opposite side of your front leg, and push your hips to the same side of your front leg. Hold for 10 to 15 seconds. Cross your other leg and repeat the exercise, bending in the opposite direction.
Note: This maneuver also stretches the lateral trunk muscles (quadratus lumborum) and lateral hip and thigh abductor muscles (gluteus medius, tensor fascia lata).

Golfercise System Stretch:

Position:	Standing
Set-up:	Connect one end of the exercise tube to position A and the other end to position B of the exercise handle.
	Secure the door hinge anchor around the top hinge side.
	Secure the exercise tube within the track of the door hinge anchor.
Action:	Grasp the exercise handle with your involved hand, raise your arm over your head, and cross your involved side leg in front of your uninvolved leg. Face sideways to the door. With your uninvolved side facing the door, move away until the exercise tube is taut. Your upper body should be pulled toward the support. Hold for 10 to 20 seconds. Repeat the stretch for the opposite side.
Note:	This maneuver also stretches the stomach obliques, the lateral trunk, and the outer thigh muscles.

Stretch-contract-relax (PNF): At the end of the stretch described above, strongly contract the muscle by pulling against the resistive tubing for 5 seconds. Then relax for 5 seconds and repeat the sequence 1 to 3 times, beginning with the stretch.

UPPER BACK MUSCLES
Latissimus Dorsi — "LATS"

STRENGTHENING EXERCISE

Free-Weight Exercise:

Lying face-down on a table with your involved arm hanging straight downward, grasp the weight, palm facing inward. Raise your arm backward, holding your arm straight as far as possible toward the table height. Your thumb should be facing downward in this position. Hold for 5 seconds and lower slowly. Repeat the exercise for the opposite side.

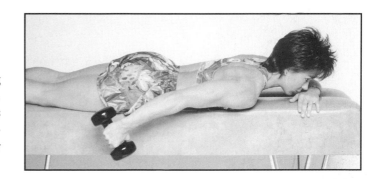

Golfercise System Exercise:

Position:	Standing
Set-up:	Connect both ends of the exercise tube to the A positions of the exercise handle.
	Secure the door hinge anchor around the top hinge.
	Secure the exercise tube within the track of the door hinge anchor.
Action:	Grasp the handle with both hands, palms down, and move away until the exercise tube is taut. This should pull your arms upward. Using both outstretched arms, pull down on the exercise handle, keeping your elbows straight. Hold for 5 to 10 seconds and return slowly.
Note:	You may exercise one side at a time by pulling with one arm.

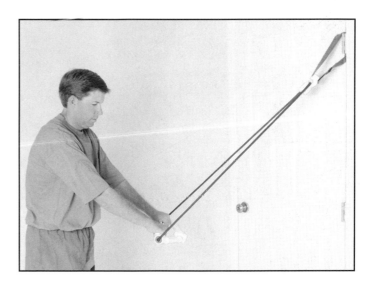

Upper Body

FOREARM AND WRIST MUSCLES
Wrist Flexors

SWING PHASE: Active in the Acceleration phase for unhinging the wrists
FUNCTION: Flexes the wrist and fingers • Stabilizes the forearms at impact

STRETCH-OUT

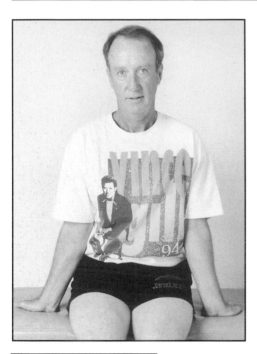

Self Stretch:

In a seated position, place the back of your hands on the chair bottom, fingers facing backward, palms down, and thumbs facing outward. Slowly move your upper body backward while keeping your hands as flat as possible. Hold for 20 to 30 seconds.

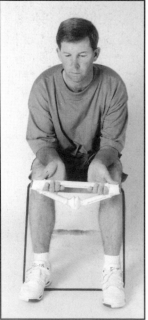

Golfercise System Stretch:

Position:	Seated
Set-up:	Connect both ends of the exercise tube to the A positions of the exercise handle. Place the exercise tube under your feet (wear exercise shoes).
Action:	Grasp the exercise handle in front of your thighs, with your palms facing upward and your forearms resting on your thighs. Raise your forearms, while allowing your wrists to bend backwards, stretching these muscles. Hold for 20 to 30 seconds.
Note:	This stretches the "wrist-cock" muscles.

Stretch-contract-relax (PNF): At the end of the stretch described above, strongly contract the muscle by pulling against the resistive tubing for 5 seconds. Then relax for 5 seconds and repeat the sequence 1 to 3 times, beginning with the stretch.

FOREARM AND WRIST MUSCLES
Wrist Flexors

STRENGTHENING EXERCISE

Free-Weight Exercise:

In a seated position with your forearm resting on your thigh, palm up, grasp the weight with your involved hand and roll your wrist upward. Hold for 2 seconds and lower slowly. Repeat the exercise for the opposite side.

Golfercise System Exercise:

Position: Seated
Set-up: Connect both ends of the exercise tube to the A positions of the exercise handle.
              Place the exercise tube under your feet (wear exercise shoes).
Action: With your forearms resting on your thighs and your palms facing upward, raise the exercise handle by rolling your wrists upward. Hold for 5 seconds and lower slowly.

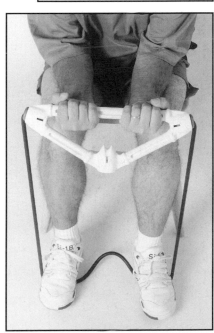

FOREARM AND WRIST MUSCLES
Wrist Extensors

SWING PHASE: Active in Takeaway phase for "wrist-cock"
FUNCTION: Extension of wrist and fingers • Stabilizes the forearms at impact

STRETCH-OUT

Self Stretch:

1. In the seated or standing position, raise both arms to shoulder height with the elbows bent and thumbs rotated facing down. Slowly straighten the elbow with thumbs rotated down and away from the body. Hold for 15 to 20 seconds.

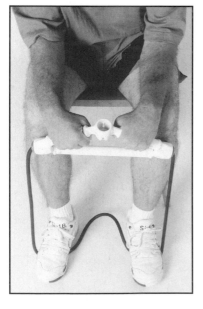

Golfercise System Stretch:

Position: Seated
Set-up: Connect both ends of the exercise tube to the A positions of the exercise handle. Place the exercise tube under your feet (wear exercise shoes).
Action: Grasp the exercise handle in front of your thighs, palms facing downward, wrists relaxed, and forearms resting on your thighs. Raise your forearms, while allowing your wrists to bend, stretching the muscles. Hold for 20 to 30 seconds.
Note: This stretches the "wrist-cock" muscles.

Stretch-contract-relax (PNF): At the end of the stretch described above, strongly contract the muscle by pulling against the resistive tubing for 5 seconds. Then relax for 5 seconds and repeat the sequence 1 to 3 times, beginning with the stretch.

FOREARM AND WRIST MUSCLES
Wrist Extensors

STRENGTHENING EXERCISE

Free-Weight Exercise:

In a seated position with your forearm resting on your thigh, grasp the weight with your involved hand, palm facing downward. Raise the weight by rolling your wrist upward. Hold for 5 seconds and lower slowly. Repeat the exercise for the opposite side.

Golfercise System Exercise:

Position: Seated
Set-up: Connect both ends of the exercise tube to the A positions of the exercise handle.
Place the exercise tube under your feet (wear exercise shoes).
Action: Grasp the exercise handle with your forearms resting on your thighs, palms facing downward. Raise the handle by rolling your wrists upward. Hold for 5 seconds and lower slowly.

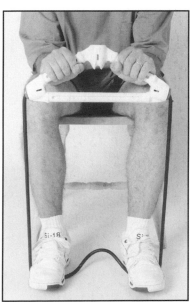

Upper Body

FOREARM AND WRIST MUSCLES
Wrist Radial Deviation

SWING PHASE: Active in Takeaway phase for "wrist-cock"
FUNCTION: Extension of wrist and fingers • Stabilizes the forearms at impact

STRETCH-OUT

Self Stretch:

1. In the seated or standing position, raise both arms to shoulder height with the elbows bent and thumbs rotated facing down. Slowly straighten the elbow with thumbs rotated down and away from the body. Hold for 15 to 20 seconds.

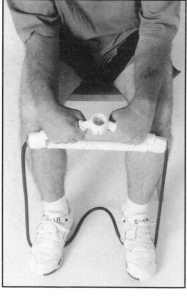

Golfercise System Stretch:

Position:	Seated
Set-up:	Connect both ends of the exercise tube to the A positions of the exercise handle. Place the exercise tube under your feet (wear exercise shoes).
Action:	Grasp the exercise handle in front of your thighs, palms facing downward, wrists relaxed, and forearms resting on your thighs. Raise your forearms, while allowing your wrists to bend, stretching the muscles. Hold for 20 to 30 seconds.
Note:	This stretches the "wrist-cock" muscles. This is the same maneuver as the wrist extensor stretch.

Stretch-contract-relax (PNF): At the end of the stretch described above, strongly contract the muscle by pulling against the resistive tubing for 5 seconds. Then relax for 5 seconds and repeat the sequence 1 to 3 times, beginning with the stretch.

FOREARM AND WRIST MUSCLES
Wrist Radial Deviation

STRENGTHENING EXERCISE

Free-Weight Exercise:

In a seated position, rest the involved forearm on your thigh with your palm facing inward. Grasp the weight and raise your wrist, with your forearm fixed on your thigh. Hold for 2 seconds and lower slowly. Repeat the exercise for the opposite side.

Golfercise System Exercise:

Position:	Seated (standing)
Set-up:	Connect one end of the exercise tube to position A and the other end to position B of the exercise handle.
	Place the exercise tube under your feet (wear exercise shoes).
Action:	Grasp the exercise handle with your palms facing inward using your golf grip to hold the handle. Rest your forearms on your thighs. With the tubing taut, raise your wrists. Hold for 5 seconds and return slowly.
Note:	For best results, use your golf grip.

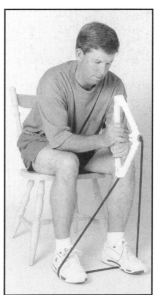

Upper Body

FOREARM AND WRIST MUSCLES
Wrist Ulnar Deviation

SWING PHASE: Active in the Acceleration phase for "unhinging" the wrists
FUNCTION: Flexes the wrist and fingers • Stabilizes the forearms at impact

STRETCH-OUT

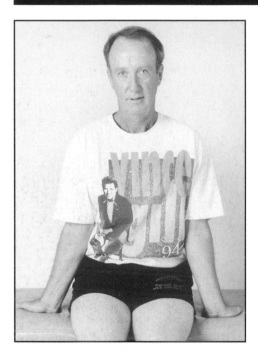

Self Stretch:

In a seated position, place the back of your hands on the chair bottom, fingers facing backward, palms down, and thumbs facing outward. Slowly move your upper body backward while keeping your hands as flat as possible. Hold for 20 to 30 seconds.

Golfercise System Stretch:

Position:	Seated
Set-up:	Connect both ends of the exercise tube to the A positions of the exercise handle. Place the exercise tube under your feet (wear exercise shoes).
Action:	Grasp the exercise handle in front of your thighs, with your palms facing upward and your forearm resting on your thighs. Raise your forearms, while allowing your wrists to bend backwards, stretching these muscles. Hold for 20 to 30 seconds.
Note:	This stretches the "wrist-cock" muscles. This is the same maneuver as the wrist flexor stretch.

Stretch-contract-relax (PNF): At the end of the stretch described above, strongly contract the muscle by pulling against the resistive tubing for 5 seconds. Then relax for 5 seconds and repeat the sequence 1 to 3 times, beginning with the stretch.

FOREARM AND WRIST MUSCLES
Wrist Ulnar Deviation

STRENGTHENING EXERCISE

Free-Weight Exercise:

While lying face up, put the involved arm over your shoulder, palm facing in. Grasp the weight and raise your wrist toward the ceiling. Hold for 5 seconds and lower slowly. Repeat the exercise for the opposite side.

Golfercise System Exercise:

Position:	Seated
Set-up:	Connect one end of the exercise tube to position A and the other end to position B of the exercise handle.
Action:	Wrap the exercise tube around your back and over your right shoulder. Grasp the exercise handle using your golf grip. Pull your wrists downward with an "uncocking" motion. Hold for 5 seconds and return slowly.
Note:	This movement will help to improve the "uncocking" of your wrists at impact.

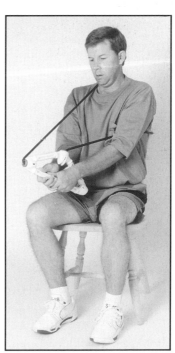

Upper Body

FOREARM AND WRIST MUSCLES
Pronation and Supination

SWING PHASE: Active in all four swing phases, primarily the Acceleration phase
FUNCTION: Pronation—downward rotation of palm, rolling wrist inward
Supination—upward rotation of palm, rolling wrist outward

STRETCH-OUT

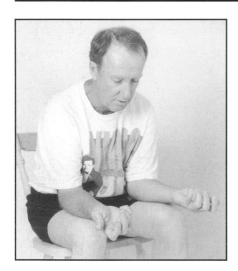

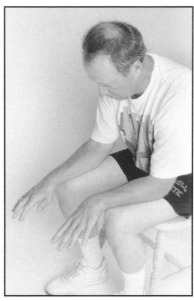

Above: Pronation (Self Stretch)
Right: Supination (Self Stretch)

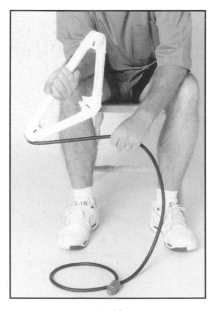

Pronation (Golfercise System)

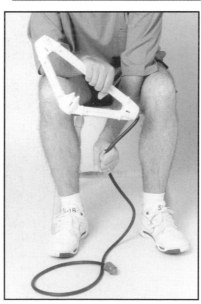

Supination (Golfercise System)

Self Stretch:

Pronation: In a seated or standing position, roll your forearms and wrists outward, keeping your elbows straight and your arms held in front of you. Hold for 5 to 10 seconds.

Supination:
1. In a seated or standing position, roll your forearms and wrists inward, keeping your elbows straight and your arms held in front of you. Hold for 5 to 10 seconds.
2. In a seated or standing position, reach backward, grasping a fence or other structure. Keep your palms facing downward at shoulder height. Move your body forward and downward until you feel a stretch in your forearm. Hold for 5 to 10 seconds.

Golfercise System Stretch:

Position: Seated
Set-up: Connect one end of the exercise tube to position A of the exercise handle.

Action:
Pronation: Grasp the exercise handle with your involved hand, palm upward. Grasp the exercise tube with your uninvolved arm and pull downward, rotating your wrist and hand outward. Repeat for the opposite side.

Supination: Grasp the exercise handle with your involved hand, palm downward. Grasp the exercise tube with your uninvolved arm and pull downward, rotating your wrist and hand inward. Repeat for the opposite side.

Stretch-contract-relax (PNF): At the end of the stretch described above, strongly contract the muscle by pulling against the resistive tubing for 5 seconds. Then relax for 5 seconds and repeat the sequence 1 to 3 times, beginning with the stretch.

FOREARM AND WRIST MUSCLES
Pronation and Supination

Upper Body

STRENGTHENING EXERCISE

Free-Weight Exercise:
In a seated position, rest your involved forearm on your thigh. Grasp the weight. Roll your wrist outward and inward. Hold for a few seconds at the end of each movement and return to the starting position. Repeat the exercise for the opposite side.

Golfercise System Exercise:

Position: Seated

Set-up: Connect one end of the exercise tube to the long strap anchor. Wrap the exercise tube around your foot.

Action:

Pronation: Grasp the strap with your involved hand, palm facing upward. Move the strap in the anchor so the looplocs are next to the anchor. The involved forearm rests on your thigh. Rotate the exercise handle so that your palm faces inward. Hold for 5 to 10 seconds. Repeat the stretch for the opposite side.

Supination: Grasp the strap with your involved hand, palm facing downward. Move the strap in the anchor so the looplocs are next to the anchor. The involved forearm rests on your thigh. Rotate the exercise handle outward so that your palm faces inward. Hold for 5 to 10 seconds. Repeat the stretch for the opposite side.

Note: Secure the exercise tube within the track for greater resistance.

Right: Pronation (Golfercise System)
Far Right: Supination (Golfercise System)

Pronation (Free Weight)   *Supination (Free Weight)*

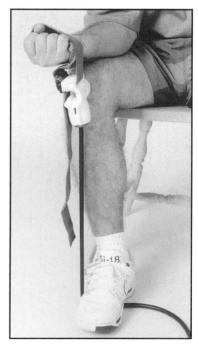

119

Secondary Stabilizing and Accessory Upper-Body Muscles

NECK MUSCLES
Flexors

SWING PHASE: Active in all swing phases
FUNCTION: Bends the head forward and downward

Upper Body	**STRETCH-OUT**

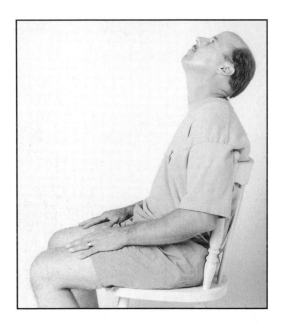

Self Stretch:

In a seated position, look back over your head as far as tolerable without causing any neck pain or discomfort. Hold for 5 to 10 seconds.
Note: If you have a previous history of neck pain or injury, perform this stretch with caution.

NECK MUSCLES
Flexors

STRENGTHENING EXERCISE

Free-Weight Exercise:

In a seated position, place the palm of one hand on your forehead. Push your head forward, resisting the movement as your head moves forward. Hold for 5 to 10 seconds.

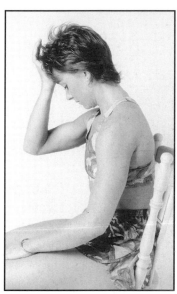

Golfercise System Exercise:

Position:	Seated
Set-up:	Connect one end of the exercise tube to the exercise tube anchor.
	Wrap the strap around the top of your head with the tubing facing backward.
Action:	Grasp the exercise tube with one hand and pull it taut. Bend your head forward. Hold for 5 seconds and return slowly.

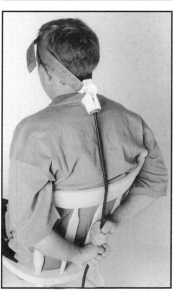

Upper Body

NECK MUSCLES
Extensors

SWING PHASE: Stabilizes the neck throughout the swing
FUNCTION: Brings the head backward

STRETCH-OUT

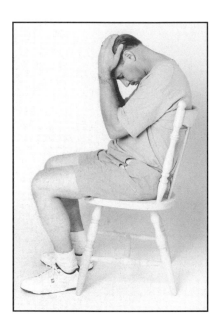

Self Stretch:

In a seated position, tuck your chin in by bending your head and neck forward. Place your hands on the top of your head and gently push your head forward toward your chin. Hold for 5 to 10 seconds.
Note: This stretch is recommended if you have a history of neck stiffness or soreness. This stretch can be done several times a day to reduce stiffness.

Upper Body

NECK MUSCLES
Extensors

STRENGTHENING EXERCISE

Free-Weight Exercise:

In a seated position, place the palm of one hand on the back of your head. Push your head backward, resisting the movement as your head moves backward. Hold for 5 to 10 seconds.

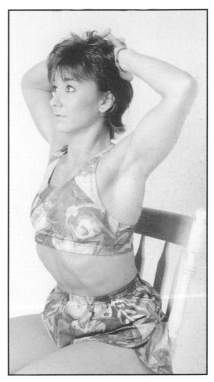

Golfercise System Exercise:

Position:	Seated
Set-up:	Connect one end of the exercise tube to the exercise tube anchor. Wrap the strap around the top of your head with the tube facing forward.
Action:	Grasp the exercise tubing with one hand and pull it taut. Bend your head backward. Hold for 5 seconds and return slowly.

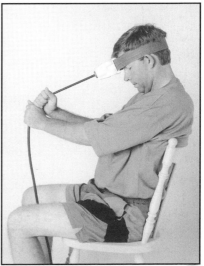

NECK MUSCLES
Lateral Bending

SWING PHASE: Stabilizes the head and neck during the swing
FUNCTION: Bends the head and neck to the side

STRETCH-OUT

Self Stretch:

In a seated or standing position, bend your head toward your right shoulder to the maximum tolerable position. Place your left hand under your buttock with your palm facing downward. Reach up with your right hand and pull your head gently toward your shoulder. Hold for 5 to 10 seconds. Repeat the stretch for the opposite side while placing your right hand under your buttock, palm facing downward.

Note: Do not pull so strenuously that pain is produced!

NECK MUSCLES
Lateral Bending

STRENGTHENING EXERCISE

Free-Weight Exercise:

In a seated position, place the palm of one hand on the side of your head. Push your head toward the side where your hand is situated, resisting the movement as your head bends laterally. Hold for 5 to 10 seconds.

Golfercise System Exercise:

Position: Seated

Set-up: Connect one end of the exercise tube anchor.
Wrap the strap around the top of your head with the tubing facing the side of your head.

Action: Grasp the exercise tubing with one hand and pull it taut. Bend your head away from the tubing. Hold for 5 seconds and return slowly. Repeat the exercise for the opposite side.

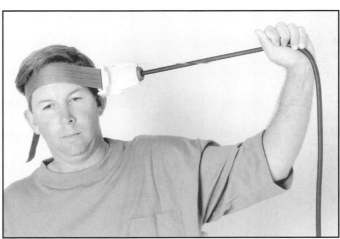

NECK MUSCLES
Rotation

SWING PHASE: Active in the Takeaway and Follow-through phases
FUNCTION: Rotates the head

STRETCH-OUT

Self Stretch:

In a seated or standing position, look to the right as far as tolerable. Place your left hand on your chin, pushing your neck farther to the right to its end range. Hold the stretch for 5 to 10 seconds. Repeat the stretch for the opposite side.

Caution: Do not push so hard that you feel pain either in your neck or jaw!

NECK MUSCLES
Rotation

STRENGTHENING EXERCISE

Free-Weight Exercise:

In a seated position, place your fingers on the side of your face while looking forward. Rotate your head to the side of your hand while resisting the movement with your hand. Repeat the exercise for the opposite side.

Upper Body

SHOULDER GIRDLE MUSCLES
Levator Scapulae and Upper Trapezius

SWING PHASE: Stabilizes shoulder throughout the swing
FUNCTION: Raises shoulder

STRETCH-OUT

Self Stretch:

In a standing position, reach behind your back with the involved side, palm facing outward. Grasp the wrist of the involved side with your uninvolved hand. While leaning your head to the opposite side, pull your involved arm downward and across your back. Hold for 10 to 15 seconds. Repeat the stretch for the opposite side.
Note: Keep your spine straight and avoid rotating your head.

Golfercise System Stretch:

Position: Standing
Set-up: Secure the door hinge anchor around the middle hinge.
Connect one end of the exercise tube to the door hinge anchor.

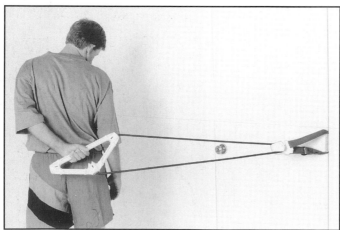

Connect the other end of the exercise tube to position B of the exercise handle.
Action: Standing sideways to the door with your involved side facing away, grasp the exercise handle with your involved arm held behind your back, palm facing outward. Move away until the tubing is taut, pulling your arm across your back. Lean your head to the opposite side. Hold for 10 to 15 seconds. Repeat the stretch for the opposite side.

Stretch-contract-relax (PNF): At the end of the stretch described above, strongly contract the muscle by pulling against the resistive tubing for 5 seconds. Then relax for 5 seconds and repeat the sequence 1 to 3 times, beginning with the stretch.

SHOULDER GIRDLE MUSCLES
Levator Scapulae and Upper Trapezius

STRENGTHENING EXERCISE

Free-Weight Exercise:

In a standing position, grasp the weight on your involved side, keeping your arm straight, resting at your side. Raise your shoulder (shoulder shrug) to maximum height while keeping your arm to your side. Hold for 10 seconds and lower slowly. Repeat the exercise for the opposite side.

Golfercise System Exercise:

Position:	Standing
Set-up:	Secure the door hinge anchor around the lower hinge.
	Connect both ends of the exercise tube to the A positions of the exercise handle.
	Place the exercise tube in the track of the door hinge anchor.
Action:	Grasp the exercise handle and raise both shoulders (shoulder shrug) to maximum height, holding your arms straight. Hold for 10 seconds and lower slowly. Repeat the exercise for the opposite side.

MID-BACK MUSCLES
Rhomboids

SWING PHASE: Stabilizes the shoulders throughout the swing
FUNCTION: Pulls the shoulder blades toward the spine • Weakness produces rounded shoulders and a bent-forward posture or hunchback

STRETCH-OUT

Self Stretch:

1. In a seated or standing position, reach across the front of your body with your involved arm while grasping your elbow with your uninvolved hand. Pull the involved arm toward the opposite shoulder. Hold for 5 to 10 seconds. Repeat the stretch for the opposite side.
   Note: This stretch is recommended for golfers with previous shoulder injuries, because it will not place undue stress on the shoulder. This maneuver also stretches the infraspinatus and supraspinatus of the rotator cuff muscles.
2. While sitting on the ground, cross your involved ankle over the opposite straight leg at the knee. Rotate your shoulders toward the involved side so that the opposite elbow is outside the involved knee. Place your other hand flat on the ground behind you. Then slowly look over your shoulder so as to rotate your trunk to the side of the involved leg as far as tolerable. At the same time, apply counterpressure with your uninvolved elbow against the bent knee. Hold for approximately 20 to 30 seconds. Reverse leg positions and stretch the other side.

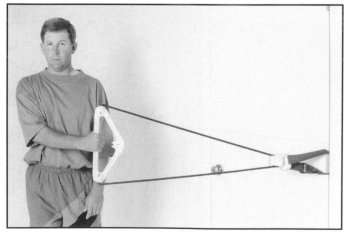

Golfercise System Stretch:

Position: Standing
Set-up: Connect both ends of the exercise tube to the A positions of the exercise handle.
Secure the door hinge anchor around the middle hinge.
Secure the exercise tube within the track of the door hinge anchor.
Action: Grasp the exercise handle and reach across your body, palm facing inward. With your uninvolved side turned toward the door, move away from the door until the tubing is taut, pulling your shoulder across your body. Rotate your chest away from the door. Hold for 10 to 15 seconds. Repeat the stretch for the opposite side.

Stretch-contract-relax (PNF): At the end of the stretch described above, strongly contract the muscle by pulling against the resistive tubing for 5 seconds. Then relax for 5 seconds and repeat the sequence 1 to 3 times, beginning with the stretch.

MID-BACK MUSCLES
Rhomboids

STRENGTHENING EXERCISE

Free-Weight Exercise:

In a standing position, bend forward at the waist, supporting your upper body with the uninvolved arm on a chair or table. With your outstretched involved arm, grasp the weight and lift your arm straight upward, bending your elbow. Hold for 10 seconds and return slowly. Repeat the exercise for the opposite side.

Golfercise System Exercise:

Position:	Standing
Set-up:	Connect both ends of the exercise tube to the A positions of the exercise handle.
	Secure the door hinge anchor around the middle hinge.
	Secure the exercise tube within the track of the door hinge anchor.
Action:	Grasp the exercise handle. Move away from the door until the resistive tubing is taut. Face the door with your arm outstretched. Pull the handle toward your side, bending your elbow. Hold for 10 seconds and return slowly. Repeat the exercise for the opposite side.

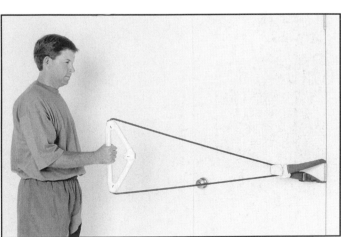

Upper Body

SHOULDER MUSCLES
Anterior Deltoid

SWING PHASE: Stabilizes the shoulder throughout the swing
FUNCTION: Shoulder abduction, raises the shoulder
Anterior medial rotation and flexion of the shoulder
Posterior lateral rotation and extension of the shoulder

STRETCH-OUT

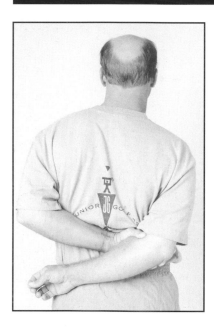

Self Stretch:

In a seated or standing position, reach down and behind your back with your involved forearm, palm facing outward. Raise your forearm toward the opposite shoulder blade as high as tolerable. To increase the stretch, reach behind your back with your opposite arm grasping just above your elbow, pulling the involved arm toward the middle of your back. Hold the stretch for 5 to 10 seconds. Repeat the stretch for the opposite side.

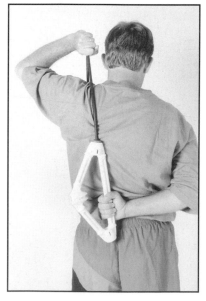

Golfercise System Stretch:

Position: Standing
Set-up: Connect one end of the exercise tube to position A of the exercise handle.
Action: Reach down and behind your back with your involved forearm and grasp the exercise handle. Then grasp the other end of the exercise tube with your opposite hand held overhead and pull upward. Hold for 5 to 10 seconds. Repeat the stretch for the opposite side.
Caution: You should not experience any pain.
Note: This stretch can also be performed using the golf-club shaft.

Stretch-contract-relax (PNF): At the end of the stretch described above, strongly contract the muscle by pulling against the resistive tubing for 5 seconds. Then relax for 5 seconds and repeat the sequence 1 to 3 times, beginning with the stretch.

SHOULDER MUSCLES
Anterior Deltoid

STRENGTHENING EXERCISE

Free-Weight Exercise:

In a standing position, grasp the weights with both arms, elbows bent less than 90°. Raise the weight with your elbows pointing forward. Hold for 10 seconds and lower slowly.

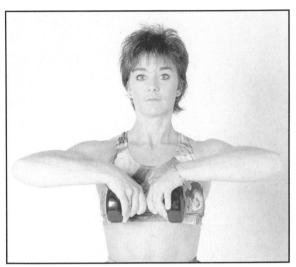

Golfercise System Exercise:

Position: Standing

Set-up: Connect both ends of the exercise tube to the A positions of the exercise handle.
Secure the door hinge anchor around the lower hinge.
Secure the exercise tube within the track of the door hinge anchor.

Action: Grasp the exercise handle while facing away from the door. Move away so that the tubing is taut. Raise your arm to just below shoulder height. Hold for 10 seconds and return slowly. Repeat the exercise for the opposite side.

Upper Body

SHOULDER MUSCLES
Middle Deltoid

SWING PHASE: Stabilizes the shoulder throughout the swing
FUNCTION: Shoulder abduction — raises arm outward

STRETCH-OUT

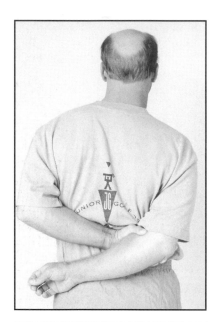

Self Stretch:

In a seated or standing position, reach down and behind your back with your involved forearm, palm facing outward. Raise your forearm toward the opposite shoulder blade as high as tolerable. To increase the stretch, reach behind your back with your opposite arm grasping just above your elbow, pulling the involved arm toward the middle of your back. Hold the stretch for 5 to 10 seconds. Repeat the stretch for the opposite side.

Golfercise System Stretch:

Position: Standing
Set-up: Connect one end of the exercise tube to position A of the exercise handle.
Action: Reach down and behind your back with your involved forearm and grasp the exercise handle. Then grasp the other end of the exercise tube with your opposite hand held overhead and pull upward. Hold for 5 to 10 seconds. Repeat the stretch for the opposite side.
Caution: You should not experience any pain.
Note: This stretch can also be performed using the golf-club shaft.

Stretch-contract-relax (PNF): At the end of the stretch described above, strongly contract the muscle by pulling against the resistive tubing for 5 seconds. Then relax for 5 seconds and repeat the sequence 1 to 3 times, beginning with the stretch.

SHOULDER MUSCLES
Middle Deltoid

STRENGTHENING EXERCISE

Free-Weight Exercise:

In a standing position, grasp the weights with both arms, elbows bent less than 90°. Raise the weight, with your elbow at your side. Hold for 10 seconds and lower slowly.

Golfercise System Exercise:

Position:	Standing
Set-up:	Connect both ends of the exercise tube to the A positions of the exercise handle.
	Secure the door hinge anchor around the lower hinge.
	Secure the exercise tube within the track of the door hinge anchor.
Action:	Stand with your involved arm away from the door, and your body at 90° with the door. Grasp the exercise handle, with your arm at your side, with your elbow bent 90°, hand held straight outward. Raise your arm to just below shoulder height. Hold for 10 seconds and return slowly. Repeat the exercise for the opposite side.

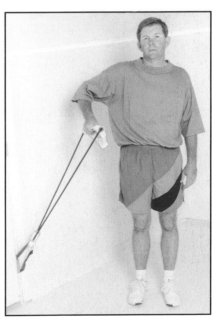

Upper Body

SHOULDER MUSCLES
Posterior Deltoid

SWING PHASE: Stabilizes the shoulder throughout the swing
FUNCTION: Shoulder abduction — raises arm outward and backward

STRETCH-OUT

Self Stretch:

In a seated or standing position, reach across the front of your body with your involved arm while grasping your elbow with your uninvolved hand. Pull the involved arm toward the opposite shoulder. Hold for 5 to 10 seconds. Repeat the stretch for the opposite side.

Note: This stretch is recommended for golfers with previous shoulder injuries, because it will not place undue stress on the shoulder. This maneuver also stretches the infraspinatus and supraspinatus of the rotator cuff muscles.

ANTERIOR ARM MUSCLES
Biceps

STRENGTHENING EXERCISE

Free-Weight Exercise:

In a standing or seated position, hold your arms against your side, palms facing inward. Grasp the weight with your involved hand and raise the weight by bending your elbows, turning your palm upward as you raise the weight. Hold for 5 seconds, then lower the weight slowly. Repeat the exercise for the opposite side.

Golfercise System Exercise:

Position:	Seated or standing
Set-up:	Connect both ends of the exercise tube to the A positions of the exercise handle.
	Secure the door hinge anchor around the bottom hinge.
	Secure the exercise tube within the track of the door hinge anchor.
Action:	While seated facing the door, grasp the exercise handle with your palms facing upward and your arms downward. If seated, move the chair so that the tubing is taut. Raise the handle toward your chest with your elbows fixed to your side. Hold for 5 seconds and return slowly.

Upper Body

POSTERIOR ARM MUSCLES
Triceps

SWING PHASE: Active in the Forward and Acceleration phases
FUNCTION: Extension of the forearm; pulls raised arm downward and backward

STRETCH-OUT

Self Stretch:

In a standing position, reach up and behind your back with the involved forearm, palm toward your back. Reach toward your opposite shoulder blade. For maximum stretch, grasp the elbow of your involved arm with your opposite hand and pull backward. Hold the stretch for 5 to 10 seconds. Repeat the stretch for the opposite side.

Golfercise System Stretch:

Position: Standing
Set-up: Connect both ends of the exercise tube to the A positions of the exercise handle.
Secure the door hinge anchor around the top hinge.
Secure the exercise tube within the track of the door hinge anchor.
Action: While facing away from the door, grasp the exercise handle with your arms raised above your head, palms facing upward. Move away from the door until the exercise tubing is taut, pulling your arms backward with your elbows bent. Stretch for 5 to 10 seconds. Repeat the stretch for the opposite side.

Stretch-contract-relax (PNF): At the end of the stretch described above, strongly contract the muscle by pulling against the resistive tubing for 5 seconds. Then relax for 5 seconds and repeat the sequence 1 to 3 times, beginning with the stretch.

POSTERIOR ARM MUSCLES
Triceps

STRENGTHENING EXERCISE

Free-Weight Exercise:

In a seated or standing position, raise your arms overhead with your elbows bent at 90°. Grasp the weight with your hands. Straighten the arms by lifting the weight toward the ceiling, elbows pointing forward while you raise the weight. Hold for 5 seconds and lower the weight slowly.

Golfercise System Exercise:

Position:	Standing
Set-up:	Connect both ends of the exercise tube to the A positions of the exercise handle.
	Secure the door hinge anchor around the top hinge.
	Secure the exercise tube within the track of the door hinge anchor.
Action:	While facing toward the door, grasp the exercise handle, palms facing downward, keeping your hands close together and your elbows fixed to your side. Move away until the exercise tubing is taut. Push the handle downward. Hold for 5 seconds and return slowly.

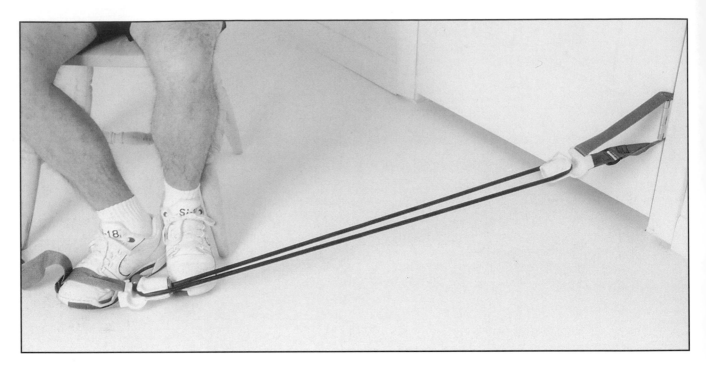

Strong lower-leg muscles are essential for proper weight transfer.

NOTE: The Golfercise System exercises described in this chapter use the unique patented design exercise equipment. This computer-designed and engineered equipment has four pieces and incorporates the revolutionary *progressive variable resistance tubing*. The equipment includes:

1. **Progressive variable resistance exercise tube**
2. **Exercise handle with exercise tube connectors at:**
   position(s) A — ends of handle and
   position B — apex of handle
3. **Exercise tube anchor with adjustable strap lock**
4. **Door hinge anchor**

Lower-Body Exercises

12

The following systematic, golf-specific stretches and exercises are designed to improve the flexibility, endurance, and strength in every muscle group of the lower body that is required for a technically correct golf swing. These exercises are designed specifically to improve your game by stretching and by increasing the endurance and strength of the golf-specific lower-body muscles. To achieve maximum benefit, perform the exercises every other day. Always remember to stretch before you exercise any muscle, using the principles of physical conditioning discussed in Chapters 2-4.

Primary Active Lower-Body Muscles

STOMACH OBLIQUE MUSCLES
Internal and External Oblique Muscles

SWING PHASE: Active during all four swing phases
FUNCTION: Bends trunk forward and rotates trunk

Lower Body | **STRETCH-OUT**

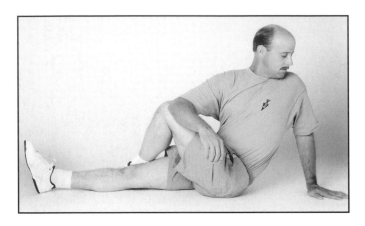

Self Stretch:

While sitting on the ground, cross your involved ankle over the opposite straight leg at the knee. Rotate your shoulders away from the involved side so that the opposite elbow is outside the involved knee. Place your other hand flat on the ground behind you. Then slowly look over your shoulder so as to rotate your trunk to the side of the involved leg as far as tolerable. At the same time, apply counterpressure with your uninvolved elbow against the bent knee. Hold for approximately 20 to 30 seconds. Reverse leg positions and stretch the other side.

Note: This maneuver will also stretch the hip muscles. This stretch is excellent for players with back problems and can be done throughout the round.

Golfercise System Stretch:

Position:	Standing
Set-up:	Connect one end of the exercise tube to position A and the other end to position B of the exercise handle.
	Secure the door hinge anchor around the top hinge.
	Secure the exercise tube within the track of the door hinge anchor.
Action:	Grasp the exercise handle with your involved hand, raise your arm over your head, and cross your involved side leg in front of your uninvolved leg. Face sideways to the door. With your uninvolved side facing the door, move away until the exercise tube is taut. Your upper body should be pulled toward the support. Hold for 10 to 20 seconds. Repeat the stretch for the opposite side.
Note:	This maneuver also stretches the lateral upper back, the lateral trunk, and the outer thigh muscles.

Stretch-contract-relax (PNF): At the end of the stretch described above, strongly contract the muscle by pulling against the resistive tubing for 5 seconds. Then relax for 5 seconds and repeat the sequence 1 to 3 times, beginning with the stretch.

STOMACH OBLIQUE MUSCLES
Internal and External Oblique Muscles

STRENGTHENING EXERCISE

Free-Weight Exercise:

Lying face-up, with your hips and knees bent approximately 45° and your feet flat on the ground, cross your chest with your arms. For a more strenuous exercise, hold weights on your chest. Raise your torso up so that your shoulder blades are just off the ground. Rotate to the right, holding for 10 seconds, and return slowly. Repeat the exercise, rotating to the left.

Golfercise System Exercise:

Position:	Seated on ground with legs underneath you
Set-up:	Connect both ends of the exercise tube to the A positions of the exercise handle. Secure the door hinge anchor around the lower hinge. Secure the exercise tube within the track of the door hinge anchor.
Note:	For increased resistance, triple wrap the tube. For an easier workout, or if sitting on the ground with your legs underneath is too difficult, sit in a chair and use the middle hinge to secure the door anchor.
Action:	Face away from the door. Place the exercise handle next to your side. Grasp the handle, with your opposite hand reaching across your chest. Rotate your body toward the opposite side of the exercise handle. Hold for 10 seconds and return slowly. Repeat the exercise for the opposite side.
Note:	Rotation of the trunk to the right exercises the right internal oblique muscle. Rotation of the trunk to the left exercises the left internal oblique muscle.

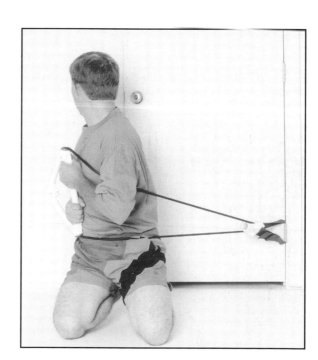

Lower Body

LATERAL TRUNK MUSCLES
Quadratus Lumborum

SWING PHASE: Active in the Acceleration and Follow-through phases
FUNCTION: Bends the trunk (spine) to the side

STRETCH-OUT

Self Stretch:

In a standing position, cross one leg over the other, and raise your arms above your head with your fingers interlaced, palms facing upward. Slowly bend your trunk to the opposite side of your front leg and push your hips to the same side of your front leg. Hold for 10 to 15 seconds. Cross your other leg and repeat the exercise, bending in the opposite direction.
Note: This maneuver also stretches the upper back (latissimus dorsi), the stomach oblique muscles, and the outer thigh muscles (tensor fascia lata and gluteus medius).

Golfercise System Stretch:

Position:	Standing
Set-up:	Connect one end of the exercise tube to position A and the other end to position B of the exercise handle.
	Secure the door hinge anchor around the top hinge.
	Secure the exercise tube within the track of the door hinge anchor.
Action:	Grasp the exercise handle with your involved hand, raise your arm over your head, and cross your involved side leg in front of your uninvolved leg. Face sideways to the door. With your uninvolved side facing the door, move away until the exercise tube is taut. Your upper body should be pulled toward the support. Hold for 10 to 20 seconds. Repeat the stretch for the opposite side.
Note:	This maneuver also stretches the lateral upper back, the stomach oblique muscles, and the outer thigh muscles.

Stretch-contract-relax (PNF): At the end of the stretch described above, strongly contract the muscle by pulling against the resistive tubing for 5 seconds. Then relax for 5 seconds and repeat the sequence 1 to 3 times, beginning with the stretch.

LATERAL TRUNK MUSCLES
Quadratus Lumborum

Lower Body

STRENGTHENING EXERCISE

Free-Weight Exercise:

In a standing position, grasp the weight on your uninvolved side. Bend your trunk to the opposite side, keeping your pelvis tucked under and your knees slightly bent. Hold for 5 seconds and return slowly. Repeat the exercise for the opposite side.

Golfercise System Exercise:

Position:	Seated or standing
Set-up:	Connect both ends of the exercise tube to the A positions of the exercise handle.
	Wrap the strap of the exercise tube anchor around the involved foot.
	Secure the exercise tube within the track of the anchor.
Action:	Grasp the exercise handle with your uninvolved hand. Bend your trunk to the opposite side. Hold for 10 seconds and return slowly. Repeat the exercise for the opposite side.

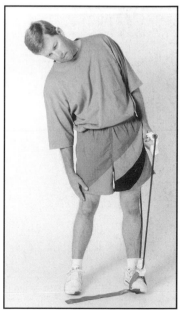

Lower Body

POSTERIOR HIP MUSCLES (Buttock)
Medial Hip and Thigh Rotator • *Gluteus Minimus*

SWING PHASE: Active in all swing phases
FUNCTION: Medial or internal rotation of hip and thigh; turns hip and thigh "in"

STRETCH-OUT

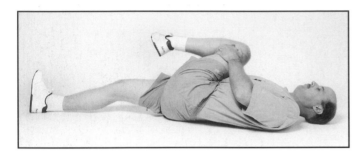

Self Stretch:

Lying face-up, pull the involved knee toward the opposite shoulder to tolerance. Hold for 15 to 20 seconds.
Note: This stretch may be performed in a seated position. Cross your involved leg over the uninvolved leg, with your ankle resting above your knee. Pull your involved knee toward the opposite shoulder to tolerance. Hold for 15 to 20 seconds.
Option: While lying face-up, bend both knees so that your feet are flat on the ground. Cross one leg over the other. Pull your bottom leg with your top leg toward the side of your top leg to the ground. This will rotate your hip and trunk. Straighten your arms out to the sides with your palms facing upward. Hold for 20 to 30 seconds. Reverse leg positions and stretch the other side.
Note: This maneuver is excellent for any player with a history of back pain.

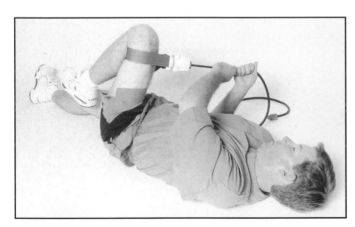

Golfercise System Stretch:

Position:	Lying face-up
Set-up:	Connect one end of the exercise tube to the exercise tube anchor.
	Wrap the strap of the exercise tube anchor around your thigh just above your knee.
Action:	Cross the involved leg over the uninvolved knee, which should be bent approximately 90°. Grasp the exercise tube and pull toward the opposite shoulder. Hold for 10 to 20 seconds. Repeat the stretch for the opposite side.

Stretch-contract-relax (PNF): At the end of the stretch described above, strongly contract the muscle by pulling against the resistive tubing for 5 seconds. Then relax for 5 seconds and repeat the sequence 1 to 3 times, beginning with the stretch.

POSTERIOR HIP MUSCLES (Buttock)
Medial Hip and Thigh Rotator • *Gluteus Minimus*

Lower Body

STRENGTHENING EXERCISE

Free-Weight Exercise:

Lying on your side, with your involved side up on the edge of a table, bend the involved hip and knee at 90°. Move your involved leg off the edge over the uninvolved, straightened leg. Raise your foot toward the ceiling while keeping your knee stationary. To maximize your performance, wear an ankle weight. Hold for 5 seconds. Repeat the exercise for the opposite side.

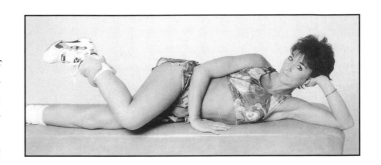

Golfercise System Exercise:

Position:	Lying face up or seated on the floor
Set-up:	Connect one end of the exercise tube to the exercise tube anchor.
	Wrap the long strap around your thigh just above your knee.
	Secure the door hinge anchor around the lower hinge.
	Connect the other end of the exercise tube to the door hinge anchor.
Note:	For extra resistance, double or triple wrap the exercise tube.
	For extra resistance, secure the door hinge anchor around the middle hinge.
Action:	Lie down or sit on the floor with your involved side next to the door. Move away until the tube is taut. Bend your involved knee so that your foot is flat on the floor. Pull your knee inward over the straightened, uninvolved leg as far as possible. Hold for 5 seconds and return slowly. Repeat the exercise for the opposite side.

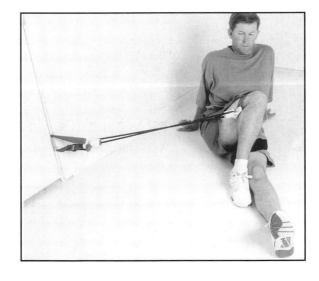

Lower Body

POSTERIOR HIP MUSCLES (Buttock)
Lateral Hip and Thigh Rotator • *Piriformis*

SWING PHASE: Active primarily in the Forward and Acceleration phases
FUNCTION: Lateral or external rotation of hip and thigh; turns hip and thigh "outward"

STRETCH-OUT

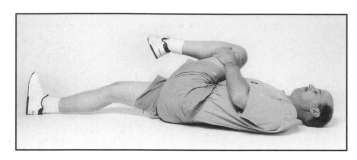

Self Stretch:

Lying face-up, pull the involved knee toward the opposite shoulder to tolerance. Hold for 15 to 20 seconds.
Note: This stretch may be performed in a seated position. Cross your involved leg over the uninvolved leg, with your ankle resting above your knee. Pull your involved knee toward the opposite shoulder to tolerance. Hold for 15 to 20 seconds.

Option: While lying face-up, bend both knees so that your feet are flat on the ground. Cross one leg over the other. Pull your bottom leg with your top leg toward the side of your top leg to the ground. This will rotate your hip and trunk. Straighten your arms out to the sides with your palms facing upward. Hold for 20 to 30 seconds. Reverse leg positions and stretch the other side.
Note: This maneuver is excellent for any player with a history of back pain.

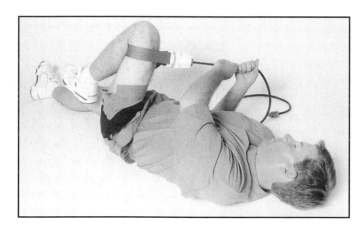

Golfercise System Stretch:

Position:	Lying face-up
Set-up:	Connect one end of the exercise tube to the exercise tube anchor. Wrap the strap of the exercise tube anchor around your thigh just above your knee.
Action:	Cross the involved leg over the uninvolved knee, which should be bent approximately 90°. Grasp the exercise tube and pull toward the opposite shoulder. Hold for 10 to 20 seconds. Repeat the stretch for the opposite side.

Stretch-contract-relax (PNF): At the end of the stretch described above, strongly contract the muscle by pulling against the resistive tubing for 5 seconds. Then relax for 5 seconds and repeat the sequence 1 to 3 times, beginning with the stretch.

POSTERIOR HIP MUSCLES (Buttock)
Lateral Hip and Thigh Rotator • *Piriformis*

STRENGTHENING EXERCISE

Free-Weight Exercise:

While lying on your side, with the involved side facing upward, flex your involved hip 90°, bend your knee 90°, and place your involved foot behind the knee of the uninvolved, straightened leg. Raise your involved knee toward the ceiling, keeping your foot secure behind the uninvolved knee. Hold for 5 seconds and return slowly. Repeat the exercise for the opposite side.

Note: For maximum results, place an ankle weight just above your knee.

Golfercise System Exercise:

Position:	Lying face-up or seated on the floor
Set-up:	Connect one end of the exercise tube to the exercise tube anchor.
	Wrap the long strap around your thigh just above your knee.
	Secure the door hinge anchor around the lower hinge.
	Connect the other end of the exercise tube to the door hinge anchor.
Note:	For extra resistance, double or triple wrap the exercise tube.
	For extra resistance, secure the door hinge anchor around the middle hinge.
Action:	Lie down or sit on the floor with the involved side away from the door. Move away until the tube is taut. Bend the involved knee with your foot flat on the floor. Pull the involved knee downward. Hold for 5 to 10 seconds and raise slowly. Repeat the exercise for the opposite side.

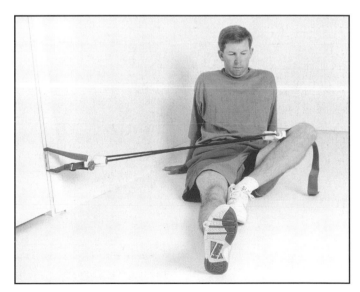

POSTERIOR HIP MUSCLES (Buttock)
Thigh Extensors • *Gluteus Maximus*

Lower Body

SWING PHASE: Active in the Acceleration and Follow-through phases
FUNCTION: Extends or brings the thigh backward

STRETCH-OUT

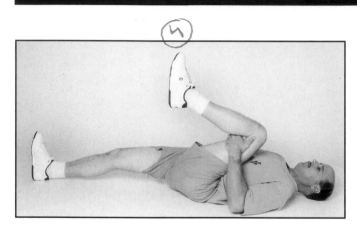

Self Stretch:

While in a sitting position or lying face-up, grasp under your leg just above your knee and pull your knee toward your chest. Keep your back and head straight or on the floor if you are lying down. Hold for 20 to 30 seconds. Repeat the stretch for the opposite side.

Note: This maneuver will also stretch your hamstrings. Do not place your hands over the top of your shin while doing this stretching maneuver, because it will place unwanted pressure on your knee and decrease the stretch.

Option: While lying face-up, place your arms under both legs just above your knees and pull your legs to your chest. Keep your back and neck flat on the floor. Hold for 20 to 30 seconds.

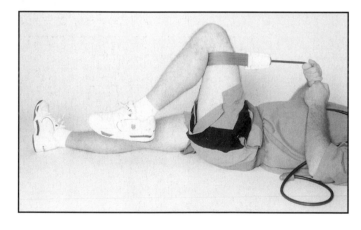

Golfercise System Stretch:

Position: Lying face-up
Set-up: Wrap the strap of the exercise tube anchor around your thigh just above your knee.
Secure the exercise tube within the track of the anchor.
Action: Grasp the end of the exercise tube and raise your leg. Your hip should be flexed, with your leg pulled toward your chest. Hold for 20 to 30 seconds. Repeat the stretch for the opposite side.

POSTERIOR HIP MUSCLES (Buttock)
Thigh Extensors • *Gluteus Maximus*

Lower Body

STRENGTHENING EXERCISE

Free-Weight Exercise:

In a standing position, step up one stair or onto a step stool with your involved foot, then step back down with your uninvolved foot. Continue the stair stepping until you feel tightness or soreness in your buttock. Repeat the exercise for the other side.
Note: This exercise can be done on a mechanical stair climber for best results. This exercise is also excellent for cardiovascular conditioning.

Golfercise System Exercise:

Position:	Standing facing the door
Set-up:	Connect one end of the exercise tube to the exercise tube anchor.
	Wrap the strap of the exercise tube anchor around your ankle.
	Secure the door hinge anchor around the lower hinge.
	Connect the other end of the exercise tube to the door hinge anchor.
Note:	For extra resistance, double or triple wrap the exercise tube.
Action:	While standing facing the door, move away until the exercise tube is taut. Pull your leg away from the door, extending your hip. Hold for 5 seconds. Repeat the exercise for the other side.

INNER THIGH MUSCLES
Medial Hip and Thigh Adductors • *Adductor Longus, Magnus, and Brevis*

SWING PHASE: Active in the Forward and Acceleration phases
FUNCTION: Brings the thigh inward

STRETCH-OUT

Self Stretch:

1. In a standing position, separate your legs, bend your uninvolved knee, and transfer your weight to this leg. Push your trunk toward the uninvolved side. This will stretch the inside of the involved leg. Hold for 20 to 30 seconds. Reverse leg positions and repeat the stretch for the other side.
2. While sitting on the floor, bend forward and grasp your feet, pulling them slowly toward your buttock. Use your arms to push your knees gently outward toward the floor. Hold for a count of 20 to 30 seconds.

INNER THIGH MUSCLES
Medial Hip and Thigh Adductors • *Adductor Longus, Magnus, and Brevis*

Lower Body

STRENGTHENING EXERCISE

Free-Weight Exercise:

Lying face-up, flex your involved hip 60° to 80°. Bend your involved knee 45°, and lower your leg toward the table. Slowly raise your knee upward so that it points to the ceiling. Hold for 5 seconds, then lower slowly. Repeat the exercise for the opposite side.

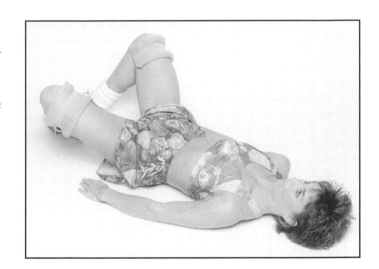

Golfercise System Exercise:

Position:	Lying face-up or seated on floor
Set-up:	Connect one end of the exercise tube to the exercise tube anchor.
	Wrap the strap of the exercise tube anchor around your thigh just above your knee.
	Secure the door hinge anchor around the lower hinge.
	Connect the other end of the exercise tube to the door hinge anchor.
Note:	For extra resistance, double or triple wrap the exercise tube.
Action:	Lie or sit on the floor with your involved side toward the door. Move away until the tube is taut. Straighten your involved leg with the leg moved away from center at approximately 45°. Pull your leg to the midline. Hold for 5 seconds and return slowly. Repeat the exercise for the opposite side.

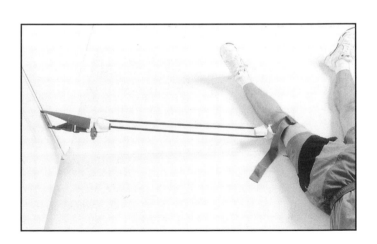

Lower Body

OUTER THIGH MUSCLES
Lateral Hip and Thigh Abductors • *Tensor Fascia Lata and Gluteus Medius*

SWING PHASE: Active in Forward, Acceleration, and early Follow-through phases
FUNCTION: Brings the thigh outward

STRETCH-OUT

Self Stretch:

In a standing position, cross one leg over the other, and raise your arms above your head with your fingers interlaced, palms facing upward. Slowly bend your trunk to the opposite side of your front leg and push your hips to the same side of your front leg. Hold for 10 to 15 seconds. Cross your other leg and repeat the exercise, bending in the opposite direction.
Note: This maneuver also stretches the lateral trunk muscles (quadratus lumborum), the stomach oblique muscles, and the upper back (latissimus dorsi).

Golfercise System Stretch:

Position:	Standing
Set-up:	Connect one end of the exercise tube to position A and the other end to position B of the exercise handle.
	Secure the door hinge anchor around the top hinge.
	Secure the exercise tube within the track of the door hinge anchor.
Action:	Grasp the exercise handle with your involved hand, raise your arm over your head, and cross the involved side leg in front of your uninvolved leg. Face sideways to the door. With your uninvolved side facing the door, move away until the exercise tube is taut. Your upper body should be pulled toward the support. Hold for 10 to 20 seconds. Repeat the stretch for the opposite side.
Note:	This maneuver also stretches the lateral upper back, the stomach oblique muscles, and the upper-back muscles.

Stretch-contract-relax (PNF): At the end of the stretch described above, strongly contract the muscle by pulling against the resistive tubing for 5 seconds. Then relax for 5 seconds and repeat the sequence 1 to 3 times, beginning with the stretch.

OUTER THIGH MUSCLES
Lateral Hip and Thigh Abductors • *Tensor Fascia Lata and Gluteus Medius*

STRENGTHENING EXERCISE

Free-Weight Exercise:

Lie down on your side, with the involved side facing upward. Wearing an ankle weight, raise the involved leg straight toward the ceiling. Hold for 5 seconds and lower slowly. Repeat the exercise for the opposite side.

Golfercise System Exercise:

Position:	Lying face-up or seated on the floor
Set-up:	Connect one end of the exercise tube to the exercise tube anchor.
	Wrap the long strap of the exercise tube anchor around your thigh just above your knee.
	Secure the door hinge anchor around the lower hinge.
	Connect the other end of the exercise tube to the door hinge anchor.
Note:	For extra resistance, double or triple wrap the exercise tube.
Action:	Lie or sit on the floor with the involved leg away from the door. Move the leg outward to approximately 45°. Hold for 5 seconds and return slowly. Repeat the exercise for the opposite side.

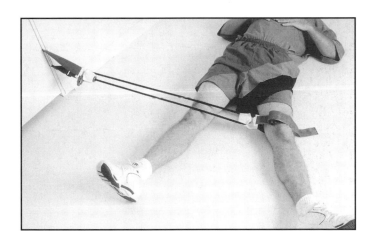

Lower Body

ANTERIOR LOWER-LEG MUSCLES
Ankle and Foot Invertors • *Anterior Tibialis*

SWING PHASE: Active throughout the swing
FUNCTION: Inversion of foot; rolls ankle outward
Aids in weight transfer and ankle "roll"

STRETCH-OUT

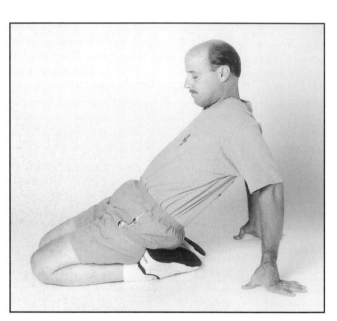

Self Stretch:

1. While sitting on the floor with your feet brought underneath with the soles of your feet facing toward the ceiling, lean backward with your hands supporting you on the ground. This stretches the quadriceps and anterior leg muscles. Your feet must not flare out during this stretch but should be together, pointing straight backward. Hold the stretch for 20 to 30 seconds.
    Note: This may be difficult for the senior player.
2. In a seated position, place the tops of your feet on the floor, toes pointing backward. Lean back in your chair, stretching the muscles of the anterior leg. Hold for 20 to 30 seconds.

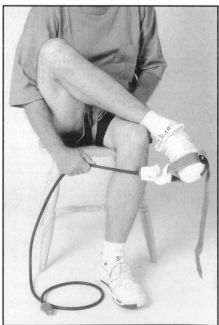

Golfercise System Stretch:

Position:	Seated
Set-up:	Connect one end of the exercise tube to the exercise tube anchor. Wrap the strap of the exercise tube anchor around your foot (wear exercise shoes) with the tube coming off of the outside of your foot.
Action:	Cross the involved ankle over the uninvolved knee. Grasp the exercise tube and pull downward. This stretches the foot invertor muscles, rolling the ankle outward. Hold for 5 to 10 seconds. Repeat the stretch for the opposite side.

Stretch-contract-relax (PNF): At the end of the stretch described above, strongly contract the muscle by pulling against the resistive tubing for 5 seconds. Then relax for 5 seconds and repeat the sequence 1 to 3 times, beginning with the stretch.

ANTERIOR LOWER-LEG MUSCLES
Ankle and Foot Invertors • *Anterior Tibialis*

STRENGTHENING EXERCISE

Free-Weight Exercise:

In a seated position, wearing an ankle weight wrapped around your fore-foot, cross your involved ankle over your uninvolved leg. Raise your foot toward the ceiling. Hold for 5 seconds and lower slowly. Repeat the exercise on the other side.

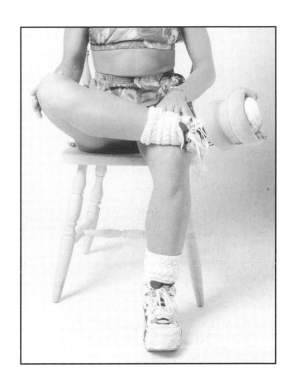

Golfercise System Exercise:

Position:	Seated
Set-up:	Connect one end of the exercise tube to the exercise tube anchor.
	Wrap the strap of the exercise tube anchor around your foot (wear exercise shoes).
	Secure the door hinge anchor around the lower hinge.
	Connect the other end of the exercise tube to the door hinge anchor.
Note:	For extra resistance, double or triple wrap the exercise tube.
Action:	With your involved foot toward the door, exercise tube taut, pull your involved foot inward (away from the door) with your heel stabilized by the chair leg. Hold for 5 seconds and return slowly. Repeat the exercise for the opposite side.

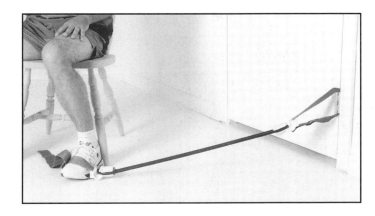

ANTERIOR LOWER-LEG MUSCLES
Ankle and Foot Evertors • *Peroneus Longus and Brevis*

SWING PHASE: Active throughout swing; aids in weight transfer and ankle "roll"
FUNCTION: Eversion of the foot; rolls ankle inward

STRETCH-OUT

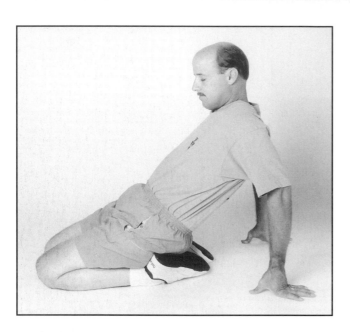

Self Stretch:

1. While sitting on the floor with your feet brought underneath with the soles of your feet facing toward the ceiling, lean backward with your hands supporting you on the ground. This stretches the quadriceps and anterior leg muscles. Your feet must not flare out during this stretch but should be together, pointing straight backward. Hold the stretch for 20 to 30 seconds.
    Note: This may be difficult for the senior player.
2. In a seated position, place the tops of your feet on the floor, toes pointing backward. Lean back in your chair, stretching the muscles of the anterior leg. Hold for 20 to 30 seconds.

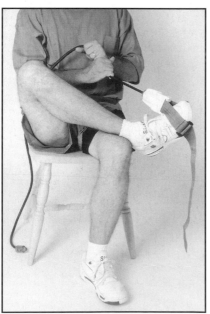

Golfercise System Stretch:

Position:	Seated
Set-up:	Connect one end of the exercise tube to the exercise tube anchor. Wrap the strap of the exercise tube anchor around your foot (wear exercise shoes) with the tube coming off of the inside of your foot.
Action:	Cross the involved leg over the uninvolved leg. Grasp the exercise tube and pull upward. This stretches the foot evertor muscles, rolling the ankle inward. Hold for 5 to 10 seconds. Repeat the stretch for the opposite side.

Stretch-contract-relax (PNF): At the end of the stretch described above, strongly contract the muscle by pulling against the resistive tubing for 5 seconds. Then relax for 5 seconds and repeat the sequence 1 to 3 times, beginning with the stretch.

ANTERIOR LOWER-LEG MUSCLES
Ankle and Foot Evertors • *Peroneus Longus and Brevis*

STRENGTHENING EXERCISE

Free-Weight Exercise:

In a seated position, wear an ankle weight wrapped around your forefoot with your involved leg slightly outstretched. Roll your ankle inward. Hold for 5 to 10 seconds and return slowly. Repeat the exercise for the opposite side.

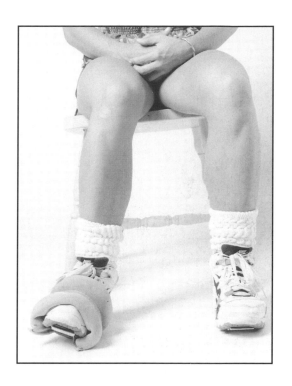

Golfercise System Exercise:

Position:	Seated
Set-up:	Connect one end of the exercise tube to the exercise tube anchor.
	Wrap the strap of the exercise tube anchor around your foot (wear exercise shoes).
	Secure the door hinge anchor around the lower hinge.
	Connect the other end of the exercise tube to the door hinge anchor.
Note:	For extra resistance, double or triple wrap the exercise tube.
Action:	With your involved foot away from the door, exercise tube taut, pull your involved foot outward (away from the door) with your heel stabilized by the leg of the chair or your other foot. Hold for 5 seconds and return slowly. Repeat the exercise for the opposite side.

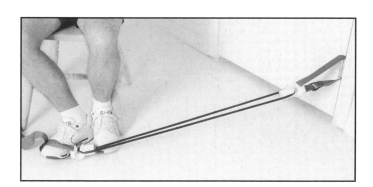

ANTERIOR LOWER-LEG MUSCLES
Ankle and Foot Dorsiflexors • *Extensor Digitorum Longus and Brevis*

SWING PHASE: Active throughout the swing; aids in balance
FUNCTION: Raises foot upward; dorsiflexion of ankle

STRETCH-OUT

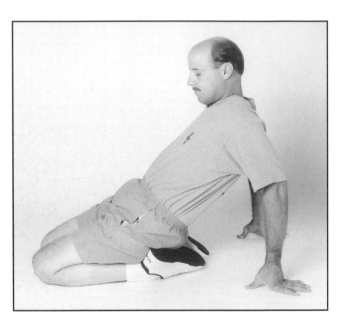

Self Stretch:

1. While sitting on the floor, with your feet brought underneath and the soles of your feet facing toward the ceiling, lean backward with your hands supporting you on the ground. This stretches the quadriceps and anterior leg muscles. Your feet must not flare out during this stretch but should be together, pointing straight backward. Hold the stretch for 20 to 30 seconds.
   Note: This may be difficult for the senior player.
2. In a seated position, place the tops of your feet on the floor, toes pointing backward. Lean back in your chair, stretching the muscles of the anterior leg. Hold for 20 to 30 seconds.

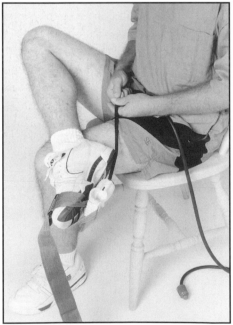

Golfercise System Stretch:

Position:	Seated
Set-up:	Connect one end of the exercise tube to the exercise tube anchor. Wrap the strap of the exercise tube around your foot (wear exercise shoes) with the tube coming off of the bottom of your foot.
Action:	Cross your involved leg over your uninvolved leg. Pull on the exercise tube, which should be under your foot and over your heel. This stretches the muscles that raise the foot (dorsiflexion). Hold for 5 to 10 seconds. Repeat the stretch for the opposite side.

Stretch-contract-relax (PNF): At the end of the stretch described above, strongly contract the muscle by pulling against the resistive tubing for 5 seconds. Then relax for 5 seconds and repeat the sequence 1 to 3 times, beginning with the stretch.

ANTERIOR LOWER-LEG MUSCLES
Ankle and Foot Dorsiflexors • *Extensor Digitorum Longus and Brevis*

Lower Body

STRENGTHENING EXERCISE

Free-Weight Exercise:

In a seated position, wearing an ankle weight wrapped around your forefoot (preferably in a chair where your feet do not touch the floor), raise your forefoot upward. Hold for 5 seconds and return slowly until your foot is pointed downward. Repeat the exercise for the opposite side.

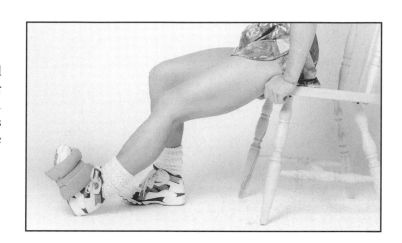

Golfercise System Exercise:

Position:	Seated on the floor
Set-up:	Connect one end of the exercise tube to the exercise tube anchor.
	Wrap the strap of the exercise tube around your foot (wear exercise shoes) with the tube coming off of the bottom of your foot.
	Secure the door hinge anchor around the lower hinge.
	Connect the other end of the exercise tube to the door hinge anchor.
Note:	For extra resistance, double or triple wrap the exercise tube.
Action:	Facing the door with the involved leg straight, move away until the exercise tube is taut. Pull the involved foot upward by bending at your ankle. Hold for 5 seconds and return slowly. Repeat the exercise for the opposite side.

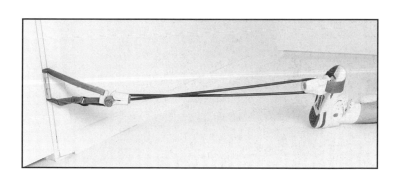

Secondary Stabilizing and Accessory Lower-Body Muscles

ABDOMINAL STOMACH MUSCLES
Rectus Abdominous

SWING PHASE: Stabilizes trunk during the swing
FUNCTION: Bends trunk forward

Lower Body

STRETCH-OUT

Self Stretch:

Note: No stretch is provided in this text, because it is very rare to have tight abdominal muscles.

ABDOMINAL STOMACH MUSCLES
Rectus Abdominous

STRENGTHENING EXERCISE

Free-Weight Exercise:

Lying face-up, with your hips and knees bent at approximately 45°, and your feet flat on the floor, cross your arms over your chest. Raise your torso so that your shoulder blades are just off the ground. Hold for 5 to 10 seconds and lower slowly.

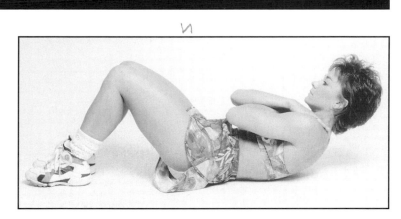

Golfercise System Exercise:

Position:	Seated in a chair
Set-up:	Connect both ends of the exercise tube to the A positions of the exercise handle.
	Secure the door hinge anchor around the top hinge.
	Secure the exercise tube within the track of the door hinge anchor.
Note:	For extra resistance, triple wrap the exercise tube.
Action:	Face away from the door. Place the exercise handle horizontally over your chest. Grasp with both palms facing outward or inward. The exercise tube should be taut. Bend forward at your waist until your chest nears your thighs. Hold for 10 seconds and return slowly.
Note:	You can also do this exercise by holding the exercise handle in both of your hands behind your neck.

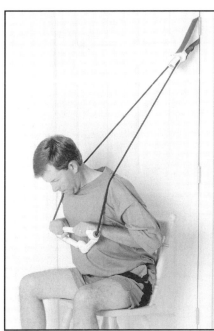

LOW-BACK MUSCLES (Trunk Extensors)
Erector Spinae Muscle (Lumbar and Thoracic)

Lower Body

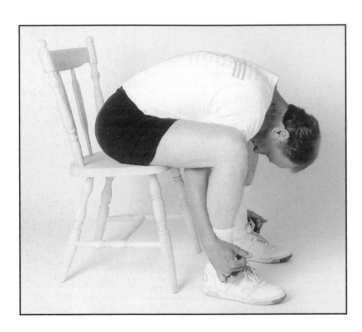

SWING PHASE: Stabilizes the trunk during the swing
FUNCTION: Extending the back, bending back to the side, and rotating trunk

STRETCH-OUT

Self Stretch:

1. In a sitting position, bend forward at your waist, bringing your shoulders and head as far forward as tolerable. To increase the stretch, reach your arms inside your legs, wrapping them around the outside of your ankles and pulling your trunk forward. Hold for 15 to 20 seconds.
   Note: This stretch is excellent for players with back problems and can be done throughout the round.

2. While sitting on the ground, cross your involved ankle over the opposite straight leg at your knee. Rotate your shoulders toward the involved side so that the opposite elbow is outside your involved knee. Place your other hand flat on the ground behind you. Then slowly look over your shoulder so as to rotate your trunk to the side of the involved leg as far as tolerable. At the same time, apply counterpressure with your uninvolved elbow against your bent knee. Hold for approximately 20 to 30 seconds. Reverse leg positions and stretch the other side.

   Note: This maneuver will also stretch the hip muscles. This stretch is excellent for players with back problems and can be done throughout the round.

3. While lying face-up, bend both knees so that your feet are flat on the ground. Cross one leg over the other. Pull your bottom leg with your top leg toward the side of your top leg to the ground. This will produce a rotation of the hip and trunk. Straighten your arms out to the sides with your palms facing upward. Hold for 20 to 30 seconds. Reverse leg positions and stretch the other side.

   Note: This maneuver will also stretch the hip muscles.

LOW-BACK MUSCLES (Trunk Extensors)
Erector Spinae Muscle (Lumbar and Thoracic)

STRENGTHENING EXERCISE

Free-Weight Exercise:

While lying flat on your stomach, arch your back by raising your shoulders off of the ground. This may be done with your arms behind your neck or resting behind your back. Hold for 3 to 5 seconds and return slowly.

Note: This exercise should not be done during episodes of low-back pain or if it produces low-back pain.

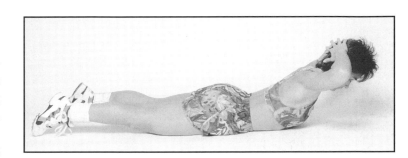

Golfercise System Exercise:

Position:	Seated
Set-up:	Connect both ends of the exercise tube to the A positions of the exercise handle.
	Secure the door hinge anchor around the lower hinge.
	Secure the exercise tube within the track of the door hinge anchor.
Note:	For extra resistance, triple wrap the exercise tube.
Action:	Hold the exercise handle against your chest while facing the door. Bend forward and move the chair away from the door until the exercise tube is taut. Raise up to a seated position. Hold for 10 seconds and lower slowly.
Note:	Stop bending backward when you are sitting straight up.

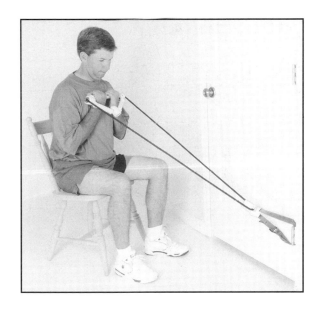

Lower Body

ANTERIOR THIGH MUSCLES
Knee Extensor • *Quadriceps Femoris*

SWING PHASE: Stabilizes the knee and leg during the swing
FUNCTION: Extends the knee

STRETCH-OUT

Self Stretch:

1. In a standing position, bring your involved foot up toward your buttock by bending your knee. Grasp your foot with your hand and pull your foot toward your buttock while at the same time rotating your hip backward. Use a chair to support yourself. Hold for 5 to 10 seconds. Repeat the stretch for the opposite side.
2. While sitting on the floor, tuck both legs underneath your buttocks with the tops of your feet flat on the ground, knees bent and together. Lean backward to tolerance. Hold for 5 to 10 seconds.
   Note: This may be difficult for the senior player.

Golfercise System Stretch:

Position: Standing
Set-up: Connect one end of the exercise tube to the exercise tube anchor.
             Wrap the strap of the exercise tube anchor around your ankle.
Action: With your knee bent backward, pull your foot toward your buttock by reaching behind, grabbing the exercise tube, and pulling it upward. Use a chair or wall to steady yourself. This will flex your knee and extend your hip. Hold for approximately 5 to 10 seconds. Repeat the stretch for the opposite side.

Stretch-contract-relax (PNF): At the end of the stretch described above, strongly contract the muscle by pulling against the resistive tubing for 5 seconds. Then relax for 5 seconds and repeat the sequence 1 to 3 times, beginning with the stretch.

ANTERIOR THIGH MUSCLES
Knee Extensor • *Quadriceps*

STRENGTHENING EXERCISE

Free-Weight Exercise:

In a seated position and while wearing an ankle weight, slowly straighten or extend your knee to 180°. Contract your quadriceps muscle strongly for 3 to 5 seconds, then lower your leg slowly. Repeat the exercise for the other side.

Note: When this exercise is done properly, you should feel a burning sensation in the region of your medial knee, just above your kneecap. This exercise is very helpful in strengthening an unstable knee.

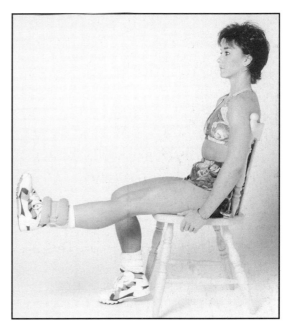

Golfercise System Exercise:

Position:	Seated (preferably in a chair high enough so that your feet do not touch the floor)
Set-up:	Connect one end of the exercise tube to the exercise tube anchor. Wrap the strap of the exercise tube anchor around your ankle. Secure the door hinge anchor around the lower hinge. Connect the other end of the exercise tube to the door hinge anchor.
Note:	For extra resistance, double or triple wrap the exercise tube.
Action:	Face away from the door. Move the chair away from the door until the exercise tube is taut. Slowly straighten your knee. Hold for 5 seconds and lower slowly. Repeat the exercise for the other side.

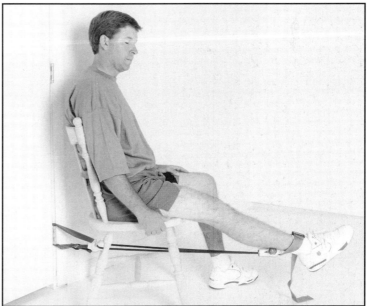

POSTERIOR THIGH MUSCLE
Knee Flexor • *Hamstrings*

SWING PHASE: Stabilizes the knee and leg throughout the swing
FUNCTION: Aids in internal and external rotation of the knee

STRETCH-OUT

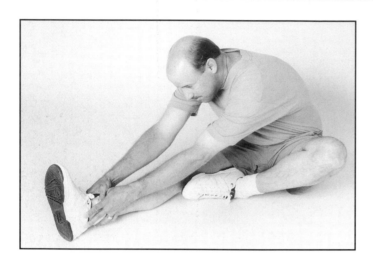

Self Stretch:

1. While sitting on the floor, straighten your involved leg out and in front of you while bending your uninvolved leg, with the bottom of your foot touching the inside of your thigh. This is the straight-leg, bent-knee position. Slowly reach forward, walking your arms down the involved straightened leg. Hold for 5 to 10 seconds. Reverse your leg position and repeat the exercise.

2. While lying face up, grasp just above your knee in the back of your leg and pull your leg toward your chest. Remain lying flat on the ground. Hold for 20 to 30 seconds. Repeat the stretch for the opposite side.

3. In a standing position, cross one leg over the other, place your arms behind your back, and bend forward at your hips, keeping your knees straight. Hold for 20 to 30 seconds. Reverse leg positions to stretch the opposite side.
   Note: This stretch should not be done if you have a history of low-back pain. Remember—never bounce!
   Option: While in the straight-leg, knee-bent position, wrap a towel around the ball of your outstretched leg, pulling your toes toward your knee. To increase the stretch, slightly lean forward at your hips. Hold for 20 to 30 seconds. Reverse leg positions and stretch the other side.

Golfercise System Stretch:

Position: Lying face-up
Set-up: Wrap the strap of the exercise tube anchor around your ankle.
Connect one end of the exercise tube to the exercise tube anchor.
Action: Grasp the end of the exercise tube and pull your straight leg upward, stretching your leg extensors or hamstring musculature.

Stretch-contract-relax (PNF): At the end of the stretch described above, strongly contract the muscle by pulling against the resistive tubing for 5 seconds. Then relax for 5 seconds and repeat the sequence 1 to 3 times, beginning with the stretch.

POSTERIOR THIGH MUSCLE
Knee Flexor • *Hamstrings*

STRENGTHENING EXERCISE

Free-Weight Exercise:

While lying face-down and wearing an ankle weight, bend your knee by bringing your heel toward your buttock. Hold for 5 seconds and slowly lower your leg. Repeat the exercise for the opposite side.

Note: If you have a history of low-back pain, place a pillow under your stomach so that your back is arched during this exercise.

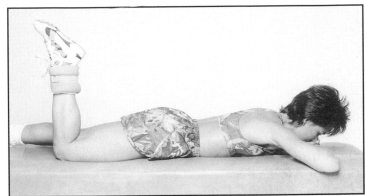

Golfercise System Exercise:

Position:	Lying face-down — facing away from the door
Set-up:	Connect one end of the exercise tube to the exercise tube anchor.
	Wrap the strap of the exercise tube anchor around your ankle.
	Secure the door hinge anchor around the lower hinge.
	Connect the other end of the exercise tube to the door hinge anchor.

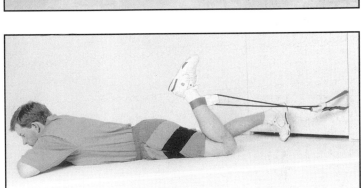

Note: For extra resistance, double or triple wrap the tube for greater resistance.

Action: While lying face-down, leg straight, move away from the door until the exercise tube is taut. Bend your knee, bringing your heel toward the buttock. Hold for 5 seconds and return slowly. Repeat the exercise for the other side.

Lower Body

POSTERIOR LEG MUSCLES
Calf • *Gastrocnemius and Soleus*

SWING PHASE: Stabilizes the knee and ankle throughout the swing
FUNCTION: Lowering or plantar flexion of the foot, knee flexion

STRETCH-OUT

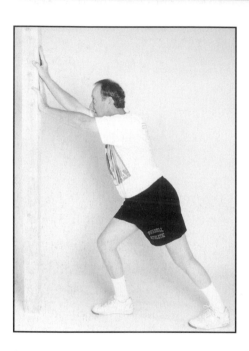

Self Stretch:

1. In a standing position, face a fence or wall against which you can lean, keeping your involved leg behind your uninvolved leg. Straighten your involved leg while bending your uninvolved leg at the knee. The uninvolved leg should be close to the wall. The involved leg should be straight, with your foot flat on the ground, pointing straight ahead. Your arms should be about chest height, with your palms on the wall. Slowly move your hips toward the wall while keeping your involved back leg straight and your foot flat. Hold for 20 to 30 seconds. Reverse leg positions and repeat the stretch on the other side.

2. While in a seated straight-leg, knee-bent position, wrap a towel around the ball of your outstretched leg, pulling your toes toward your knee. To increase the stretch, lean forward slightly at the hips. Hold for 20 to 30 seconds. Reverse leg positions and stretch the other side.

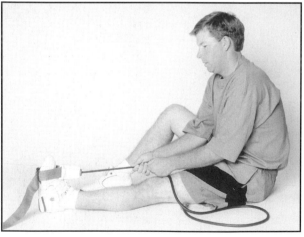

Golfercise System Stretch:

Position:	Seated on floor
Set-up:	Connect one end of the exercise tube to the exercise tube anchor.
	Wrap the strap of the exercise tube anchor around your foot (wear exercise shoes).
Action:	Grasp the exercise tube and pull so that your foot bends upward or toward your knee. Hold for 20 to 30 seconds. Repeat the stretch for the other side.

POSTERIOR LEG MUSCLES
Calf

STRENGTHENING EXERCISE

Free-Weight Exercise:

In a standing position with the balls of your feet resting on a 2x4 or edge of a stair, lower your heels below the stair and then maximally rise up on your toes. Hold for 5 to 10 seconds and lower slowly.

Golfercise System Exercise:

Position:	Seated on floor
Set-up:	Connect one end of the exercise tube to the exercise tube anchor.
	Wrap the strap of the exercise tube anchor around your foot (wear exercise shoes) with the tube coming off of the top.
Note:	For extra resistance, double or triple wrap the exercise tube.
Action:	While seated, push foot forward by bending at the ankle. Hold for 5 to 10 seconds and return slowly. Repeat the exer-cise for the opposite side.

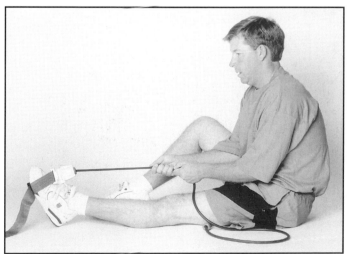

A golf-specific strength and conditioning program will give you the "edge" you are looking for.

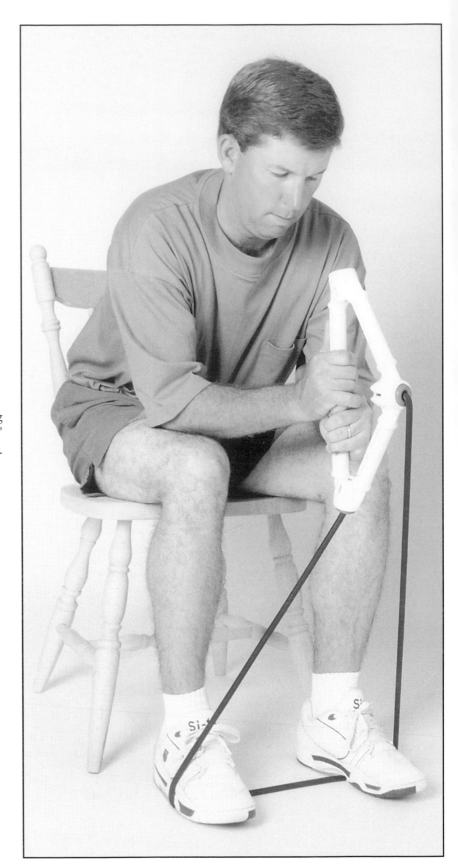

Top-Ten Exercise Routines

13

T he following exercise routine will exercise the primary muscle groups necessary for proper swing biomechanics. This routine is divided into exercises for the upper body and lower body. It will improve your flexibility, your endurance strength, and, most important, your rapid strength contraction.

The routines are divided into three levels. Level I is designed for the deconditioned or out-of-shape golfer, for the golfer who is coming off of an injury, or for the golfer of any age who is just beginning to exercise. Level II is designed primarily for endurance and increased strength. This level also aids in prevention and rehabilitation of injured muscles. Level III, the most intense level, is designed to maximize strength and endurance and to improve rapid strength, which is so vital for proper swing biomechanics.

Level I exercises are to be performed in a slow manner with light resistance and through a decreased range of motion. Each exercise is done in short ranges, not throughout the full range of motion, and is performed slowly (0° to 60° per second). Approximately 30° of movement per second is recommended in this level. This motion is designed to improve healing of injured muscles, tendons, or joints, to strengthen weakened tendons, ligaments, and muscles, and to prepare muscles and joints for a more aggressive exercise program that will improve strength.

Level II exercises are designed to increase muscle strength and endurance through performance at a slow pace with gradually increasing resistance. Exercising at this level will prevent injuries as well as rehabilitate weakened muscles and ligaments following Level I exercises. Level II exercises will improve muscle contraction efficiency, increase nourishment to the joint for joint strength and stability, improve muscle girth or strength throughout the range of motion, increase the velocity at which the muscle contracts, and aid in the overall agility of the muscle group being exercised. The exercises should be performed slowly in both the concentric (muscle-shortening) and eccentric (muscle-lengthening) motions. In *rehabilitating* any muscle group, I recommend that you wait approximately 90 seconds between sets. However, to prevent injuries, and to increase strength and endurance, you should only wait approximately 30 to 45 seconds between sets for maximum results.

Level III is the most robust and demanding exercise routine. This level will maximize muscle strength and endurance and develop rapid muscle strength. Rapid muscle strength refers to the ability of a muscle to contract instantaneously and explosively through the range of motion. This muscle activity is necessary for proper swing biomechanics during the forward and acceleration swing phases. The exercises in this level are to be performed rapidly and with maximum resistance, utilizing the overload principle (see Chapters 2 and 1). The repetitions are done rapidly during the concentric (muscle-shortening) motion. This rapid contraction of the muscle will improve the functional and rapid-strength capabilities of the muscle. The time between sets should be no longer than 30 to 45 seconds. If you experience any pain while exercising in Level III, simply move to the Level II routine for the painful muscle group.

LEVEL	I	II	III
Speed of Contraction Concentric (Contract) Eccentric (Relax)	Slow Slow	Slow Slow	Rapid Slow
Range of Motion	Short	Full	Full
Resistance	Mild — > Moderate	Moderate — > Full	Maximum

Prior to exercising, stretch out each muscle group to be exercised. These stretches will properly prepare the muscle groups for the ensuing exercise. In addition, they will improve flexibility of the joint, decrease the potential for minor injury during the exercise routine, and optimally prepare the muscle group for the exercise activity. This will improve the overall benefits from your exercise routine. At no point should you disregard stretching prior to your exercise workout.

Caution: If you experience an injury that produces pain during a Level I exercise routine, consult your doctor. Certain types of injuries require medical intervention and temporarily discontinuing your conditioning program.

SHOULDER ROTATOR CUFF MUSCLES
1. Internal Shoulder Rotator • *Subscapularis*

SWING PHASE: Active in all phases, primarily Forward and Acceleration
FUNCTION: Internally rotates and adducts the arm.

**Upper-Body
Routine**

STRETCH-OUT

Top Ten / Upper Body

Position:	Standing
Set-up:	Connect one end of the exercise tube to position A of the exercise handle.
Action:	Reach up and behind your back with the involved arm and grasp the exercise handle. With your uninvolved arm, reach down and behind your back, grasp the exercise tube, and pull down gently. Hold for 5 to 10 seconds. Repeat the stretch for the opposite side.
Caution:	You should not experience any pain.
Note:	This stretch can also be performed using the golf-club shaft.

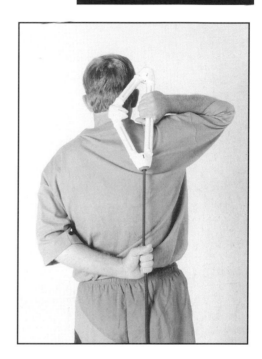

EXERCISE

Position:	Standing
Set-up:	Connect both ends of the exercise tube to the A positions of the exercise handle. Secure the door hinge anchor around the middle hinge. Secure the exercise tube within the track of the door hinge anchor.
Action:	Grasp the handle with your involved side, moving away until the tubing is taut, with your involved side facing the door. Pull the handle toward your stomach, with your palm facing inward and your elbow bent at 90° and fixed to your side. Hold for 5 seconds and return slowly. Repeat the exercise for the opposite side.
Note:	This same maneuver can be performed by grasping the exercise handle connected to the exercise tube, palm facing upward.

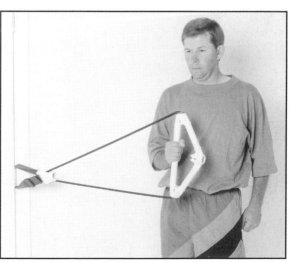

SHOULDER ROTATOR CUFF MUSCLES
2. Arm and Shoulder Abduction • *Supraspinatus*

SWING PHASE: Active during Takeaway and Follow-through
FUNCTION: Raises arm and shoulder upward (abductor)

Top Ten / Upper Body

STRETCH-OUT

Position: Standing
Set-up: Connect one end of the exercise tube to position A of the exercise handle.
Action: Reach down and behind your back with your involved forearm and grasp the exercise handle. Then grasp the other end of the exercise tube with your opposite hand held overhead and pull upward. Hold for 5 to 10 seconds. Repeat the stretch for the opposite side.
Caution: You should not experience any pain.
Note: This stretch can be performed using the golf-club shaft.

EXERCISE

Position: Standing
Set-up: Connect one end of the exercise tube to position A and the other end to position B of the exercise handle.
Secure the door hinge anchor around the lower hinge.
Secure the exercise tube within the track of the door hinge anchor.
Action: Grasp the exercise handle and move away until the resistive tubing is taut, with your uninvolved side toward the door. With your arm in the center of your body, raise your arm to just below shoulder level while keeping your elbow straight and your thumb down. Hold for 5 seconds and lower slowly. Repeat the exercise for the opposite side.
Caution: Do not raise your arm above shoulder height, because this may cause muscle injury.

SHOULDER ROTATOR CUFF MUSCLES
3. External Shoulder Rotator • *Infraspinatus*

SWING PHASE: Active during Takeaway and Follow-through
FUNCTION: Externally rotates the arm

STRETCH-OUT

Position:	Standing
Set-up:	Connect one end of the exercise tube to position A of the exercise handle.
Action:	Reach down and behind your back with your involved forearm and grasp the exercise handle. Then grasp the other end of the exercise tube with your opposite hand held overhead and pull upward. Hold for 5 to 10 seconds. Repeat the stretch for the opposite side.
Caution:	You should not experience any pain.
Note:	This stretch can also be performed using the golf-club shaft.

EXERCISE

Position:	Standing
Set-up:	Connect both ends of the exercise tube to the A positions of the exercise handle. Secure the door hinge anchor around the middle hinge. Secure the exercise tube within the track of the door hinge anchor.
Action:	Grasp the exercise handle with your involved hand and move away until the tubing is taut. Your involved arm should be across the front of your body and your uninvolved side should be facing the door. Pull the exercise handle out and away from your body, with your palm facing toward the door and your elbow bent at 90° and fixed to your side. Hold for 5 seconds and return slowly. Repeat the exercise for the opposite side.
Note:	This same maneuver can be performed by grasping the exercise handle connected to the exercise tube, palm facing down, and using a correct golf grip.

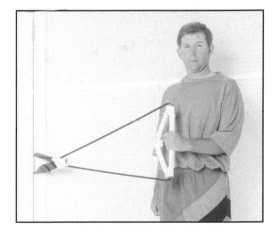

Shoulder Rotator Cuff Routine			
	Level I	**Level II**	**Level III**
Stretch-Out	1 Repetition Hold for 5-10 seconds	2 Repetitions Hold for 5-10 seconds	3 Repetitions Stretch-contract-relax
Strengthening Exercise	1 Set 8-10 reps per arm	2 Sets 8-10 reps per arm	3 Sets 8-10 reps per arm

CHEST AND UPPER-BACK MUSCLES
4. Anterior Chest • *"Pecs"*

SWING PHASE: Active during Forward, Acceleration, and Follow-through
FUNCTION: Internal rotation of the arm • Adduction of raised arm

STRETCH-OUT

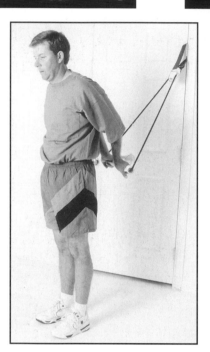

Position:	Standing
Set-up:	Connect both ends of the exercise tube to the A positions of the exercise handle. Secure the door hinge anchor around the top hinge. Secure the exercise tube within the track of the door hinge anchor.
Action:	Face away from the door. Grasp the handle, with both hands behind you at the small of your back, palms facing downward. Move away from the door or support until the exercise tube is taut, pulling on the anterior chest muscles. Your arms should be straight, extending backward. Stretch for 15 to 20 seconds and relax.

EXERCISE

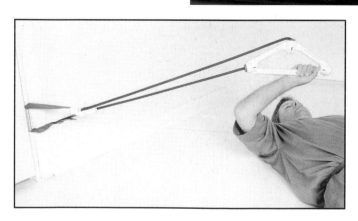

Position:	Lying face-up
Set-up:	Connect one end of the exercise tube to position A and the other to position B of the exercise handle. Secure the door hinge anchor around the lower hinge. Secure the exercise tube within the track of the door hinge anchor.
Action:	Lying face-up with the involved side toward the door, grasp the handle. Pull the handle in front and across your body. Hold for 5 seconds and return slowly. Repeat the exercise for the opposite side.

CHEST AND UPPER-BACK MUSCLES
5. Upper Back • *"Lats"*

SWING PHASE: Active during Forward, Acceleration, and early Follow-through
FUNCTION: Pulls arms down • Aids in internal rotation of arm

STRETCH-OUT	
Position:	Standing
Set-up:	Connect both ends of the exercise tube to position A and position B of the exercise handle. Secure the door hinge anchor around the top hinge side. Secure the exercise tube within the track of the door hinge anchor.
Action:	Grasp the exercise handle with your involved hand, raise your arm over your head, and cross your involved side leg in front of your uninvolved leg. Face sideways to the door. With your uninvolved side facing the door, move away until the exercise tube is taut. Your upper body should be pulled toward the support. Hold for 10 to 20 seconds. Repeat the stretch for the opposite side.
Note:	This maneuver also stretches the stomach obliques, the lateral trunk, and the outer thigh muscles.

EXERCISE	
Position:	Standing
Set-up:	Connect both ends of the exercise tube to the A positions of the exercise handle. Secure the door hinge anchor around the top hinge. Secure the exercise tube within the track of the door hinge anchor.
Action:	Grasp the handle with both hands, palms down, and move away until the exercise tube is taut. This should pull your arms upward. Using both outstretched arms, pull down on the exercise handle, keeping your elbows straight. Hold for 5 to 10 seconds and return slowly.
Note:	You may exercise one side at a time by pulling with one arm.

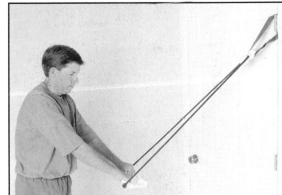

Chest and Upper Back Routine			
	Level I	**Level II**	**Level III**
Stretch-Out	1 Repetition Hold for 5-10 seconds	2 Repetitions Hold for 5-10 seconds	3 Repetitions Stretch-contract-relax
Strengthening Exercise	1 Set 8-10 reps per arm	2 Sets 8-10 reps per arm	3 Sets 8-10 reps per arm

FOREARM AND WRIST MUSCLES
6. Wrist Flexor

SWING PHASE: Active during Acceleration
FUNCTION: Flexes wrist and fingers • Grip strength • "Unhinging" at impact

STRETCH-OUT

Position:	Seated
Set-up:	Connect both ends of the exercise tube to the A positions of the exercise handle.
	Place the exercise tube under your feet (wear exercise shoes).
Action:	Grasp the exercise handle in front of your thighs, with your palms facing upward and your forearms resting on your thighs. Raise your forearms, while allowing your wrists to bend backwards, stretching these muscles. Hold for 20 to 30 seconds.
Note:	This stretches the "wrist-cock" muscles.

EXERCISE

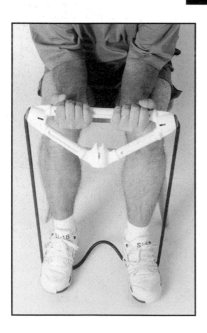

Position:	Seated
Set-up:	Connect both ends of the exercise tube to the A positions of the exercise handle.
	Place the exercise tube under your feet (wear exercise shoes).
Action:	With your forearms resting on your thighs and your palms facing upward, raise the exercise handle by rolling your wrists upward. Hold for 5 seconds and lower slowly.

FOREARM AND WRIST MUSCLES
7. Wrist Extensors

SWING PHASE: Active during Takeaway
FUNCTION: Extends the wrist and fingers • Aids the "wrist-cock"

STRETCH-OUT

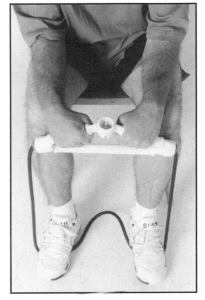

Position:	Seated
Set-up:	Connect both ends of the exercise tube to the A positions of the exercise handle.
	Place the exercise tube under your feet (wear exercise shoes).
Action:	Grasp the exercise handle in front of your thighs, palms facing downward, wrists relaxed, and forearms resting on your thighs. Raise your forearms, while allowing your wrists to bend, stretching the muscles. Hold for 20 to 30 seconds.
Note:	This stretches the "wrist-cock" muscles.

EXERCISE

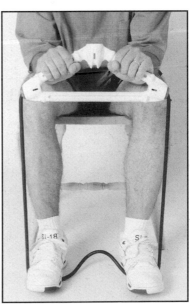

Position:	Seated
Set-up:	Connect both ends of the exercise tube to the A positions of the exercise handle.
	Place the exercise tube under your feet (wear exercise shoes).
Action:	Grasp the exercise handle with your forearms resting on your thighs, palms facing downward. Raise the handle by rolling your wrists upward. Hold for 5 seconds and lower slowly.

FOREARM AND WRIST MUSCLES
8. Radial Wrist Deviation

SWING PHASE: Active during Takeaway
FUNCTION: Deviates the wrist toward the thumb side • "Wrist-cock"
Aids in extension of the wrist and fingers

Top Ten / Upper Body

STRETCH-OUT

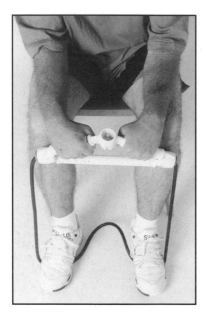

Position:	Seated
Set-up:	Connect both ends of the exercise tube to the A positions of the exercise handle.
	Place the exercise tube under your feet (wear exercise shoes).
Action:	Grasp the exercise handle in front of your thighs, palms facing downward, wrists relaxed, and forearms resting on your thighs. Raise your forearms, while allowing your wrists to bend, stretching the muscles. Hold for 20 to 30 seconds.
Note:	This stretches the "wrist-cock" muscles. This is the same maneuver as the wrist extensor stretch.

EXERCISE

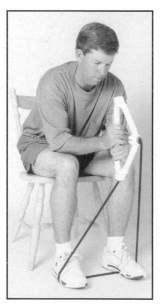

Position:	Seated or standing
Set-up:	Connect one end of the exercise tube to position B and the other end to position A.
	Place the exercise tube under your feet (wear exercise shoes).
Action:	Grasp the exercise handle with your palms facing inward, using your golf grip to hold the handle. Rest your forearms on your thighs. With the tube taut, raise your wrists. Hold for 5 seconds and return slowly.
Note:	For best results, use your golf grip.

FOREARM AND WRIST MUSCLES
9. Ulnar Wrist Deviation

SWING PHASE: Active during Acceleration
FUNCTION: Deviates the wrist toward little finger • "Uncocks" wrist at impact
Aids in flexion of the wrist and fingers

STRETCH-OUT

Position:	Seated
Set-up:	Connect both ends of the exercise tube to the A positions of the exercise handle.
	Place the exercise tube under your feet (wear exercise shoes).
Action:	Grasp the exercise handle in front of your thighs, with your palms facing upward and your forearms resting on your thighs. Raise your forearms, while allowing your wrists to bend backwards, stretching these muscles. Hold for 20 to 30 seconds.
Note:	This stretches the "wrist-cock" muscles. This is the same maneuver as the wrist flexor stretch.

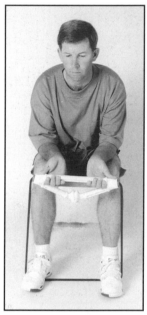

EXERCISE

Position:	Seated
Set-up:	Connect one end of the exercise tube to position A and the other to position B of the exercise handle.
Action:	Wrap the exercise tube around your back and over your right shoulder. Grasp the exercise handle using your golf grip. Pull your wrists downward with an "uncocking" motion. Hold for 5 seconds and return slowly.
Note:	This movement will help to improve the "uncocking" of your wrists at impact.

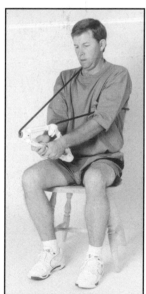

FOREARM AND WRIST MUSCLES
10. Forearm and Wrist Pronator/Supinator

SWING PHASE: Active in all phases, primarily Acceleration
FUNCTION: Pronation—Downward rotation of hand; rolls wrist "inward"
Supination—Upward rotation of hand; rolls wrist "outward"

STRETCH-OUT

Position: Seated

Set-up: Connect one end of the exercise tube to position A of the exercise handle.

Action:

Pronation: Grasp the exercise handle with your involved hand, palm upward. Grasp the exercise tube with your uninvolved arm and pull downward, rotating your wrist and hand outward. Repeat for the opposite side.

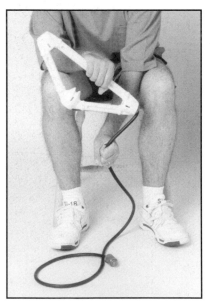

Supination: Grasp the exercise handle with your involved hand, palm downward. Grasp the exercise tube with your uninvolved arm and pull downward, rotating your wrist and hand inward. Repeat for the opposite side.

Stretch-contract-relax (PNF): At the end of the stretch described, strongly contract the muscle by pulling against the resistive tubing for 5 seconds. Then relax for 5 seconds and repeat the sequence 1 to 3 times, beginning with the stretch.

FOREARM AND WRIST MUSCLES
10. Forearm and Wrist Pronator/Supinator
(Continued)

EXERCISE

Position:	Seated
Set-up:	Connect one end of the exercise tube to the long strap anchor. Wrap the exercise tube around your foot.
Action:	

Pronation: Grasp the strap with your involved hand, palm facing upward. Move the strap in the anchor so the looplocs are next to the anchor. The involved forearm rests on your thigh. Rotate the exercise handle so that your palm faces inward. Hold for 5 to 10 seconds. Repeat the stretch for the opposite side.

Supination: Grasp the strap with your involved hand, palm facing downward. Move the strap in the anchor so the looplocs are next to the anchor. The involved forearm rests on your thigh. Rotate the exercise handle outward so that your palm faces inward. Hold for 5 to 10 seconds. Repeat the stretch for the opposite side.

Note: Secure the exercise tube within the track for greater resistance.

Forearm and Wrist Muscles Routine			
	Level I	**Level II**	**Level III**
Stretch-Out	1 Repetition Hold for 20-30 seconds	2 Repetitions Hold for 20-30 seconds	3 Repetitions Stretch-contract-relax
Strengthening Exercises	1 Set 8-10 reps per muscle group	2 Sets 8-10 reps per muscle group	3 Sets 8-10 reps per muscle group

Lower-Body Routine

Top Ten Lower Body

STOMACH AND TRUNK MUSCLES
1. Abdominal Internal and External Obliques

SWING PHASE: Active in all phases
FUNCTION: Bends trunk forward • Internal—Rotates trunk to opposite side
External—Rotates trunk to same side

STRETCH-OUT

Position:	Standing
Set-up:	Connect one end of the exercise tube to position A and the other end to position B of the exercise handle.
	Secure the door hinge anchor around the top hinge.
	Secure the exercise tube within the track of the door hinge anchor.
Action:	Grasp the exercise handle with your involved hand, raise your arm over your head, and cross the involved side leg in front of the uninvolved leg. Face sideways to the door. With your uninvolved side facing the door, move away until the exercise tube is taut. Your upper body should be pulled toward the support. Hold for 10 to 20 seconds. Repeat the stretch for the opposite side.
Note:	This maneuver will help maintain flexibility of your trunk turn during cold days and when under stress. This maneuver also stretches the lateral upper back, the lateral trunk, and the outer thigh muscles. It can be performed during play, with your partner holding the strap.

EXERCISE

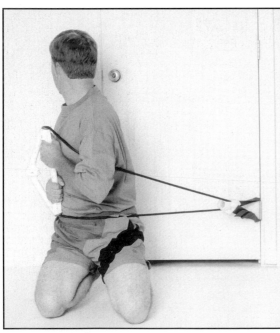

Position:	Seated on ground with legs underneath you
Set-up:	Connect both ends of the exercise tube to the A positions of the exercise handle.
	Secure the door hinge anchor around the lower hinge.
	Secure the exercise tube within the track of the door hinge anchor.
Note:	For increased resistance, triple wrap the tube. For an easier workout, or if sitting on the ground with your legs underneath is too difficult, sit in a chair and use the middle hinge to secure the door anchor.
Action:	Face away from the door. Place the exercise handle next to your side. Grasp the handle, with your opposite hand reaching across your chest. Rotate your body toward the opposite side of the exercise handle. Hold for 10 seconds and return slowly. Repeat the exercise for the opposite side.
Note:	Rotation of the trunk to the right exercises the right internal oblique muscle. Rotation of the trunk to the left exercises the left internal oblique muscle.

STOMACH AND TRUNK MUSCLES
2. Lateral Trunk • *Quadratus Lumborum*

SWING PHASE: Active during Acceleration and Follow-through
FUNCTION: Bends trunk to the side

STRETCH-OUT

Top Ten / Lower Body

Position:	Standing
Set-up:	Connect one end of the exercise tube to position A and the other end to position B of the exercise handle.
	Secure the door hinge anchor around the top hinge.
	Secure the exercise tube within the track of the door hinge anchor.
Action:	Grasp the exercise handle with your involved hand, raise your arm over your head, and cross your involved side leg in front of your uninvolved leg. Face sideways to the door. With your uninvolved side facing the door, move away until the exercise tube is taut. Your upper body should be pulled toward the support. Hold for 10 to 20 seconds. Repeat the stretch for the opposite side.
Note:	This maneuver will help maintain flexibility of your trunk turn during cold days and when under stress. This maneuver also stretches the lateral upper back, the stomach oblique muscles, and the outer thigh muscles.

EXERCISE

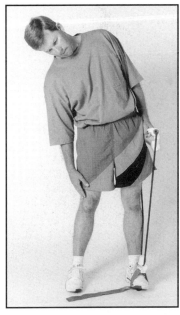

Position:	Seated or standing
Set-up:	Connect both ends of the exercise tube to the A positions of the exercise handle.
	Wrap the strap of the exercise tube anchor around the uninvolved foot.
	Secure the exercise tube within the track of the anchor.
Action:	Grasp the exercise handle with your uninvolved hand. Bend your trunk to the opposite side. Hold for 10 seconds and return slowly. Repeat the exercise for the opposite side.

STOMACH AND TRUNK MUSCLES
3. Low-Back Muscles • Trunk Extensor

SWING PHASE: Active in all phases
FUNCTION: Extends the back • Stabilizes trunk during swing and putting

Top Ten / Lower Body

STRETCH-OUT

Position:	Seated
Set-up:	None
Action:	In a sitting position, bend forward at your waist, bringing your shoulders and head as far forward as tolerable. To increase the stretch, reach your arms inside your legs, wrapping them around the outside of your ankles and pulling your trunk forward. Hold for 15 to 20 seconds.
Note:	This stretch is excellent for players with back problems and can be done throughout the round.

EXERCISE

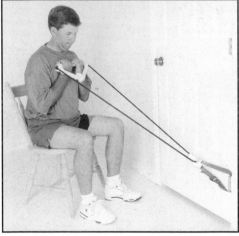

Position:	Seated
Set-up:	Connect both ends of the exercise tube to the A positions of the exercise handle. Secure the door hinge anchor around the lower hinge. Secure the exercise tube within the track of the door hinge anchor.
Note:	For extra resistance, triple wrap the exercise tube.
Action:	Hold the exercise handle against your chest while facing the door. Bend forward and move the chair away from the door until the exercise tube is taut. Raise up to a seated position. Hold for 10 seconds and lower slowly.
Note:	Stop bending backward when you are sitting straight up.

Stomach and Low-Back Routine			
	Level I	**Level II**	**Level III**
Stretch-Out	1 Repetition Hold for 20-30 seconds	2 Repetitions Hold for 20-30 seconds	3 Repetitions Hold for 20-30 seconds
Strengthening Exercise	1 Set 8-12 repetitions	2 Sets 10-15 repetitions	3 Sets 10-15 repetitions

BUTTOCK MUSCLES
4. Medial Hip and Thigh Rotator • *Gluteus Minimus*

SWING PHASE: Active in all phases
FUNCTION: Medial rotation of hip and thigh • Rotates thigh "in"

STRETCH-OUT	Top Ten / Lower Body

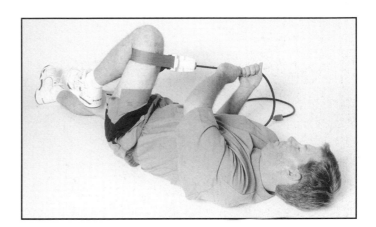

Position:	Lying face-up
Set-up:	Connect one end of the exercise tube to the exercise tube anchor.
	Wrap the strap of the exercise tube anchor around your thigh just above your knee.
Action:	Cross the involved leg over the uninvolved knee, which should be bent approximately 90°. Grasp the exercise tube and pull toward the opposite shoulder. Hold for 10 to 20 seconds. Repeat the stretch for the opposite side.

EXERCISE

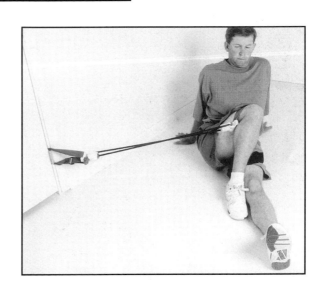

Position:	Lying face-up or seated on the floor.
Set-up:	Connect one end of the exercise tube to the exercise tube anchor.
	Wrap the long strap around your thigh just above your knee.
	Secure the door hinge anchor around the lower hinge.
	Connect the other end of the exercise tube to the door hinge anchor.
Note:	For extra resistance, double or triple wrap the exercise tube.
	For extra resistance, secure the door hinge anchor around the middle hinge.
Action:	Lie down or sit on the floor with your involved side next to the door. Move away until the tube is taut. Bend your involved knee so that your foot is flat on the floor. Pull your knee inward over the straightened, uninvolved leg as far as possible. Hold for 5 seconds and return slowly. Repeat the exercise for the opposite side.

BUTTOCK MUSCLES
5. Lateral Hip and Thigh Rotator • *Piriformis*

SWING PHASE: Active during Forward and Acceleration
FUNCTION: Lateral rotation of hip and thigh • Rotation of thigh "out"

Top Ten / Lower Body

STRETCH-OUT

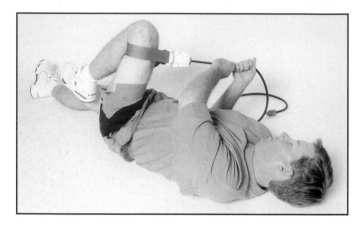

Position: Lying face-up
Set-up: Connect one end of the exercise tube to the exercise tube anchor.
Wrap the strap of the exercise tube anchor around your thigh just above your knee.
Action: Cross the involved leg over the uninvolved knee, which should be bent approximately 90°. Grasp the exercise tube and pull toward the opposite shoulder. Hold for 10 to 20 seconds. Repeat the stretch for the opposite side.

EXERCISE

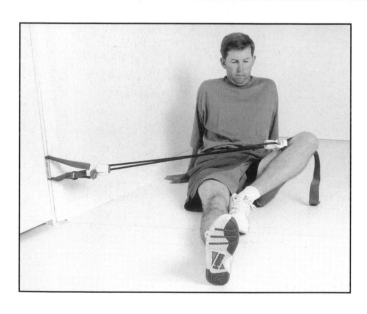

Position: Lying face-up or seated on the floor.
Set-up: Connect one end of the exercise tube to the exercise tube anchor.
Wrap the long strap around your thigh just above your knee.
Secure the door hinge anchor around the lower hinge.
Connect the other end of the exercise tube to the door hinge anchor.
Note: For extra resistance, double or triple wrap the exercise tube.
For extra resistance, secure the door hinge anchor around the middle hinge.
Action: Lie down or sit on the floor with the involved side away from the door. Move away until the tube is taut. Bend the involved knee with your foot flat on the floor. Pull the involved knee downward. Hold for 5 to 10 seconds and raise slowly. Repeat the exercise for the opposite side.

BUTTOCK MUSCLES
6. Thigh and Hip Extensor • *Gluteus Maximus*

SWING PHASE: Active in Acceleration and Follow-through
FUNCTION: Extends or brings the thigh backward

STRETCH-OUT	Top Ten / Lower Body

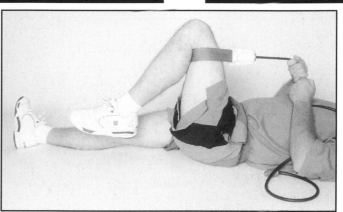

Position:	Lying face-up
Set-up:	Connect one end of the exercise tube to the exercise tube anchor. Wrap the strap of the exercise tube anchor around your thigh just above your knee.
Action:	Grasp the end of the exercise tube and raise your leg. Your hip should be flexed, with your leg pulled toward your chest. Hold for 20 to 30 seconds. Repeat the stretch for the opposite side.

EXERCISE

Position:	Standing facing the door
Set-up:	Connect one end of the exercise tube to the exercise tube anchor. Wrap the strap of the exercise tube anchor around your ankle. Secure the door hinge anchor around the lower hinge. Connect the other end of the exercise tube to the door hinge anchor.
Note:	For extra resistance, double or triple wrap the exercise tube.
Action:	While standing facing the door, move away until the exercise tube is taut. Pull your leg away from the door, extending your hip. Hold for 5 seconds. Repeat the exercise for the other side.

Buttock Muscles Routine			
	Level I	**Level II**	**Level III**
Stretch-Out	1 Repetition Hold for 15-20 seconds	2 Repetitions Hold for 15-20 seconds	3 Repetitions Stretch-contract-relax
Strengthening Exercise	1 Set 8-10 reps per hip	2 Sets 8-10 reps per hip	3 Sets 8-10 reps per hip

THIGH MUSCLES
7. Inner Thigh Muscles — Medial Hip and Thigh Adductors
Adductor Longus, Magnus, and Brevis

SWING PHASE: Active during Forward and Acceleration
FUNCTION: Brings the thigh inward (adductor) • Aids in weight transfer

Top Ten / Lower Body

STRETCH-OUT

Position: Standing
Set-up: Separate your legs, looking straight ahead.
Bend your involved knee, then transfer your weight to this side.
Action: Push your trunk toward the involved side, stretching your inner thigh. Hold for 20 to 30 seconds. Reverse leg positions and repeat the stretch for the other side.

EXERCISE

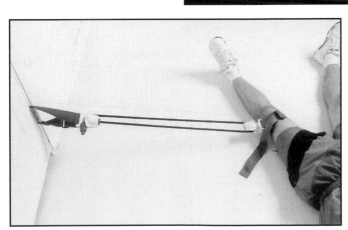

Position: Lying face-up or seated on floor
Set-up: Connect one end of the exercise tube to the exercise tube anchor.
Wrap the strap of the exercise tube anchor around your thigh just above your knee.
Secure the door hinge anchor around the lower hinge.
Connect the other end of the exercise tube to the door hinge anchor.
Note: For extra resistance, double or triple wrap the exercise tube.
Action: Lie or sit on the floor with your involved side toward the door. Move away until the tube is taut. Straighten your involved leg with the leg moved away from center at approximately 45°. Pull your leg to the midline. Hold for 5 seconds and return slowly. Repeat the exercise for the opposite side.

THIGH MUSCLES
8. Outer Thigh Muscles — Lateral Hip and Thigh Abductors
Tensor Fascia Lata and Gluteus Medius

SWING PHASE: Active in Forward, Acceleration, and early Follow-through
FUNCTION: Brings the thigh outward (abductor) • Aids in weight transfer

STRETCH-OUT	Top Ten / Lower Body

Position:	Standing
Set-up:	Connect one end of the exercise tube to position A and the other end to position B of the exercise handle.
	Secure the door hinge anchor around the top hinge.
	Secure the exercise tube within the track of the door hinge anchor.
Action:	Grasp the exercise handle with your involved hand, raise your arm over your head, and cross your involved side leg in front of your uninvolved leg. Face sideways to the door. With your uninvolved side facing the door, move away until the exercise tube is taut. Your upper body should be pulled toward the support. Hold for 10 to 20 seconds. Repeat the stretch for the opposite side.
Note:	This maneuver also stretches the lateral upper back, the stomach oblique muscles, and the outer thigh muscles.

EXERCISE

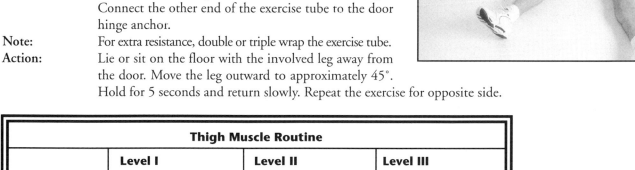

Position:	Lying facc-up or seated on the floor
Set-up:	Connect one end of the exercise tube to the exercise tube anchor.
	Wrap the long strap of the exercise tube anchor around your thigh just above your knee.
	Secure the door hinge anchor around the lower hinge.
	Connect the other end of the exercise tube to the door hinge anchor.
Note:	For extra resistance, double or triple wrap the exercise tube.
Action:	Lie or sit on the floor with the involved leg away from the door. Move the leg outward to approximately 45°.
	Hold for 5 seconds and return slowly. Repeat the exercise for opposite side.

Thigh Muscle Routine			
	Level I	**Level II**	**Level III**
Stretch-Out	1 Repetition Hold for 15-20 seconds	2 Repetitions Hold for 15-20 seconds	3 Repetitions Stretch-contract-relax
Strengthening Exercise	1 Set 8-10 reps per thigh	2 Sets 8-10 reps per thigh	3 Sets 8-10 reps per thigh

ANTERIOR LOWER-LEG MUSCLES
9. Ankle and Foot Inversion
Anterior Tibialis

SWING PHASE: Active in all phases
FUNCTION: Inverts the foot • Rolls the ankle outward • Aids in weight transfer

STRETCH-OUT

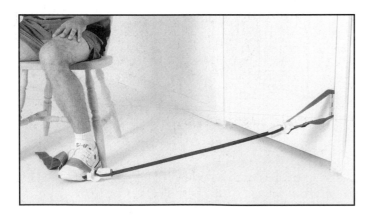

Position:	Seated
Set-up:	Connect one end of the exercise tube to the exercise tube anchor. Wrap the strap of the exercise tube anchor around your foot (wear exercise shoes) with the tubing coming off of the outside of your foot.
Action:	Cross the involved ankle over the uninvolved knee. Grasp the exercise tube and pull downward. This stretches the foot invertor muscles, rolling the ankle outward. Hold for 5 to 10 seconds. Repeat the stretch for the opposite side.

EXERCISE

Position:	Seated
Set-up:	Connect one end of the exercise tube to the exercise tube anchor. Wrap the strap of the exercise tube anchor around your foot (wear exercise shoes). Secure the door hinge anchor around the lower hinge. Connect the other end of the exercise tube to the door hinge anchor.
Note:	For extra resistance, double or triple wrap the exercise tube.
Action:	With your involved foot toward the door, exercise tube taut, pull your involved foot inward (away from the door) with your heel stabilized by the chair leg. Hold for 5 seconds and return slowly. Repeat the exercise for the opposite side.

ANTERIOR LOWER-LEG MUSCLES
10. Ankle and Foot Eversion
Peroneus Longus and Brevis

SWING PHASE: Active in all phases
FUNCTION: Everts the foot • Rolls the ankle inward • Aids in weight transfer

<table>
<tr><td style="background:black; color:white">STRETCH-OUT</td></tr>
</table>

Top Ten / Lower Body	

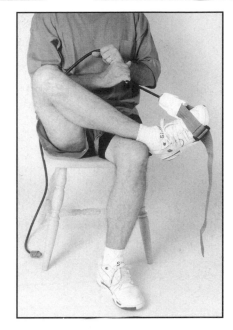

Position: Seated
Set-up: Connect one end of the exercise tube to the exercise tube anchor. Wrap the strap of the exercise tube anchor around your foot (wear exercise shoes) with the tubing coming off of the inside of your foot.
Action: Cross the involved leg over the uninvolved leg. Grasp the exercise tube and pull upward. This stretches the foot evertor muscles, rolling the ankle inward. Hold for 5 to 10 seconds. Repeat the stretch for the opposite side.

<table>
<tr><td style="background:black; color:white">EXERCISE</td></tr>
</table>

Position: Seated
Set-up: Connect one end of the exercise tube to the exercise tube anchor. Wrap the strap of the exercise tube anchor around your foot (wear exercise shoes).
Secure the door hinge anchor around the lower hinge.
Connect the other end of the exercise tube to the door hinge anchor.
Note: For extra resistance, double or triple wrap the exercise tube.
Action: With your involved foot away from the door, exercise tube taut, pull your involved foot outward (away from the door) with your heel stabilized by the leg of the chair or other foot. Hold for 5 seconds and return slowly. Repeat the exercise for the opposite side.

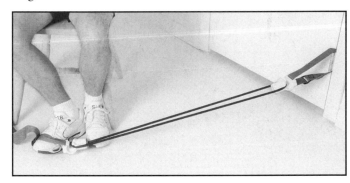

Anterior Lower-Leg Muscle Routine			
	Level I	**Level II**	**Level III**
Stretch-Out	1 Repetition Hold for 5-10 seconds	2 Repetitions Hold for 5-10 seconds	3 Repetitions Stretch-contract-relax
Strengthening Exercise	1 Set 8-10 reps per leg	2 Sets 8-10 reps per leg	3 Sets 8-10 reps per leg

I recommend that you "split" your exercise routine so as to work the upper and lower body on alternating days. In order to accomplish maximum improvement in strength and endurance, you should perform your routine every other day. The upper- and lower-body exercises can be performed easily in a six-day routine. For example, work the upper body on Monday, Wednesday, and Friday and the lower body on Tuesday, Thursday, and Saturday. When exercising in Levels II or III, you should exercise to the point of fatigue. It is important that the muscle groups being exercised become completely fatigued at the end of the third set. Do not exercise muscle groups on consecutive days because this will tend to decrease your strength and improvement by overfatiguing your muscles and greatly increasing your chances for injury.

By using the Golfercise System and exercising the specific muscles used in the exercise swing, you can expect to achieve the following results:

1. Increased joint flexibility.
2. Decreased time away from play following injury.
3. Decreased potential for injury.
4. Increased muscle strength.
5. Increased muscle endurance.
6. An increase in the explosive contractibility of the muscle (rapid strength).
7. Improved coordination.
8. Improved quality of play overall.

And I believe that you will see a direct relationship between lowered scores as you improve your conditioning of these specific golf muscles.

You should chart the level of exercise, the total time for your exercise, the date on which the exercises were performed, the number of repetitions, and the number of sets. This will help you to set goals toward improvement.

Your game will improve considerably by performing a structured pre-swing warm-up routine prior to play.

Pre-Swing Warm-Up Routine

14

**Prime-The-Pump
Stretch-Out
Warm-Up**

How important is it to warm up prior to play? If you are serious about improving your game and decreasing your chance of injury, the answer is very simple. Although I rarely, if ever, see amateur golfers going through a structured warm-up routine, <u>everyone's</u> game would improve considerably if he or she would do a warm-up. Most injuries of the shoulder, elbow, and back are due to poor conditioning or a lack of pre-play warm-up exercises.

Can you envision an athletic trainer for a professional team allowing his players to begin play without first warming up? No, never! However, most amateur golfers, and many professional players, do not engage in a proper warm-up routine <u>prior</u> to swinging the club. It is not enough to do a few stretching maneuvers prior to hitting balls on the driving range or teeing off. You simply cannot begin your round by doing a couple of nonspecific stretching maneuvers and expect your body to warm up, let alone warm up the golf-specific muscles. The end result of <u>not</u> preparing your body for any athletic event, including golf, is decreased performance and increased chance of injury to your joints and muscles.

Practicing on the driving range prior to teeing off is highly recommended. But this practice does not take the place of a warm-up routine that prepares your golf muscles for play. You should instead see it as a means to fine-tune your swing by reestablishing your muscle "memory." Prior to any practice session or pre-game session, your muscles must be ready for play. This is true not only for golf, but for all athletic activities. Whether you are practicing on the driving range or playing your round, you <u>must</u> first warm up your golf muscles and joints properly! This cannot be done without a specific pre-swing warm-up routine that 1) increases overall body metabolism, 2) increases the blood flow to the muscles, which will bring needed oxygen, 3) stretches the muscles and joints to improve flexibility, and 4) exercises the specific muscles involved in the activity so that they can perform at their optimal level prior to teeing off.

Just think how foolish it would be for a professional football player to suit up in full pads, take the field, tackle a few of his teammates at 25 percent speed, then at 50 percent speed, and finally at 100 percent speed a couple of times just prior to kick-off without any pre-game warm-up routine. If you saw this on television, you would be highly critical of this team's coaching methods. Yet golfers, from the touring professional down through the amateur ranks, continually disregard the warm-up routine of their game. Think about golf as an athletic event and prepare properly for play. This cannot be done without warming up <u>prior</u> to swinging the club.

The pre-swing warm-up routine in this chapter is designed specifically to stretch and warm up the golf-specific muscles. The pre-swing warm-up consists of three basic components:

1. **PRIME-THE-PUMP**
2. **STRETCH-OUT**
3. **WARM-UP**

These three components are designed to: 1) provide a general body warm-up, 2) stretch the golf muscles and joints, and 3) warm up the golf muscles.

The general warm-up is meant to increase the body temperature and blood flow to the muscles so as to raise your body metabolism in preparation for play. I call this section "**prime-the-pump**," which is the first segment of the pre-swing warm-up routine. The name comes from the fact that the general warm-up is meant to increase cardiac output. When "the pump" is primed, your pulse rate will rise due to increased blood flow to your muscles. This is done through a general exercise routine that includes any activity that increases your heart rate, such as stair climbing, rapidly walking in place, or calisthenics. Any activity that increases your heart rate and breathing for approximately 3 to 5 minutes should achieve the desired results. Your goal is to increase your heart rate by 60 percent of your maximum heart rate (maximum heart rate is calculated by subtracting your age from 220) or by increasing your pulse rate by approximately 15 to 20 beats per minute.

The second category of the warm-up, the "**stretch-out**," focuses on stretching to increase the flexibility of the muscles used for the golf swing, allowing a smooth, rhythmic, technically correct swing.

The third category of the routine is the specific muscle "**warm-up**," which prepares the golf-specific muscles for play. A proper pre-swing routine generally takes approximately 7 to 12 minutes. More time may be required on colder days.

Performing a structured pre-swing warm-up drill will properly and specifically warm up your muscles and joints prior to addressing the ball on the first tee or practicing on the driving range. This routine will greatly enhance your performance, as well as decrease your potential for injuries. The stretching and muscle routine includes preparing some 20 major golf-specific muscles for play. The pre-swing warm-up flows in a logical sequence so as to decrease the time required to go from one stretch/exercise to the next. This warm-up routine will maximize results while minimizing the time required.

PRE-SWING WARM-UP ROUTINE
(7 to 12 minutes)

I. PRIME-THE-PUMP

Purpose:

Prime-the-pump is the <u>general</u> warm-up of the pre-swing routine, the purpose of which is to increase your heart rate (pulse) by at least 60 percent of your maximum heart rate (220 minus your age) or to increase your resting heart rate by approximately 15 to 20 beats. This will increase your body's temperature by 1) increasing the blood flow to the muscles, 2) increasing oxygen to the muscles, and 3) increasing muscle metabolism. These are all required for optimal muscle performance. Increased heart rate is achieved by performing a continuous and rhythmic exercise for 3 to 5 minutes.

Activity:

This can be done by light, short-distance running or jogging, stair climbing, fast walking, swinging two and three clubs slowly and rhythmically **without** going through the complete range of motion, or by using the Golfercise System equipment to warm up the large muscles of the upper and lower body. This <u>general</u> warm-up will mobilize your body for action and prepare it for stretching and golf-specific warm-up exercises. You should not develop marked fatigue during this section of the pre-swing routine. The time required for a satisfactory general warm-up varies with individuals, age, and weather. On cooler days, prime-the-pump will take more time. On cold days, warm clothing should be worn during the pre-swing routine. This will decrease the general warm-up time. For the younger golfer, the ideal is to just break a light sweat. For the senior golfer, the ideal is to become slightly winded. If you have any cardiovascular problems, consult your doctor for recommendations.

II. STRETCH-OUT AND WARM-UP ROUTINES

Purpose of Stretch-Out:

The golf-specific muscles should be stretched using either basic stretch techniques or the stretch-contract-relax (PNF) technique. Stretching improves the flexibility of muscles and joints that is so necessary for a smooth, rhythmic swing and for achieving proper shoulder and hip turn. Stretching also decreases the chance of injury. For the senior player, basic stretch techniques are generally recommended over the stretch-contract-relax maneuvers, particularly on a cooler day.

The stretching portion of the pre-swing routine should take approximately 4 to 7 minutes to stretch properly the primary upper- and lower-body muscles used in the golf swing. The time will vary depending on the weather and your overall physical condition. On cooler days, you should devote more time to stretching than on hot days. It is necessary to remember that, during a stretching routine, whether you are using the basic stretch or stretch-contract-relax (PNF) maneuvers, the stretch should not produce any pain. Rather, you should feel a mild, pulling sensation. At no time should you bounce or jerk during the stretch. Perform the stretch in a slow, controlled manner. Never do stretching maneuvers by rapidly rotating your upper body, holding the club behind your back or neck, because it can injure your shoulder ligaments and tendons and aggravate a back condition.

Purpose of Warm-Up:

The golf-specific warm-up follows the general warm-up, or prime-the-pump, and the stretch-out routine. The specific warm-up routine exercises the muscles that are sports-specific, including the major muscle groups used in the four phases of the golf swing. These exercises will prepare the golf muscles for play. By properly warming up these muscles, you will be able to approach the first tee or the driving range with your golf muscles in a state of readiness.

The main purpose of the specific warm-up exercises is to increase the temperature and amount of blood flow to the primary muscles used during the golf swing. By increasing the temperature of these golf-specific muscles, each muscle receives more oxygen, and your muscle coordination is improved. Increased metabolism achieved through the golf-specific warm-up exercises also enables your muscles to increase their contractibility, which improves muscle performance. Other benefits of a golf-specific warm-up routine are decreased muscle tension, improved muscle and tendon flexibility, and improved joint mobility.

The effects of the warm-up will persist for approximately 30 to 45 minutes. However, the closer the warm-up period to teeing off, the more beneficial it will be. In order to obtain maximum benefits from the pre-swing warm-up, I recommend that you not allow more than 15 minutes to pass between completion of the pre-swing warm-up and beginning your play.

Note: The golf-specific warm-up exercise routine is designed to be done at the same time as the stretch-out routine. Begin in a standing position, then proceed to sitting on a chair or bench, followed by sitting on the ground. For correct sequence, refer to the pictures at the end of this chapter.

STRETCH-OUT AND WARM-UP COMPONENTS

STANDING SECTION

A. LATERAL UPPER BACK ("LATS"), FOREARMS, STOMACH OBLIQUES, LATERAL TRUNK, AND OUTER THIGH MUSCLES
   These muscles are stretched out as a unit and warmed up separately.

Stretch-Out:

In a standing position, cross one leg over the other, raise your arms above your head with your fingers interlaced, and your palms facing upward. Slowly bend your trunk to the opposite side of your front leg and push your hips to the same side of your front leg. Hold for 10 to 15 seconds. Cross your other leg and repeat the exercise, bending in the opposite direction.

B. SHOULDER ROTATOR CUFF MUSCLES

Stretch-Out:
1. Shoulder and Arm Abduction
   In a standing position, raise your arm above your head with your involved side while grasping just above your elbow with your other hand. Pull your involved arm across your body and over your head with your uninvolved hand. Hold the stretch for 5 to 10 seconds. Repeat the stretch for the opposite side.
   Optional: In a standing position, reach down and behind your back with your involved forearm, palm facing outward. Raise your forearm toward your opposite shoulder blade as high as tolerable. To increase the stretch, reach behind your back with your opposite arm, grasping just above your elbow and pulling your involved arm toward the middle of your back. Hold the stretch for 5 to 10 seconds. Repeat the stretch for the opposite side.
   Caution: If you experience any pain, decrease the pull or discontinue.

2. Internal Shoulder Rotation
In a standing position, reach across the front of your chest with your involved side while grasping just above your elbow with your other hand. Pull your involved arm across your body with your uninvolved hand. Hold the stretch for 5 to 10 seconds. Repeat the stretch for the opposite side.

Note: This is the preferred method for seniors or for anyone with previous shoulder injuries. This maneuver also stretches the posterior shoulder capsule ligament.

3. External Shoulder Rotation
In a standing position, place your involved hand against your side with your palm facing outward. With your involved elbow at about 90°, rotate your elbow forward. Grasp above your elbow with your uninvolved hand and pull across and downward. Hold the stretch for 5 to 10 seconds. Repeat the stretch for the opposite side.

Caution: If you experience any pain, decrease the pull or discontinue.

Warm-Up:
1. Internal Shoulder Rotator
In a standing position, place your involved arm against your side with your elbow bent at 90° facing forward, thumb up. Grasp your wrist with your opposite hand. Push the involved arm toward your stomach while resisting with the other hand. Repeat this maneuver 3 to 5 times. Repeat the maneuver for the opposite side.

2. External Shoulder Rotator
In a standing position, place your involved arm next to your side with your elbow bent at 90° and your arm resting against your stomach. Grasp your wrist with the opposite hand. Pull your involved arm outward against resistance. Repeat this maneuver 3 to 5 times. Repeat the maneuver for the opposite side.

3. Shoulder Abductor
In a standing position with your involved arm resting toward your side, and your elbow straight, grasp your wrist with your uninvolved hand. Raise your involved arm straight out, thumb down, while resisting with the uninvolved hand. Repeat this maneuver 3 to 5 times. Repeat the maneuver for the opposite side.

C. ANTERIOR CHEST MUSCLES: *Pectoralis Muscles, "Pecs"*

Stretch-Out:

In a standing position, raise one arm against a fence, door jamb, or other support and rotate your body forward to stretch the anterior shoulder muscle. You may want to bring your opposite arm behind your back and grab the fence to aid in rotating your torso and shoulders. Hold 5 to 10 seconds. Repeat the stretch for the opposite side.

Warm-Up:

In a standing position, interlock your fingers with your arms raised at chest height. With the involved side, push your arm across your body while resisting with the uninvolved side. Push while resisting back and forth 3 to 5 times.

D. INNER THIGH MUSCLES:

Medial Hip and Thigh Adductor • *Adductor Longus, Magnus, and Brevis*

Stretch-Out:

In a standing position, separate your legs, bend the uninvolved knee, and, with your weight transferred to this leg, push your trunk toward the uninvolved side. This will stretch the inside of the involved leg. Hold for 20 to 30 seconds. Reverse leg positions and repeat on the other side.

E. ANTERIOR THIGH AND LEG MUSCLES:

Knee Extensor, Ankle Inversion, and Eversion
Quadriceps, Anterior Tibialis, Peroneus Longus and Brevis

Stretch-Out:

In a standing position, bring the involved foot up toward your buttock by bending your knee. Grasp your foot with your hand and pull it toward your buttock while at the same time keeping your stomach flat. Use a bench to support yourself. Hold for 5 to 10 seconds. Repeat the stretch for the opposite side.

F. CALVES

Stretch-Out:

In a standing position, face a fence or wall against which you can lean. Keep your involved leg behind your uninvolved leg. Straighten your involved leg while bending your uninvolved leg at the knee. The uninvolved leg should be close to the wall. The involved leg should be straight, with your foot flat on the ground, pointing straight ahead. Your arms should be about chest height with your palms on the wall. Slowly move your hips toward the wall while keeping your involved back leg straight and your foot flat. Hold for 20 to 30 seconds. Reverse leg positions and repeat the stretch to the other side.

G. UPPER BACK: *"LATS"*

Warm-Up:

In a standing position, raise your involved arm to shoulder height with your elbow bent. With your other hand, grasp underneath your elbow. Push your involved arm down, with your elbow coming to the side of your body while resisting with your uninvolved hand. Repeat the maneuver for the opposite side.

Pre-Swing Warm-Up

H. POSTERIOR ARM MUSCLES: *Triceps*

Warm-Up:

In a standing position, keep your involved arm resting on your side, and your elbow bent at 90°, arm facing outward. With your other hand, grasp the wrist of your involved arm. Push your wrist downward against resistance. Perform this maneuver 3 to 5 times. Repeat the maneuver for the opposite side.

I. FOREARM MUSCLES: *Forearm Extensor Muscles*

Stretch-Out:

In a standing position, with your arms outstretched in front of your chest, roll your thumbs inward and downward to maximum rotation, bending your wrists so that your fingers point outward. Hold the stretch for 5 to 10 seconds.

Warm-Up:

In a standing position, place your palms together with your fingers outstretched, and facing away from your body. Keeping your arms in one place, bend your wrists back and forth against resistance. Repeat this maneuver 5 to 10 times.

J. STOMACH OBLIQUE MUSCLES:
Internal and External Abdominal Obliques

Warm-Up:

In a standing position, hold the shaft of a club against your chest with your palms facing inward. Place the end of the shaft against a support (tree, fence post, or held by a partner). Rotate your trunk against the resisted golf shaft. Perform the maneuver 3 to 5 times. Repeat the maneuver for the opposite side.

SEATED ROUTINE IN A CHAIR OR BENCH

A. NECK MUSCLES

Note: If you have a history of neck pain, perform the extension maneuver with caution.

Stretch-Out:

1. Neck Flexion

   In a seated position, tuck your chin in by bending your head and neck forward. Place your hands on the top of your head and gently push your head forward toward your chin. Hold for 5 to 10 seconds.

   Note: This stretch is recommended if you have a history of neck stiffness/soreness. You can do this stretch several times a day to reduce stiffness.

2. Neck Extension

   In a seated position, look back over your head as far as tolerable without causing any neck pain or discomfort. Hold for 5 to 10 seconds.

   Note: If you have a previous history of neck pain or injury, perform this stretch with caution.

3. Neck Bending

   In a seated position, bend your head toward your right chest. Place your hands on the top of your head and gently push your head forward toward the chest. Hold for 5 to 10 seconds. Repeat the stretch for the opposite side.

   Note: Do not pull so strenuously that pain is produced!

4. Neck Rotation

   In a seated position, look to the right as far as tolerable. Place your left hand on your chin, pushing your neck farther to the right of its end range. Hold the stretch for 5 to 10 seconds. Repeat the stretch for the opposite side.

   Note: Do not push so as to produce pain either in your neck or jaw!

B. LOW-BACK MUSCLES

Stretch-Out:

In a sitting position, bend forward at your waist, bringing your shoulders and head forward as far as tolerable. To increase the stretch, reach your arms inside your legs, wrapping them around the outside of your ankles and pulling your trunk forward. Hold for 15 to 20 seconds.

Pre-Swing Warm-Up

Warm-Up:
While in a seated position, bending forward and grabbing your ankles, pull up with your back while resisting with your hands on your ankles. Repeat this maneuver 3 to 5 times.
Caution: Do not use maximum pulling force, because it may aggravate the low-back muscles. If you have high blood pressure, do not do this maneuver without consulting your doctor!

C. ANTERIOR LOWER-LEG MUSCLES

Warm-Up:
While in a seated position, cross one leg over the other with your ankle above your knee. Grasp the involved foot with your uninvolved hand. Raise your foot (not your ankle) upward while resisting with your hand. Lower your foot while resisting with your hand. Perform this maneuver 3 to 5 times. Repeat the maneuver for the opposite side.

SEATED ROUTINE ON THE GROUND OR FLOOR

A. POSTERIOR HIP MUSCLES (BUTTOCKS)
Medial and Lateral Hip and Thigh Rotator Muscles
Gluteus Minimus, Piriformis

Stretch-Out:
Grasp the involved thigh near your knee. Pull your thigh toward the opposite shoulder with both arms. Hold the stretch for 10 to 15 seconds. Repeat the stretch for the opposite side.

Warm-Up:
Grasp the involved thigh near your knee. Pull your thigh toward the opposite shoulder with both hands. Rotate your thigh and knee outward while resisting. Then rotate your thigh and knee inward while resisting. Perform this maneuver 3 to 5 times. Repeat the maneuver for the opposite side.
Note: Grasp the involved thigh near the knee. Never grasp below the knee.

B. GENERAL HIP, LOW BACK, STOMACH, AND SHOULDER

Self Stretch:
While sitting on the ground, cross your involved ankle over your opposite straight leg at the knee. Rotate your shoulders toward the involved side so that the opposite elbow is outside the involved knee. Place your other hand flat on the ground behind you. Then slowly look over your shoulder so as to rotate your trunk to the side of the involved leg as far as tolerable. At the same time, apply counterpressure with your uninvolved elbow against the bent knee. Hold for approximately 20 to 30 seconds. Reverse leg positions and stretch the other side.
Note: This stretch is excellent for players with back problems and can be done throughout the round.

PRE-SWING WARM-UP ROUTINE

I. **Prime-the-Pump**
  A. **General Full-Body Activity**
  Fast Paced Walking
  Stair Climbing
  Calisthenics — Jumping Jacks, Run In Place, Jog, etc.
  B. **Goal**
  Increase Heart Rate Approximately 15-20 Beats/Second
  Increase Blood Flow to Muscles

II. **Stretch-Out and Warm-Up**
  Stretch-Out: Hold Each Stretch for 5 Seconds (Recommend PNF Methods)
  Warm-Up: Exercise (contract) Each Muscle 3 to 5 times through Full Range of Motion
  A. **Standing**
  1. Upper Back, Forearms, Stomach Obliques, Lateral Trunk, and Outer Thigh
  Stretch-Out:
  Interlock Fingers - Raise Arms Overhead, Palms Up - Cross Legs - Lean to Opposite Side of Front Leg
  2. Shoulder Rotator Cuff
  Stretch-Out:
  Arm Behind Head
  Arm Across Chest
  Wrist Against Waist, Palm Out - Pull Elbow In
  Warm-Up:
  Internal Shoulder Rotator
    Elbow to Side - Pull Arm IN Against Resistance
  External Shoulder Rotator
    Elbow to Side - Pull Arm OUT Against Resistance
  Shoulder Abductor
    Arm Down, Thumb Facing Down, Raise Arm OUT and UP Against Resistance
  3. Chest
  Stretch-Out:
  Arm Up Against Door Jamb or Support
  Arms Up - Lean into Corner
  Warm-Up:
  Interlock Fingers - Push Arms Across Body Against Resistance
  4. Inner Thighs
  Stretch-Out:
  Legs Far Apart, Lean to One Side with Knees Bent

5. Anterior Thigh and Leg
    <u>Stretch-Out:</u>
    Grab Top of Foot, Pull Heel to Buttock
6. Calves
    <u>Stretch-Out:</u>
    With Back Leg Straight, Lean Forward Against a Support
7. Upper Back
    <u>Warm-Up:</u>
    Push Elbow Down Against Resistance
8. Posterior Arm
    <u>Warm-Up:</u>
    Elbow to Side, Arm Bent, Push Down Against Resistance
9. Forearms
    <u>Stretch-Out:</u>
    Arms Outstretched in Front, Roll Thumbs In and Down, Bend Wrists so Fingers Point Outward
    <u>Warm-Up:</u>
    Palms Together - Bend Wrists Back and Forth Against Resistance
10. Stomach Obliques
    <u>Warm-Up:</u>
    Hold Club Shaft Against Chest, Place Shaft Against Support, Rotate Trunk

B. Seated Routine on a Chair or Bench

1. Neck
    <u>Stretch-Out:</u>
    Bend Forward, Backward, to both sides (45°), and Rotate
2. Low Back
    <u>Stretch-Out:</u>
    Bend Forward, Grab Ankles
    <u>Warm-Up:</u>
    Pull Up While Resisting with Hands on Ankles (see caution page 210)
3. Anterior Lower Leg
    <u>Warm-Up:</u>
    Cross Leg - Grasp Foot, Resist Movement of Foot Up and Down

C. Seated Routine on the Ground or Floor

1. Medial and Lateral Hip and Thigh Rotator Muscles
    <u>Stretch-Out:</u>
    Lying - Pull Thigh and Knee to Opposite Side
    <u>Warm-Up:</u>
    Knee Bent - Resist Outward Movement/Inward Movement
2. General Hip, Low Back, Stomach, and Shoulder
    <u>Stretch-Out:</u>
    Cross Leg, Knee Bent, Rotate Opposite Side Facing Backward with Elbow Inside of Knee

The pre-swing warm-up routine will prepare you for golf by warming up the golf-specific muscles and joints prior to play. The routine will take approximately 7 to 12 minutes, depending on the length of time you hold the stretch and the number of warm-up repetitions you perform. The senior golfer should spend more time on the stretching portion of this routine, while the younger golfer should spend more time on the specific warm-up exercises. This systematic pre-swing routine will properly warm up your body and the golf-specific muscles so that you are physically prepared when approaching the first tee. I believe that if you use this pre-swing warm-up routine religiously prior to teeing off or practicing on the driving range, the results will be dramatic, not only in lowering your score, but in preventing injuries as well. The amateur player will notice this most in the quality of play in the first few holes. If you take a short break at the turn, I recommend using the stretching segment of the pre-swing routine prior to teeing off on the tenth hole. This will keep you limber and loose for the back nine.

Pre-Swing Warm-Up

A majority of amateur players, as well as some touring professionals, go from the practice green to the driving range and begin hitting balls without so much as doing even a basic stretch-out routine. If you take the time to prepare your body for play, your game will improve greatly and you'll have much less chance of sustaining an injury.

The following pages provide a comprehensive series of photos depicting the Pre-Swing Warm-Up Routine

PRE-SWING WARM-UP ROUTINE

<u>STANDING</u>

Pre-Swing Warm-Up

Left:
Generalized Warm-Up
(Running in Place,
Stair Stepping,
Jumping Jacks,
Fast Walking, etc.)

Right:
Check Pulse
(approximately 15-20 beats
increase from resting)

RIGHT SIDE MANEUVERS

**Stretch for Upper Back,
Forearms, Stomach
Obliques, Lateral Trunk,
and Outer Thigh**

LEFT SIDE MANEUVERS

RIGHT SIDE MANEUVERS

LEFT SIDE MANEUVERS

Pre-Swing Warm-Up

Stretch for Shoulder Rotator
Cuff Muscles (Upper)

Stretch for Shoulder Rotator
Cuff Muscles (Middle)

Stretch for Shoulder Rotator
Cuff Muscles (Lower)

RIGHT SIDE MANEUVERS

LEFT SIDE MANEUVERS

Pre-Swing Warm-Up

**Warm-up for
Internal Shoulder
Rotator Cuff Muscle**

**Warm-up for
External Shoulder
Rotator Cuff Muscle**

**Warm-up for
Shoulder Abductor
Rotator Cuff Muscle**

RIGHT SIDE MANEUVERS

LEFT SIDE MANEUVERS

Stretch for
Chest Muscles

Warm-up for
Chest Muscles

Stretch for
Inner Thigh
Muscles

RIGHT SIDE MANEUVERS

LEFT SIDE MANEUVERS

Pre-Swing Warm-Up

**Stretch for
Anterior Thigh
and Leg Muscles**

**Stretch for
Calf Muscles**

**Warm-up for
Upper Back
Muscles**

RIGHT SIDE MANEUVERS

LEFT SIDE MANEUVERS

Warm-up for
Posterior Arm
Muscles

Pre-Swing Warm-Up

Stretch for
Forearm
Muscles

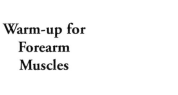

Warm-up for
Forearm
Muscles

RIGHT SIDE MANEUVERS

LEFT SIDE MANEUVERS

**Warm-up for
Stomach
Oblique
Muscles**

Pre-Swing Warm-Up

SITTING ROUTINE IN A CHAIR OR BENCH

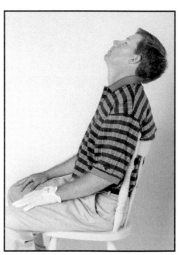

Neck Stretch
Left Photo: **Forward**
Right Photo: **Backward**

**Neck Stretch
(turn head 45°)**

RIGHT SIDE MANEUVERS

LEFT SIDE MANEUVERS

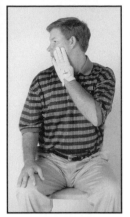

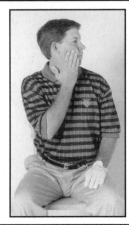

Neck
Rotation
Stretch

Pre-Swing Warm-Up

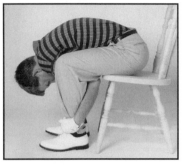

Low Back
Left Photo:
Stretch
Right Photo:
Warm-up

Warm-up for
Anterior
Lower Leg
Muscles
Raise Foot Up
Against
Resistance

Warm-up for
Anterior
Lower Leg
Muscles
Push Foot Down
Against
Resistance

SEATED ROUTINE ON GROUND OR FLOOR

RIGHT SIDE MANEUVERS		LEFT SIDE MANEUVERS

Pre-Swing Warm-Up

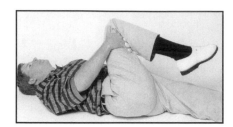

Stretch for Medial and Lateral Hip and Thigh Rotator Muscles

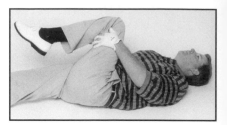

Warm-up for Medial and Lateral Hip and Thigh Rotator Muscles

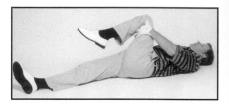

General Stretch for Hip, Low Back, and Stomach Mucles

Glossary

● ●

Abduction:
Movement away from midline.

Acceleration:
To increase the velocity of the club head during the impact phase.

Acceleration Swing Phase:
The acceleration phase begins when the shaft of the club is in the horizontal position during the downswing and ends just after impact with the ball.

Adduction:
Movement toward midline.

Adductor Magnus, Longus, and Brevis:
Hip and thigh adductor muscles.

Agility:
The ability to make rapid and coordinated muscle movements.

Angular Momentum:
The change in angular velocity of a body divided by the time over which change occurs.

Ankle Eversion:
Rolls the ankle inward.

Ankle Inversion:
Rolls the ankle outward.

Anterior Thigh Muscles (Knee Extension):
Quadratus femoris.

Biceps:
Anterior arm muscles. Flexes the forearm.

Biomechanics:
The study of mechanical motion in a biological system.

Centripetal Force:
The inward force exerted on the shaft necessary to keep the club head moving in a circular motion. This force is increased with increased club speed (centripetal acceleration).

Cervical Spine:
The joints of the neck.

Classic Golf Swing:
Upright posture with little extension and rotation of the low back at the end of the follow-through.

Concentric Contraction:
The muscle is being shortened during the contraction (positive contraction).

Decelerate:
To slow the club-head speed during the impact phase.

Deconditioned:
Out of shape, in poor physical condition.

Deltoid (Anterior, Middle, and Posterior):
Shoulder muscles.

Dorsiflexion:
Bend the foot and ankle in a dorsal (upward) direction.

Dynamic Rapid Strength Training:
Individual exercise routines performed with high to maximal resistance with the exercise performed at or near maximum speed. This exercise method improves strength, endurance, and rapid strength.

Dynamic Slow Strength Training:
Exercises performed at high or maximum resistance with slow, steady movements. This training technique improves strength and endurance but is not suited for improving rapid strength, which is necessary to improve golf-swing mechanics.

Eccentric Contraction:
The muscle is being lengthened (negative contraction) during the contraction.

Endurance:
The ability of a muscle to perform work by holding a maximum contraction for a given length of time or by continuing to move at submaximal levels. Denotes the fatigue resistance to long-lasting or repetitive applications of strength.

Erector Spinae:
Low-back muscles. Extends and bends the low back.

Extension:
To straighten or unbend a joint where the angle increases.

Extensor Digitorum Longus:
Ankle and foot dorsiflexion. Anterior lower-leg muscle.

Extensor Hallucis Longus:
Ankle and foot dorsiflexion. Anterior lower-leg muscle.

External Oblique:
Part of the stomach muscles.

Fatigue:
Decreased strength caused by repeated or prolonged muscle contraction.

Flexion:
To bend a joint where the angle decreases.

Follow-Through Swing Phase:
Follow-through begins after impact with the ball and ends with the club at the top at the end of motion.

Forward Swing Phase:
The forward swing begins at initiation of the downswing and ends when the club shaft is horizontal.

Gastrocnemius and Soleus Muscles:
Posterior leg muscles.

Gluteus Maximus:
Posterior hip muscle. Hip extensor.

Gluteus Medius:
Hip and thigh abductor muscle.

Gluteus Minimus:
Posterior hip muscle. Medial hip rotators.

Golfercise System:
A unique exercise system that stretches and strengthens the golf-specific muscles.

Hamstrings (Knee Flexor):
   Posterior thigh muscles.

Infraspinatus:
   Rotator cuff shoulder muscle (internal shoulder rotation).

Inside-Out Swing:
   When the arc of the club begins inside the target line and ends outside the target line. Common in hookers.

Internal Oblique:
   Part of the stomach muscles.

Isokinetic Exercise:
   An exercise where the joint motion occurs at a controlled rate of speed and where the muscle contracts at a variable resistance. (Joint motion fixed; muscle resistance variable.)

Isometric Exercise:
   Exercise that is performed with the muscle being exercised; maintains a fixed length and without joint motion. (Joint motion fixed; muscle resistance fixed.)

Isotonic Exercise:
   Exercise performed by contracting or shortening the muscle, causing movement of the joint to which it is attached. (Joint motion variable; muscle resistance fixed.)

Latissimus Dorsi (Lats):
   Upper-back muscle.

Levator Scapula:
   Part of the shoulder girdle muscles.

Ligament Instability:
   Joint hypermobility (abnormal motion) due to ligament laxity.

Lumbar Spine:
   The joints of the low back.

Modern Golf Swing:
   "C" posture with low-back extension and rotation at the end of the follow-through.

Muscle Balance:
   Equal tone and muscle strength between one side of the body and the other.

Muscle Memory:
   Ability to repeat the same biomechanical movement without conscious thought.

Muscle Tightness:
   Tight muscles that do not allow for full joint motion and/or smooth fluid joint motion.

Outside-In Swing:
   When the arc of the club begins outside the target line and ends inside the target line. Common in players that often slice the ball.

Pectoralis Minor and Major:
   Anterior chest muscles.

Peroneus Longus and Brevis:
   Ankle and foot eversion (rolls the ankle inward). Anterior lower-leg muscles.

Piriformis:
   Posterior hip muscle. Lateral hip rotators.

PNF:
   See Proprioceptive Neurofacilitation.

Power:
   The ability to release muscular work as a function of time. Necessary for distance.

Primary Muscle Groups:
   The main or most active muscle during the four phases of the golf swing.

Proprioceptive Neurofacilitation (PNF):
Stretching by using the stretch-contract-relax method.
Quadratus Lumborum:
Lateral trunk muscle. Bends trunk to side.
Radial Deviation:
Wrist movement toward the thumb.
Range of Motion (ROM):
The full extent of movement and/or rotation of a joint.
Rectus Abdominous:
Part of the stomach muscles.
Rhomboid Minor and Major:
Mid-back muscles.
Rhythmic Swing:
Smooth, non-jerky.
ROM:
See Range of Motion.
Stabilizing Muscles:
Muscles that support the primary muscles during the swing.
Strength:
The maximum voluntary force exerted in a single muscular contraction.
Subscapularis:
Rotator cuff shoulder muscle (external shoulder rotation).
Supraspinatus:
Rotator cuff shoulder muscle (shoulder abduction).
Takeaway Swing Phase:
The takeaway begins when you address the ball and ends at the top of the backswing.
Tensor Fascia Lata:
Hip and thigh abductor muscle.
Teres Minor:
Rotator cuff shoulder muscle (internal shoulder rotation, shoulder adduction).
Thoracic Spine:
The joints of the mid back.
Tibialis Anterior:
Ankle and foot inversion (rolls the ankle outward). Anterior lower leg muscle.
Triceps:
Posterior arm muscle.
Ulnar Deviation:
Wrist movement toward the little finger.
Upper Trapezius:
Part of the shoulder girdle muscles.

Index

thigh extensors, exercise for, 152-153, 193
thigh muscles, 51, 54, 70, 78, 79, 85-86, 88, 146, 207
    anterior, 168-169
    inner, exercise for, 154-155, 194
    outer, exercise, 156-157, 195
    posterior, 170-171
    routine for, 195
thigh rotators, exercise for, 148-150, 191-192
thoracic scoliosis, 44
thoracic spine, 54, 166-167
timing, 82
Top-Ten conditioning program, 6-7
    exercise routines, 175-198
    objective of, 7
triceps muscle, 38, 41, 68, 76, 84
    exercise for, 140-141
trunk
    bending, 55
    muscles, 29, 50, 51, 54, 79, 87, 88, 89, 90, 95, 96, 108, 146-147, 189-190
    rotation, 55, 67, 78, 87
    turn, 50, 77, 87, 95, 96
trunk extensors, 166-167, 190
twisting motion, and injuries, 4

U
ulnar deviator, 38, 47, 84, 116-117, 185
"uncocking" of wrist, 81, 83, 117, 185
"uncoiling" effect, 73, 74
"unhinging," of wrists, 116
Universal (machine), 34
upper-back muscles, 38, 68, 92, 93, 94, 146
    exercise for, 108-109, 181
    range of motion in, 42-43, 44
    routine, 181
    See also latissimus dorsi
upper body
    evaluation of range of motion of joints, 42
    golf muscles of, 38-41
    joints involved in acceleration swing phase, 82-89
    joints involved in follow-through swing phase, 94-96
    joints involved in forward swing phase, 75-79
    joints involved in takeaway phase, 66068
    joints of, 41
    muscles involved in acceleration swing phase, 82-89
    muscles involved in follow-through swing phase, 92-94
    muscles involved in forward swing phase, 75-76
    muscles involved in takeaway phase, 66-68
    pictorial diagram of (anterior view), 39
    pictorial diagram of (posterior view), 40
    primary muscles of, 38
    self-evaluation of joints and muscles of, 41-42
    stabilizing muscles of, 41
    top-ten routine for, 177-187
upper trapezius, 41, 68, 128-129

V
volume, of an exercise program, 18

W
warm-up, 202
    components of, 205-210
    purpose of, 204
warm-up routine, 4-5, 12-13, 201-222
    and isotonic conditioning program, 33
    purpose of, 12, 201-2-2
    See also pre-swing warm-up routine
Watkins, De Lormen, 33
weight, amount of to increase strength, 17
weight-conditioning programs, generic, 89
weight distribution, 70, 92
weights, use of, 33. See also free weights, use of
weight transfer, 49, 50, 72, 77, 78, 158
    during acceleration swing phase, 85-86, 87
    right-to-left, 73, 76
wrist, 92
    as site of injury, 3, 4
    deviators, 184
    exercise for, 110-119, 182-187
    extensors, 67, 76, 84, 112-113, 183
    flexors, 38, 67, 76, 84, 110-111, 187
    joints, 41
    muscles, 68
    pronation, 84
    radial deviation, 114-115
    range of motion in, 47
    routine, exercise, 187
    squared with ball, 84
    supination, 46, 84
    ulnar deviation, 116-117

Y
Yocum, L., 3

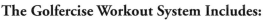

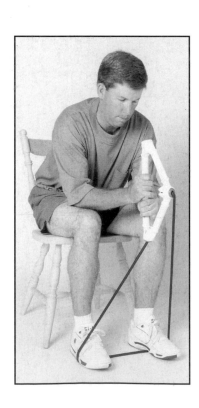